JUSTIFICATION

LINWOOD JACKSON, JR.

PUBLISHED BY FIDELI PUBLISHING, INC.

ISBN: 978-1-60414-752-0 (hardcover)
978-1-60414-660-8 (paperback)

Cover art and design by Fatima Azhar

For information, email the author at

LinwoodJackson@hotmail.com

or visit linwoodjacksonjr.com

Published by

Fideli Publishing, Inc.

www.FideliPublishing.com

Man will believe any *thing* over positive affirmation,
But the living God's wisdom is sure,
And that wisdom's *voice* is immutable,
So who is justified to reject that wisdom's *breath*?

Wherein is one right to disbelieve what cannot fail?
He says, "I am here,
I am ever present:
I know you.

"I am here," *He* says,
"I am here,
Wherefore stumble due to a lack of faith?
I am here, and I know you.
Although the *seas* roar and the *heavens* close their *mouth*,
Though the *earth* is dry and the *air* is thin,
I am here despite what may be,
I am ever present to inform you:
You are not forgotten.

"I am here," *He* again says,
"I am here,
And no *thing* is without My approval.
There will be no *thing* framed which cannot be broken;
Before it touches you,
It touches Me,
And as it grinds you,
It breaks Me,
So where is your faith?

"Hear My *voice*," *He* says,
"And know no *thing* else;
I am here.

"If the captain of the ship does lift up his eyes,
And in lifting up to check the stars,
Will he not return his eyes back down to the ocean?
Will he not direct the boat at his will?

"Why then believe that *I* cannot see?
And if I am, for a moment, away from you,
Why believe that My hearing has ceased?
A creature searching for food will enter into a garden,
Not knowing what he will find,
Yet he enters and searches with no mind of desire,
But what he sets his eye on,
He devours,
And what he finds,
He eats with no question,
For what is found is sufficient for the time,
Making his search beneficial.

"Will you refuse words because you think I refuse to answer?
Will you quit faith to pick up undocumented confidence?
I am here,
I am ever with you,
Produce your faith."

Man would rather consume doubt than perplexity,
And would rather digest sorrow than chastisement,
But know this,
His Wisdom is Creator,
And by that Saying,
I will be made whole.

L

Contents

Introduction

1. Our faith, so long as we educate it, is intelligent. To hear, "Thy faith hath made thee whole,"[1] and, "According to your faith be it unto you,"[2] bears witness to the fact that within faith is an intelligent substance capable of bringing into existence whatsoever the heart and mind will cultivate. The only issue is on what to have faith on, and why.

2. When once faith's "what" and "why" is answered, the question of how to have faith will never surface, because when we hear, "Believe ye that I am able to do this?"[3] having a faith already nurtured on an established hope, "Yea, Lord,"[4] we will confidently and comfortably reply. Faith is easy and involves no thought when once the heart and mind are together engaged on a desire, but faith's "what" and "why" is difficult to grasp, because what can I have faith in without any knowledge of what to spend the energy of my faith on, and why should I spend that energy without knowing or personally understanding why I should spend my self?

3. Faith is not empty or negligent, but faith has an appetite that must be fed, and the regimen of every personal faith revolves around experimenting with hope to acquire knowledge of what to exercise faith on, and why. If it then says, "Have faith in God,"[5] it is crucial to our faith's development that we understand why we are to have faith in "God," and in what context. The ninth division of the book of Matthew opens up our understanding to what our faith should rest on, and why, to the end our conversation may operate as a sure creature of creation's wisdom.

---

1   Matthew 9:22
2   Matthew 9:29
3   Matthew 9:28
4   Matthew 9:28
5   Mark 11:22

4. What to have faith on is clearly revealed to us in the ninth division of the book of Matthew. When once an issue of *blood* has, within our conscience, come to our knowledge, or if we mentally or spiritually sleep and that slumber has come to our knowledge, or if we are inwardly blind to how to care for self and that blindness has come to our knowledge, then it is time to take the *body* of that knowledge on the living God's religious character for wisdom to apply for refreshing our spiritual understanding.

5. Because creation is the end of the Bible's science, when once our need for newness of thought and feeling has dawned upon our conscience, it is time to not only trust that we can know liberation from our character defects, but that we can also learn how to refrain from that defect to remain free from self-cultivated or inherited *illness*. It is for this reason that Paul, understanding the end of *heaven's* will, counsels, "Believe on him that raised up Jesus our Lord from the dead,"[6] and, "If the Spirit of him that raised up Jesus from the dead dwell in you, he that raised up Christ from the dead shall also quicken your mortal bodies by his Spirit."[7]

6. Our faith has the ability to make or to create our conversation's mind whole because its attention is placed on the living God's wisdom, making it well to remember that "God is a Spirit."[8] To hear, "Have faith in God,"[9] is to hear, "Have faith in what is spirit," meaning that there is given to us some promise of His mind to believe on for a certain manner of creation. If we have faith on this mind's counsel then "we might receive the promise of the Spirit through faith,"[10] and that promise is plainly deliverance from mental and spiritual issues of *blood*, *sleep*, and *blindness*, making it imperative to understand that "through knowledge shall the just be delivered."[11]

---

6   Romans 4:23
7   Romans 8:11
8   John 4:24
9   Mark 11:22
10   Galatians 3:14
11   Proverbs 11:9

7. In every case within the ninth division of the book of Mathew, a promise believed on by hope resulted in the end of that hope when exercised by faith.

8. While one priest spoke to the living God's chief apostle about his sick daughter, "a woman, which was diseased with an issue of blood twelve years, came behind him, and touched the hem of his garment: for she said within herself, If I may but touch his garment, I shall be whole."[12]

9. The goal for this *woman* was to receive clean blood to better purify her brain and organs from impurities, which impurities kept her lame and unable to function without discomfort, seeing as how she "had spent all her living upon physicians, neither could be healed of any."[13] But for this woman, the force behind the garment of this minister, she believed, afforded her a better lifestyle.

10. She believed that her God's life-current flowed from His throne and into the very clothes of His messenger, therefore they must give off some *good thing* by them, seeing as how they were so close to his person. Hence, the call of living God's Physician went forth, was heard and then accepted by one who was willing to endure self-humiliation and self-denial for self-possession. The clothes or the flesh of the man had no power to heal any one, but by faith on the perceived hope, "the power of the Lord was present to heal them."[14] That healing is "by the power of the Spirit of God,"[15] and that "power" is "Christ the power of God, and the wisdom of God."[16]

11. Now, "your faith should not stand in the wisdom of men, but in the power of God,"[17] and seeing as how "God is a Spirit,"[18] the *power* of the Spirit is "Christ the power of God, and the wisdom of God."[19] Therefore seeing as how the living God "hath made the earth by his

---

12   Matthew 9:20,21
13   Luke 8:43
14   Luke 5:17
15   Romans 15:19
16   1 Corinthians 1:24
17   1 Corinthians 2:5
18   John 4:24
19   1 Corinthians 1:24

power, he hath established the world by his wisdom,"[20] it is that, by the creative power of His present wisdom, our faith's mind is to confess, "The Spirit of God hath made me."[21]

12. Creation is the end of faith, and since there is no physical garment for us to touch, our thoughts must rise higher when hopeful to discern what commandment we are to apply self to, and why, seeing as how "God requireth that which is past."[22] The assignment of old, to faithfully touch this man's garment, still stands, but it is our responsibility to put our labor in right context. By touching his garment, "immediately her issue of blood stanched,"[23] therefore if we also care to have our diseased *blood* halted and exchanged for a pure and sober mind, and with better circulation than ever, it is well to know to handle his *garment*.

13. "Blood," as it is here mentioned, should not be thought of as literal blood, for "the life of the flesh is in the blood."[24] The force behind this man's garment is for rescuing our "flesh," or our devotional conversation, from the "life" within our "blood," and that "life" is the means whereby we ignorantly enjoy the *works* and "lusts of our flesh, fulfilling the desires of the flesh and of the mind."[25]

14. In Matthew, we may find the historian reviewing a scene in the life of the living God's chief apostle, but the meaning behind the story is for our spiritual learning, that we might "through the Spirit wait for the hope of righteousness by faith."[26] This woman did not believe in emptiness, but her faith centered around the *garment* of the living God's minister, that by actively engaging her self with it, she might obtain the end of her faith, which end should be newness through exercising faith on her hope; this lesson is for us.

15. The living God's righteousness is revealed in this scene, that by our intimate encounter with His wisdom, we "might be filled with

---

20   Jeremiah 10:12
21   Job 33:4
22   Ecclesiastes 3:15
23   Luke 8:44
24   Leviticus 17:11
25   Ephesians 2:3
26   Galatians 5:5

the knowledge of his will in all wisdom and spiritual understanding"[27] to experience the promised inward deliverance, which is why it says, "Thou desirest truth in the inward parts: and in the hidden part thou shalt make me to know wisdom."[28]

16. In order to have good "blood", it is necessary to personally handle, and to bring into "the body of the sins of the flesh,"[29] His mind's wisdom, which is why it says, "Every spirit that confesseth that Jesus Christ is come in the flesh is of God."[30] "Jesus Christ" must come in to the conversation's *body* for the construction of a new nature to govern the members and organs of the heart and mind, and seeing as how this act of creation is not literal, it is well to understand that, in proper context language, "the Lord Jesus Christ our Saviour"[31] is "the commandment of God our Saviour."[32]

17. The garment, or the covering of this man, is the *name* or counsel of his doctrine, which "name" is called, "Jesus Christ," or as it says, "They shall call his name Emman'uel, which being interpreted is, God with us."[33]

18. "Name" does not equate to a literal name, but refers to the doctrine or saying of one's religious character, even like as it says, "Hast kept my word, and hast not denied my name,"[34] and, "Thou holdest fast my name, and hast not denied my faith."[35] The *name* of "Jesus Christ" is the counsel or wisdom of the living God's spiritual understanding, and for us to touch the *garment* of this man, it is that our conversation's conscience must closely examine and execute the counsel of this doctrine, which is why it says, "Ye are clean through the word which I have spoken unto you."[36]

---

27   Colossians 1:9
28   Psalm 51:6
29   Colossians 2:11
30   1 John 4:2
31   Titus 1:4
32   Titus 1:3
33   Matthew 1:23
34   Revelation 3:8
35   Revelation 2:13
36   John 15:3

19. The "word" spoken to us by this minister is the doctrine or wisdom of the living God with or within our conversation's mind. The only way for this transaction to occur is by bringing that wisdom into the spirit of our mind, which is why it says, "That which is born of the Spirit is spirit,"[37] and, "Renew a right spirit within me,"[38] and, "Be renewed in the spirit of your mind."[39]

20. The aim of *heaven's* science is the benevolent law of the living God's righteousness working within the heart of our conversation's character, even "the law of the Spirit of life."[40] This law is the brightness of the living Gods throne, even as it says, "Thou art clothed with honour and majesty. Who coverest thyself with light as with a garment."[41] For this cause, it is well to know that "the commandment is a lamp; and the law is light";[42] and that "we have received a commandment from the Father"[43] that we might know "the kindness and love of God our Saviour toward man."[44]

21. When once our conversation can handle creation's present commandment, our faith may have credible knowledge of what to have faith on, and why. We are all born with a form of contaminated *blood* possessing and directing our thoughts and feelings; both personal and devotional; wherefore we should know that "without shedding of blood is no remission."[45]

22. In order to obtain healthy *blood* for a sober conversation in heavenly *things*, it is that the life of our naturally contaminated *blood* must find itself pouring out from us, for the *body* of the conversation's mind must suffer a wound by the *body* of the living God's knowledge. Naturally the life of the flesh is in the blood, but in reality, "a sound

---

37   John 3:6
38   Psalm 51:10
39   Ephesians 4:23
40   Romans 8:2
41   Psalm 104:1,2
42   Proverbs 6:23
43   2 John 1:4
44   Titus 3:4
45   Hebrews 9:22

heart is the life of the flesh."[46] If it is that we care to own a sane, vibrant, and stable religious character, it is then that a resurrection and circumcision of the inward person's conscience is necessary, "and circumcision is that of the heart, in the spirit."[47]

23. If we are "circumcised with the circumcision made without hands, in putting off the body of the sins of the flesh by the circumcision of Christ,"[48] as we set our faith's mind and *body* to examine and do "the law of the Spirit of life in Christ,"[49] knowledge of what to have faith on will satisfy our involvement with it, and for achieving the reason as to why we should keep on exercising faith on "life's" law. Without knowledge of what to have faith on, or of what to hope for, it will be impossible to understand the living God's thoughts and concerns for our conversation's conscience.

24. Because we need better "blood" with a better "life" to enjoy *heaven's* present kindness, "Put off concerning the former conversation...and be renewed in the spirit of your mind,"[50] it says. One's "life," in proper context of language, is one's personal devotional conversation, and the religious character within it. As the baby comes from the womb, as the butterfly is liberated from its holding, and as the plant breaks the ground to meet its environment, so too every mind, being born and raised within an worldly religious tradition, is to "have escaped the pollutions of the world through the knowledge of the Lord and Saviour Jesus Christ."[51] Thus, if the living God's student says, "It pleased God, who separated me from my mother's womb,"[52] then this experience is for our learning that we too may know the same conception.

25. Our faith, like a baby in the womb of his or her mother, needs more than what our religious tradition can offer it. The greatest test for every newly born child is breathing on his or her own, and this also is the greatest challenge for personal faith. Our faith needs to learn how

---

46   Proverbs 14:30
47   Romans 2:29
48   Colossians 2:11
49   Romans 8:2
50   Ephesians 4:22,23
51   2 Peter 2:20
52   Galatians 1:15

to live for its own good, which is why it says, "Let thine heart retain my words: keep my commandments, and live."[53]

26. A commandment has gone out from the living God concerning the *name* of His will; it is our responsibility to handle that *name* to own a *name* similar to it. A law has gone out from His religious character concerning the will of His present wisdom; it is our responsibility to examine and prove that character to own that character. The greater our effort to do this wisdom's will, the better chance we have of understanding what that will is, to take courage on it for good mental and spiritual wellbeing.

27. This is why it says, "Whosoever will save his life shall lose it: and whosoever will lose his life for my sake shall find it,"[54] and, "He that loveth his life shall lose it; and he that hateth his life in this world shall keep it unto life eternal."[55]

28. In order to properly have a well educated faith, the natural "life" of our spiritual upbringing must find itself sacrificed for a new and better conversation. We cannot advance in *heaven's* wisdom while entertaining the *earth's*. There is a will of *heaven* and a doctrinal intention within the *earth*, and seeing as how it says of that false religion plaguing *earth*, "He was cast out into the earth,"[56] "seek those things which are above, where Christ sitteth on the right hand of God. Set your affection on things above, not on things on the earth."[57]

29. Doctrinal and spiritual blindness occurs to the *eyes* due to a heart feeding on the *earth's* resources, and not the natural eyes in the head of our physical body, but "the eyes of your understanding."[58] Blind *eyes* equate to a dead mind of understanding, for if the wisdom of His mind cultivates the spirit of our mind, then without this counsel there is only the development of the *flesh*, and "flesh and blood cannot inherit the kingdom of God."[59] A spurious *kingdom* is preached and

---

53   Proverbs 4:4
54   Matthew 16:25
55   John 12:25
56   Revelation 12:9
57   Colossians 3:1,2
58   Ephesians 1:18
59   1 Corinthians 15:50

passed in to by them that will not regenerate their mind by *heaven's* wisdom to reform their conversation's conscience, which is why "they that are in the flesh cannot please God."[60] For this cause, such a flesh-based conversation leads to premature *death*, making Paul's counsel applicable: "Many are weak and sickly among you, and many sleep."[61]

30. This "sleep" is not literal, but is, for the stubbornness of the person's heart to prove the Bible's words above relying on handwritten religious dogma. Blindness of the *eyes* happens when failing to comprehend the Bible's spiritual understanding, which is why the recovering mind prays, "Lighten mine eyes, lest I sleep the sleep of death."[62] Because we willingly and consciously fail to learn of and do the law of His mind's will, the slumbering of the eyes and the decaying of the faith's confidence will commence until we "are as water spilt on the ground, which cannot be gathered up again."[63] Nevertheless, "Lighten our eyes, and give us a little reviving in our bondage,"[64] prays the reformer from self and the religious world, to the end they may experience "the mystery of his will, according to his good pleasure which he hath purposed in himself."[65]

31. Again, "the law is light,"[66] and when once this Spirit's law; which law is "the light of the knowledge of the glory of God in the face of Jesus Christ";[67] shines upon the conscience of the conversation, this wisdom will "purge your conscience from dead works to serve the living God."[68] Liberation from dead or pointless devotional works is therefore this wisdom's concern, "for this is the will of God, even your sanctification, that ye should abstain from fornication: that every one of you should know how to possess his vessel in sanctification and honour."[69] Hence,

---

60   Romans 8:8
61   1 Corinthians 11:30
62   Psalm 13:3
63   2 Samuel 14:14
64   Ezra 9:8
65   Ephesians 1:9
66   Proverbs 6:23
67   2 Corinthians 4:6
68   Hebrews 9:14
69   1 Thessalonians 4:3,4

our deliverance from fermented blood, from blindness on heavenly *things*, and from a mind dead to the *voice* of *heaven's* wisdom, along with the true condition of self without that *voice*, is based upon our willingness to let our faith exercise its self on the hope decreed for it.

32. In order to properly chase *heaven's* hope, it is crucial to our faith's development that we take knowledge of what that hope is, to understand why it is supposed to matter. Naturally, we have no knowledge of what the Bible's benevolent will is. As natural products of sensual spiritual institutions, our understanding on spiritual things is compromised from its *conception*. We have retained whatever we have retained on the Bible however we have retained it, but it is well to understand that what we have retained from the religious world is not the full end, or is not even the complete beginning of *heaven's* doctrine, seeing as how "the whole world lieth in wickedness."[70]

33. It is then right, with what we have in understanding, to bring it to the Bible, and in its nakedness, so that we may not only receive correction on manners of worship and service, but that we may receive clothing, or knowledge, to cover our faith's confidence, even like as it says, "I have caused thine iniquity to pass from thee, and I will clothe thee with change of raiment."[71]

34. The inherited religious policy that is naturally handled, or the doctrines or theories of our religious tradition that we innocently adopt, along with the added self-cultivated notions derived from that persuasion, stains our faith and decays our spiritual understanding. When we allow our faith to take close and personal knowledge of *heaven's* tongue, the muck of natural spiritual ignorance will pass away to leave the *body* of our faith clean for fresh *apparel*. This is how belief is knowledgeably developed. When personal wisdom strengthens our faith, "Now we believe...for we have heard him ourselves, and know that this is indeed the Christ,"[72] we will say.

35. We have to know that the living God's wisdom is that Savior for self and for the religious world's philosophy, and the first step is

---

70   1 John 5:19
71   Zechariah 3:4
72   John 4:42

to cultivate faith in the judgment and commandment it preaches. Our faith must hear its voice, and there is no such thing as catching this wisdom's full impression from another mouth. The commandment is private and individual, saying, "Ye are clean through the word which I have spoken";[73] faith is as personal to every mind as is the heart to every body.

36. All have a body, and within that body, all have a heart functioning only for their individual body's good. Likewise every spiritual *body* has a faith only for that *body*, and the neglecting of that personal faith means the deterioration of that *body* and its *organs*. Our faith is a living organism that needs to be treated as such. Because "the LORD is a God of knowledge, and by him actions are weighed";[74] only through knowledge acquired by an experimental faith can the person experience the decreed inward alleviation.

37. If our faith and its spiritual understanding stubbornly remains on *earth* and within the religious world; despite the fact that this wisdom says, "I leave the world, and go to the Father";[75] we will experience sickness of *blood* with a certain blindness leading to a peculiar pre-mature *death* in personal and spiritual understanding. This is why our faith must remain confident on the fact that "if the Spirit of him that raised up Jesus from the dead dwell in you, he that raised up Christ from the dead shall also quicken your mortal bodies by his Spirit."[76]

38. We need knowledge on the living God's compassionate act. It is for this reason that our faith's higher learning should not find itself delayed. Our spiritual wisdom must continually develop if we should ever hope for a faith to govern our natural and spiritual bodies. Our faith's organs remain functioning as they have material to exercise and prove, and by mentally and physically examining creation's law; as it says of His faithful, "In his law doth he meditate day and night";[77] we

---

73   John 15:3
74   1 Samuel 2:3
75   John 16:28
76   Romans 8:11
77   Psalm 1:2

open up our inward person to obtain knowledge for transforming its faculties to advance positive connections to the members of the heart. 39. This connection reforms the heart's organs to better fill up the emptiness within the natural *body's* mind with a translated wisdom of the mind derived from the living God's wisdom. When once the heart begins to embrace conversational reform by His wisdom's knowledge and experience, it is that the limbs of the body will be encouraged to act out the vibration of the heart's purified instruments, encouraging the development of faith as the mind and body exercise the life of its newly acquired wisdom. *Heaven's* will therefore cleanses our inward person from all personal and devotional illness, but it is on us to immerse our mind in it for the beautifying of our faith's character.

1

Life By Means Of Death

1. "I through the law am dead to the law, that I might live unto God."[78]

2. The honest conversation maintains sufficiency not "through the law, but through the righteousness of faith."[79] Such a conversation is to mentally and physically pass away from consenting to have its conscience ruled by the judgment of ancient and modern "philosophy and vain deceit, after the tradition of men."[80] In order to honor the living God's spiritual understanding, the conversation must no longer think and feel for natural traditional religious laws and doctrines. "The world is crucified unto me,"[81] says the reformer, for they confess loyalty to creation's science through the knowledge acquired when learning of and proving salvation's law.

3. Creation's new covenant commandment, and not the religion of Moses, is the decreed course for mental and spiritual health. The religion of old declared a man to be *justified* by handwritten religious laws.

---

78   Galatians 2:19
79   Romans 4:13
80   Colossians 2:8
81   Galatians 6:14

But seeing as how "without faith it is impossible to please him,"[82] we do well to know that "the law is not of faith."[83]

4. The living God's chief apostle *died* and *revived* that, for the purpose of the conversation's spiritual re-education, the reformer may, for the spirit of doctrinal liberty, submit their heart to *heaven's* course of learning. The living God's wisdom is to be "life unto those that find them, and health to all their flesh."[84]

5. Having begun in the living God's mind of edifying, the conversation should not be drawn to handwritten religious precepts. We are told, "The Spirit is life,"[85] and "the law of the Spirit of life"[86] declares, "We through the Spirit wait for the hope of righteousness by faith."[87] "If there had been a law given which could have given life, verily righteousness should have been by the law,"[88] yet justification is by "the grace of God: for if righteousness come by the law, then Christ is dead in vain."[89] Thus, "if Christ be not raised, your faith is vain; ye are yet in your sins,"[90] but "by the righteousness of one the free gift came upon all men unto justification of life."[91]

6. For a reminder of what "sin" presently is, it says, "The strength of sin is the law."[92] All in that ancient time saw perfection, "as pertaining to the conscience,"[93] through the "precepts, statutes, and laws, by the hand of Moses."[94] The purpose of *heaven's* new covenant wisdom is to draw minds away from self-cultivated religious opinion and to the living God through it, "wherefore henceforth know we no man after

---

82   Hebrews 11:6
83   Galatians 3:12
84   Proverbs 4:22
85   Romans 8:10
86   Romans 8:2
87   Galatians 5:5
88   Galatians 3:21
89   Galatians 2:21
90   1 Corinthians 15:17
91   Romans 5:18
92   1 Corinthians 15:56
93   Hebrews 9:9
94   Nehemiah 9:14

the flesh."[95] So then, when considering the mistake of ancient Israel to take *justification* by the philosophy of the religious law, "are ye now made perfect through the flesh?"[96]

7. Although the Jewish economy was based upon the hand of Moses, that routine of blessing through "meats and drinks, and diverse washings, and carnal ordinances,"[97] was to prepare the observer for a service without them, even like as it says, "The law was our schoolmaster to bring us unto Christ, that we might be justified by faith."[98] Before the living God's man pronounced *heaven's* will and wisdom, the commandment that should come was removed from the people, yet after having established the living God's spiritual understanding, it is counseled, "Live according to God in the spirit."[99]

8. "I serve with my spirit in the gospel of his Son,"[100] reports the apostle, for which cause he advises, "Be renewed in the spirit of your mind."[101]

9. The mind, which is another term for "the spirit," becomes the true and current house for *heaven's* commandments, and those precepts firmly situated when first learning of and obeying the precepts of His throne's religion. *Heaven's* doctrine leads to the conversation honoring the Creator's voice. The religion of Moses is based upon doing religious works to honor the hand that wrote them. The conversation's mind is to become a reflection of the living God's religious character, and this is not accomplished by centering the belief on handwritten religious *wisdom*, for it says, "The just shall live by faith."[102]

10. The just live by faith of what? We are counseled to experiment with "faith in his blood,"[103] seeing as how by faith on a living experience

---

95   2 Corinthians 5:16
96   Galatians 3:3
97   Hebrews 9:10
98   Galatians 3:24
99   1 Peter 4:6
100   Romans 1:9
101   Ephesians 4:23
102   Romans 1:17
103   Romans 3:25

without Moses' religion we are "justified by his blood,"[104] meaning, the believer trusts that they are "reconciled to God by the death of his Son"[105] to experience *heaven's* intention. Therefore being justified by faith to commune with *heaven's* Sanctuary to have the living God's religious character formed within our conversation's conscience, we are "justified freely by his grace through the redemption that is in Christ."[106] How, then, is justification perfected? It further says, "By his knowledge shall my righteous servant justify many."[107]

11. The "blood" of his chief apostle is the knowledge of his conversation's experience. If justified by his conversation's knowledge, then justification is better defined as mental and spiritual sanctification. *Heaven's* doctrine is the living God's pleasure on the conversation's inward parts, where it is not that one follows handwritten guidelines of what to eat, wear, say, think, and live, but through *heaven's* knowledge, the believer is "to be strengthened with might by his Spirit in the inner man,"[108] confessing, "I delight in the law of God after the inward man."[109] Hereafter self-regulation may support a new spiritual constitution.

12. The spirit of the conversation's mind is to receive the living God's commandments through exercising faith on *heaven's* doctrine, to the end that spirit would fill the will with the power of grace to work with an already active desire to fulfill a good service through sincere affection. Justification is then the key to living a truly honest and innovative personal and devotional life. When justified, our faith's mind is experiencing liberty from religious error, confessing to us the living God's intention, that our joy in His person should be happy, healthy, and perfect, and "perfect, as pertaining to the conscience."[110] This is why it says, "With the mind I myself serve the law of God."[111]

---

104 Romans 5:9
105 Romans 5:10
106 Romans 3:24
107 Isaiah 53:11
108 Ephesians 3:16
109 Romans 7:22
110 Hebrews 9:9
111 Romans 7:25

13. When correctly honoring *heaven's* will and wisdom, the conversation no longer abides by "the flesh to the lusts of men, but to the will of God."[112] To be of the living God's religious character, the reformer must say, "That I may know him,"[113] refraining from self-cultivated and inherited spiritual thought to personal experience His words, even like as it says, "Be ye transformed by the renewing of your mind, that ye may prove what is that good, and acceptable, and perfect, will of God."[114] Seeing as how we don't know the living God as we ought, we do well to hear how it says, "I saw, and considered it well: I looked upon it, and received instruction."[115] Thus, only from possessing a living experience outside of religious tradition and superstition may we ever confess, "Our hands have handled."[116]

14. What does the living God ask of us? It says, "Reach hither thy hand, and thrush it into my side: and be not faithless, but believing."[117] This is indeed the definition of a living experience in heavenly things.

15. These words are living and breathing words for us to employ. The philosophy of the religious law, with His man "having abolished in his flesh the enmity, even the law of commandments contained in ordinances,"[118] is become the definition of "sin," letting us know that "the law was our schoolmaster to bring us unto Christ,"[119] "but after that faith is come, we are no longer under a schoolmaster,"[120] but are rather "justified by faith."[121] And what does Moses say about this? He says, "The LORD thy God will raise up unto thee a Prophet from the midst of thee, of thy brethren, like unto me."[122] For this cause He says,

---

112   1 Peter 3:18
113   Philippians 3:10
114   Romans 12:2
115   Proverbs 24:32
116   1 John 1:2
117   John 20:27
118   Ephesians 2:15
119   Galatians 3:24
120   Galatians 3:25
121   Galatians 3:24
122   Deuteronomy 18:15

"Whosoever will not hearken unto my words which he shall speak in my name, I will require it of him."[123]

16. The living God counsels, "Let thine heart retain my words: keep my commandments, and live."[124] The reformer is to obtain wisdom "through the faith of Christ, the righteousness which is of God by faith,"[125] for through faith, "the righteousness of the law might be fulfilled in us, who walk not after the flesh, but after the Spirit."[126]

17. As Paul wrote, "Be filled with the Spirit,"[127] it is that he directs the believer to "be filled with all the fullness of God."[128] This fullness shines through creation's doctrine "to the praise of the glory of his grace,"[129] "for by grace are ye saved through faith."[130] This is why the apostle wrote, "I do not frustrate the grace of God,"[131] and, "Grieve not the holy Spirit."[132]

18. Heaven's knowledge places grace into the soul of the conversation for the health of its conscience. From personally studying *heaven's* doctrine, and allowing that knowledge to assimilate with the experience, the believer is to encounter the living God's religious character, even as it says, "When it pleased God, who separated me...and called me by his grace."[133]

19. This doctrine is the ordained Priest over *heaven's* Sanctuary for "bringing many sons unto glory."[134] The conversation is saved, recovered, or revived by a process of mind and soul regeneration through the Bible's spiritual understanding. The words of His chief messenger are to become the living reformer's diet, to the end they may confess,

---

123   Deuteronomy 18:19
124   Proverbs 4:4
125   Philippians 3:9
126   Romans 8:4
127   Ephesians 5:18
128   Ephesians 3:19
129   Ephesians 1:6
130   Ephesians 2:8
131   Galatians 2:21
132   Ephesians 4:30
133   Galatians 1:15
134   Hebrews 2:10

"I through the law am dead to the law, that I might live unto God."[135] Thus, being justified by the knowledge of *heaven's* will, "I through the law of creation am *dead* and raised to *life* by the law of creation," they confess, "that the reality of the living God's intention should keep me in the presence of His wisdom 'while I have my being.'"[136]

135   Galatians 2:19
136   Psalms 104:33

2

Life And Liberty

1. Says scripture, "Stand fast therefore in the liberty wherewith Christ hath made us free, and be not entangled again with the yoke of bondage."[137]

2. The reformer is "justified by the faith of Jesus Christ."[138] Paul's language is important, because if justified by "the faith of," then justification is, in reality, "of the faith, and of the knowledge of the Son of God."[139] The knowledge of *heaven's* wisdom, and no thing else, justifies, cleanses, or purifies the conversation's inwards, making it then true that the reformer should "run well"[140] and "obey the truth,"[141] which "truth" is that "God would justify the heathen through faith,"[142] that is, through "the faith of the Son of God."[143]

3. "The soul of the righteous"[144] is beautified through faith's exercise, and that justification through "the promise of the Spirit."[145] For this

---

137   Galatians 5:1
138   Galatians 2:16
139   Ephesians 4:13
140   Galatians 5:7
141   Galatians 5:7
142   Galatians 3:8
143   Galatians 2:20
144   Psalms 94:21
145   Galatians 3:14

cause it is said, "Through the Spirit wait for the hope of righteousness by faith,"[146] for the conversation is adopted to the living God by His wisdom through faith, and that adoption maintained through the "communion of the Holy Ghost."[147]

4. The living God would have every believing conversation actively exercising faith on His chief apostle's *name*, to the end "he might be just, and the justifier of him which believeth in Jesus."[148] The conversation is made perfect by His wisdom's pleasure, righteousness, or kindness, and not by any thing else. His man was sent to "redeem them that were under the law,"[149] that is, to rescue the conversation "made of a woman, made under the law."[150]

5. The doctrine of the living God's man was sent to redeem or rescue conversations under "law of commandments contained in ordinances";[151] them that were made of a *woman*, "called the Circumcision in the flesh made by hands,"[152] that is, "By the hands of artificers."[153] Yet according to the living God's spiritual understanding, the reformer is "circumcised with the circumcision made without hands,"[154] seeing as how "our conversation is in heaven"[155] by "a greater and more perfect tabernacle, not made withhands."[156]

6. "Christ as a son over his own house"[157] is within "heaven itself, now to appear in the presence of God for us,"[158] that we may hear, "Jerusalem which is above is free."[159] Through *heaven's* new covenant doctrine, the believing conversation is redeemed and delivered from the philosophy

---

146   Galatians 5:5
147   2 Corinthians 13:14
148   Romans 3:26
149   Galatians 4:5
150   Galatians 4:4
151   Ephesians 2:15
152   Ephesians 2:11
153   1 Chronicles 29:5
154   Colossians 2:11
155   Philippians 3:20
156   Hebrews 9:11
157   Hebrews 3:6
158   Hebrews 9:24
159   Galatians 4:26

of the religious law to be freed from *women*, or from the speculation of religious tradition, moving that conversation to say, "God, who separated me from my mother's womb...to reveal his Son in me,"[160] "hath redeemed my soul out of all distress."[161]

7. Again, "stand fast in the liberty wherewith Christ hath made us free."[162] There is no liberty in a mind "made of a woman,"[163] for who can tell a heart the way of its affection? What commandments may fasten a heart in honest and sincere devotion? Can repentance come by way of simulated order? "If there had been a law given which could have given life, verily righteousness should have been by the law,"[164] yet let the professor consider how it says, "The law of the Spirit of life in Christ Jesus hath made me free."[165]

8. There is a law decreed to move the heart to confess, "Thou didst make me hope when I was upon my mother's breasts. I was cast upon thee from the womb."[166] True communion with the Father and His wisdom will cause a separation from the *womb*, moving the separated to say, "To reveal his Son in me."[167]

9. As the conversation is separated from whatever *woman* gave birth to them, "if God permit,"[168] they are to become perfect, and "perfect, as pertaining to the conscience."[169] Through *heaven's* faith, by the regeneration of that wisdom upon the conversation's conscience, the believer should continue "holding faith, and a good conscience,"[170] which is not possible to do through "gifts and sacrifices."[171] "God would justify the

---

160 Galatians 1:15,16
161 1 Kings 1:29
162 Galatians 5:1
163 Galatians 4:4
164 Galatians 3:21
165 Romans 8:2
166 Psalms 22:9,10
167 Galatians 1:16
168 Hebrews 6:3
169 Hebrews 9:9
170 1 Timothy 1:19
171 Hebrews 8:3

heathen through faith,"[172] "not by the works of the law"[173] "after the commandments and doctrines of men."[174] This is why it says, "Carry your conversation according to God in the spirit of your mind."[175] If we would know heaven's kindness, "Worship the Father in spirit and in truth,"[176] we are counseled.

10. The liberty of "Christ," or rather the blessing of the living God's wisdom, is processed and discerned by His Spirit or Wisdom, for "where the Spirit of the Lord is, there is liberty."[177] Who is then in *bondage* but the conversation maintaining the tradition of another mind? Who is in *bondage* but the conversation fearful to break the written code of their heart, and that of *men*, in order to lift up the face to *heaven* without reproach?

11. In the fullness of time, "God sent forth his Son, made of a woman, made under the law,"[178] "that we might live through him."[179] What is written? It says, "There is none other name under heaven given among men, whereby we must be saved,"[180] howbeit every man "taken from among men is ordained for men in things pertaining to God."[181] "Was Paul crucified for you? or were ye baptized (purified) in the name of Paul?"[182] This same Paul confesses, "The gospel which was preached of me is not after man."[183]

12. "Our liberty which we have in Christ"[184] is "according to the truth of the gospel."[185] "They which be of faith are blessed with"[186] "the

---

172   Galatians 3:8
173   Galatians 2:16
174   Colossians 2:22
175   1 Peter 4:6
176   John 4:23
177   2 Corinthians 3:17
178   Galatians 4:4
179   1 John 4:9
180   Acts 4:12
181   Hebrews 5:1
182   1 Corinthians 1:13
183   Galatians 1:11
184   Galatians 2:4
185   Galatians 2:14
186   Galatians 3:9

promise of the Spirit through faith,"[187] that is, edified not "through the law, but through the righteousness of faith."[188] The righteousness of *heaven's* doctrine comes by intelligently believing "on him that raised up Jesus our Lord from the dead,"[189] even "the Spirit that raised up Jesus from the dead."[190]

13. "The Spirit is life,"[191] moving its student to say, "The law of the Spirit of life in Christ Jesus hath made me free."[192] "Free" from what? "From the law of sin and death,"[193] even that "law in my members, warring against the law of my mind."[194]

14. The force of the living God's wisdom cancels the power of hand-written religious laws from the conversation's conscience. The heart cares to please the *flesh*, or rather, the personal religion's *body*, and the impulse of the heart is to gratify spiritual appetite, yet when subject to *heaven's* law, the members are silenced and given health to become tools for uplifting. Without belief on creation's Spirit there is no portal for health, but should the believer hear "him that justifieth the ungodly, his faith is counted for righteousness."[195]

15. Through *heaven's* doctrine, all who would execute the living God's will and wisdom "have been called unto liberty."[196] The purpose of mental liberty is to produce a people with a "godly" conversation. Thus, should any remain "justified by the law; ye are fallen from grace."[197]

16. It is that "I through the law am dead to the law, that I might live unto God,"[198] yet if *life* is sought through what increases *death*, wherein is there growth and justification? "We are not under the law, but under

187 Galatians 3:14
188 Romans 4:13
189 Romans 4:24
190 Romans 8:11
191 Romans 8:10
192 Romans 8:2
193 Romans 8:2
194 Romans 7:23
195 Romans 4:4
196 Galatians 5:13
197 Galatians 5:4
198 Galatians 2:19

grace,"[199] and it is by the Spirit or Wisdom of life that "the grace of life"[200] "redeemeth thy life from destruction,"[201] for it is said, "Justified by his grace."[202]

---

199   Romans 6:15
200   1 Peter 3:7
201   Psalms 103:4
202   Titus 3:7

3

The Seed Of Faith

1. Says scripture, "He saith, A new covenant, he hath made the first old."[203]

2. That routing maintaining the spiritual structure of the ancient dispensation is passed away and forgotten, seeing as how the living God "preached before the gospel unto Abraham."[204] That practice ultimately defining acceptable service to *heaven* would find place within Abraham, for the apostle teaches that "God would justify"[205] through "the blessing of Abraham."[206]

3. That which came by Moses was "to bring us to Christ,"[207] yet through an unsanctified heart, it was declared of old, and is yet still rehearsed, "Abraham was one, and he inherited the land: but we are many; the land is given us for inheritance."[208] The *land*, the structure of denominated religion, became the idol of the ancient Israelites, and that curse still takes effect. Thus, "If ye were Abraham's children, ye

203   Hebrews 8:13
204   Galatians 3:8
205   Galatians 3:8
206   Galatians 3:14
207   Galatians 3:24
208   Ezekiel 33:24

would do the works of Abraham,"[209] says *heaven*. "Abraham believed God, and it was accounted to him for righteousness,"[210] which is why "they which be of faith are blessed."[211]

4. Herein we find *heaven's* promise, that "they which be of faith are blessed":[212] "if the inheritance be of the law, it is no more of promise,"[213] because "the law is not of faith."[214] It was said to Abraham, "I will bless thee, and make thy name great; and thou shalt be a blessing."[215] "In thee shall all families of the earth be blessed."[216] As it was said, "I will bless *you*," it is that the *name* of Abraham should be that practice bringing blessing, for God promised, "And make thy name great."[217] The name of Abraham therefore procures the blessing of the new covenant, for it says, "My covenant between me (my *name*) and thee (thy *name*), and thy seed after thee,"[218] for it says, "He saith not, And to seeds, as of many; but as of one, And to thy seed, which is Christ."[219]

5. The living God's true covenant is established between the *name* of the living God and the *name* of His chief apostle, through Abraham's *name*, for all "children of the stock of Abraham."[220] Indeed this covenant, "I will bless thee, and make thy name great,"[221] and, "I will bless them that bless thee,"[222] was confirmed in that He said, "For an everlasting covenant,"[223] which is why says, "Through the blood of the everlasting covenant."[224]

---

209   John 8:39
210   Galatians 3:6
211   Galatians 3:9
212   Galatians 3:9
213   Galatians 3:18
214   Galatians 3:12
215   Genesis 12:2
216   Galatians 12:3
217   Genesis 12:2
218   Genesis 17:7
219   Galatians 3:16
220   Acts 13:26
221   Genesis 12:2
222   Genesis 12:3
223   Genesis 17:7
224   Hebrews 13:20

6. The *name* of Abraham will cause the believer to hear, "He that loveth me shall be loved of my Father, and I will love him,"[225] "and we will come unto him, and make our abode with him."[226] It is the "stock" of Abraham to whom the promises of God are concerned. So then what is the "name" of Abraham that procures such a communion? "When God made promise to Abraham,"[227] it is not that He made an oath with him because of anything about him, but it was done because of his religious character, which is why "they which be of faith are blessed,"[228] for his *name* was established not "through the law, but through the righteousness of faith."[229]

7. As was said to Abraham, "I will bless them that honor you," it is that "the blessing of Abraham might come"[230] on them "which are of faith."[231] The *name* of Abraham is "the hope of righteousness by faith,"[232] but the former covenant, honoring the conditions of the law of Moses, remained "till the seed should come to whom the promise was made."[233] We know "that the Son of God is come,"[234] and that it says, "To thy seed, which is Christ,"[235] therefore it is not that "Christ" came, but rather "faith came,"[236] and "after faith is come,"[237] "we draw nigh unto God."[238]

8. So then "through the faith of Christ, the righteousness which is of God by faith,"[239] they which honor and assimilate the *name* of Abraham into their conversation's conscience, "the same are the children of

---

225   John 14:21
226   John 14:23
227   Hebrews 6:13
228   Galatians 3:9
229   Romans 4:13
230   Genesis 3:14
231   Galatians 3:7
232   Galatians 5:5
233   Galatians 3:19
234   1 John 5:20
235   Galatians 3:16
236   Galatians 3:23
237   Galatians 3:25
238   Hebrews 7:19
239   Philippians 3:9

Abraham."[240] That blessing of Abraham is truly that blessing of faith's edification, and it is ordained through creation's wisdom "that we might receive the promise of the Spirit through faith,"[241] for God said, "I am thy shield, and thy exceeding great reward."[242]

9. "Now to him that worketh is the reward not reckoned of grace,"[243] for the reformed conversation is defined grace, and by "the Spirit of grace"[244] "faith is counted for righteousness,"[245] leaving it that "by grace are ye saved through faith."[246] This is why it says, "The promise by faith of Jesus Christ might be given to them that believe,"[247] and, "He that believeth and is baptized shall be saved."[248]

10. "The steps of that faith of our father Abraham"[249] are for righteousness' blessing, for He said, "Thou shalt be a blessing,"[250] and, "In thee shall all families of the earth be blessed."[251] The conversations going forward "not weak in faith"[252] nor hardened "at the promise of God through unbelief,"[253] these "are blessed with faithful Abraham."[254] "Therefore it is of faith, that it might be by grace; to the end the promise might be sure to all the seed"[255] "of the faith of Abraham."[256]

11. Seeing as how "faith was reckoned to Abraham for righteousness,"[257] the living God's promise through the mind of Abraham is "for us also, to whom it shall be imputed, if we believe on

---

240 Galatians 3:7
241 Galatians 3:14
242 Genesis 15:1
243 Romans 4:4
244 Hebrews 10:29
245 Hebrews 10:29
246 Ephesians 2:8
247 Galatians 3:22
248 Mark 16:16
249 Romans 4:12
250 Genesis 12:2
251 Genesis 12:3
252 Romans 4:19
253 Romans 4:20
254 Galatians 3:9
255 Romans 4:16
256 Romans 4:16
257 Romans 4:9

him that raised up Jesus,"²⁵⁸ even on "the Spirit of him that raised up Jesus."²⁵⁹ Through *heaven's* wisdom, it is that "God would justify"²⁶⁰ by "the promise of the Spirit through faith."²⁶¹ This is why "to Abraham and his seed were the promises made,"²⁶² to the end that edification gives every conversation the opportunity "be justified by the faith of Christ, and not by the works of the law."²⁶³

12. It is that by faith in the virtue of the *blood* shed for the confirmation of the everlasting covenant that grace is to be administered by faith to recover the conversation's conscience. By faith, the conscience is purged and the conversation uplifted to match *heaven's religious* character. As "the Spirit is life,"²⁶⁴ it is that by *Him* that rose up "Christ," the believer receives "the grace of life"²⁶⁵ that they "should serve in newness of spirit,"²⁶⁶ for "the spirit giveth life."²⁶⁷ The birth of the new mind will have the conversation hearing the counsel, "That Abraham obeyed my voice, and kept my charge, my commandments, my statutes, and my laws,"²⁶⁸ leaving it that the one born of *heaven's House* will consider how it says, "This is my beloved Son: hear him."²⁶⁹

13. The blessing of faith comes by "the Spirit of truth, which proceedeth from the Father,"²⁷⁰ even "the anointing which ye have received of him"²⁷¹ "after that ye heard the word of truth."²⁷² Therefore "no man is justified by the law in the sight of God,"²⁷³ nor is spiritual innocence reckoned to the *name* of any "after the law of a carnal

---

258 Romans 4:29
259 Romans 8:11
260 Galatians 3:8
261 Galatians 3:14
262 Galatians 3:16
263 Galatians 2:16
264 Romans 8:10
265 1 Peter 3:7
266 Romans 7:6
267 2 Corinthians 3:6
268 Genesis 26:5
269 Mark 9:7
270 John 15:26
271 1 John 2:25
272 Ephesians 1:13
273 Galatians 3:11

commandment,"[274] which rule and precept cannot "make him that did the service perfect, as pertaining to the conscience."[275]

14. Yet it is only by faith in *heaven's* doctrine that it may be said, "Purge your conscience from dead works to serve the living God."[276] "Jewish fables, and commandments of men, that turn from the truth,"[277] are laid to rest by *heaven's* spiritual understanding, which is why it says, "I live by the faith of the Son of God."[278] This spiritual understanding "preached before the gospel unto Abraham, saying, In thee shall all nations be blessed,"[279] which is why it says, "Through the Spirit wait for the hope of righteousness by faith."[280]

15. The conversation is justified by "the righteousness which is of faith,"[281] and that righteousness made certain by His Wisdom or Spirit, because "it is the Spirit that beareth witness."[282] "The Spirit beareth witness with our spirit, that we are the children of God,"[283] and that witness our faith's acceptance of the atonement to *heaven's* Sanctuary so that it is known, "They which are of faith, the same are the children of Abraham,"[284] and, "Abraham's seed, and heirs according to the promise."[285]

16. So then "they which be of faith are blessed with faithful Abraham"[286] and not through him that said, "I stood between the LORD and you."[287] "It is Christ that died, yea rather, that is risen again, who is even at the right hand of God, who also maketh intercession for us."[288] "By him all that believe are justified from all things, from which

274   Hebrews 7:16
275   Hebrews 9:9
276   Hebrews 9:14
277   Titus 1:14
278   Galatians 2:20
279   Galatians 3:8
280   Galatians 5:5
281   Romans 10:6
282   1 John 5:6
283   Romans 8:16
284   Galatians 3:7
285   Galatians 3:29
286   Galatians 3:9
287   Deuteronomy 5:5
288   Romans 8:34

ye could not be justified by the law of Moses,"[289] which is why it says, "The law is not of faith,"[290] and, "Ye also are become dead to the law by the body of Christ."[291]

17. By salvation's commandment, the Christian is given newness of devotional structure to fulfill the saying, "Walk before me, and be thou perfect";[292] for as this was told to Abraham, and he did it, so too by *heaven's* promise many conversations should be made perfect by His wisdom's righteousness. The conversation is to then be "perfect, as pertaining to the conscience,"[293] and "not by works of righteousness which we have done,"[294] but rather through "the work of righteousness."[295]

18. Conversations professing the *name* of the living God's chief messenger are to "be made perfect,"[296] having "no more conscience of sins."[297] They that honor the *name* of Abraham will be just as blessed as he was, for it is that as "God having provided some better thing for us,"[298] He, observing the *death* haunting the ages, determined that "the seal of circumcision, a seal of the righteousness of the faith,"[299] should fall "unto all and upon all them that believe: for there is no difference."[300] Thus, "being justified freely by his grace through the redemption that is in Christ,"[301] "ye are all one in Christ,"[302] "and Christ is God's."[303]

19. Again, "They which be of faith are blessed with faithful Abraham."[304] As Abraham "believed in the LORD: and he counted it

289   Acts 13:39
290   Galatians 3:12
291   Romans 7:4
292   Genesis 17:1
293   Hebrews 9:9
294   Titus 3:5
295   Isaiah 32:17
296   Hebrews 11:40
297   Hebrews 10:2
298   Hebrews 11:40
299   Romans 4:11
300   Romans 3:22
301   Romans 3:24
302   Galatians 3:28
303   1 Corinthians 3:23
304   Galatians 3:9

to him for righteousness,"[305] even so they that "believeth on him that justifieth the ungodly, his faith is counted for righteousness,"[306] even as it says, "God imputeth righteousness without works."[307] Herein it is well to know that "he that hath the Son hath life,"[308] and that "your life is hid with Christ in God."[309]

20. "The Spirit is life,"[310] therefore the wisdom of the living God is given that we "might believe that Jesus is the Christ, the Son of God; and that believing ye might have life through his name."[311] "As many as received him (his *name*), to them gave he power to become the sons of God, even to them that believe on his name,"[312] which is why it is said, "Because ye are sons, God hath sent forth the Spirit of his Son into your hearts."[313] "Abraham believed God, and it was imputed unto him for righteousness,"[314] therefore His chief messenger said, "Ye believe in God, believe also in me."[315] The Christian is justified by the Spirit or Wisdom of His grace to honor the living God's *name*, awakening the heart to hear how it says, "Ye are washed, but ye are sanctified, but ye are justified in the name of the Lord Jesus, and by the Spirit of our God."[316]

21. Abraham believed the doctrine given to him, and in that act he was fit to receive that doctrine's promise. If the reformer should, through creation's present wisdom, believe on the fact of their atonement to the living God's religious character, faithfully learning of and proving that conviction, they will receive the *life* of *heaven* to renew and wash their spiritual intelligence.

---

305   Genesis 15:6
306   Romans 4:5
307   Romans 4:6
308   1 John 5:12
309   Colossians 3:3
310   Romans 8:10
311   John 20:31
312   John 1:12
313   Galatians 4:6
314   James 2:23
315   John 14:1
316   1 Corinthians 6:11

4

Grace

1. So then what is the actual measure for justification? Justification occurs by faith on *heaven's* new covenant commandment, yet if faith on *heaven's* science "justifies," then that faith must lead to the ultimate intention of faith, which is why it says, "Being justified by his grace, we should be made heirs according to the hope of eternal life."[317]

2. There is a two step process to justification: first, the exercising of faith on *heaven's* new covenant science; second, after faith on *heaven's* commandment occurs, receive and embrace grace to seal up the experience. Justification is imperfectly completed without "grace." Grace is the key to the fulfilling of *heaven's* science, which is why it says, "Abundance of grace and of the gift of righteousness."[318]

3. The end of *heaven's* commandment is the revelation of the living God's righteousness, which righteousness is "the kindness and love of God our Saviour toward man."[319] This "kindness" or "righteousness" is "all the good pleasure of his goodness, and the work of faith with

---

317   Titus 3:7
318   Romans 5:17
319   Titus 3:4

power: that the name of our Lord Jesus Christ may be glorified in you, and ye in him, according to the grace of our God and the Lord Jesus Christ."[320]

4. We have to be careful about the language Paul uses to explain grace's consolation. Grace's endeavor is through "power," and the kind of "power" found in the saying, "Not by might, nor by power, but by my spirit, saith the LORD of hosts."[321] The "power" of grace is through the living God's spirit, making justification no literal or natural work, but rather a task occurring within the spirit of the conversation, making it well for us to remember how it says, "That which is born of the Spirit is spirit."[322]

5. What is termed "spirit" is, according to the Bible, defined by the mind, even as it says, "Be renewed in the spirit of your mind."[323] When hearing the term "spirit," we therefore ought to think of "mind," for the two are synonymous terms.

6. This brief breakdown of language is important because *heaven's* will is to have "the Lord Jesus Christ" within the conversation's conscience, even like as it says, "Be ye transformed by the renewing of your mind,"[324] and, "Purge your conscience from dead works to serve the living God."[325] Seeing as how this transformation is mental and spiritual, occurring within conversation's inwards, to hear that the goal of grace is to have "the Lord Jesus Christ" within our faith's mind is to evidently hear of a transaction more profound than the words convey.

7. This transformation through justification is by the living God's spirit, and we do well to remember that "a spirit hath not flesh and bones."[326] The Bible immediately confirms to us that the fulfilling of its new covenant science is through no literal thing, or through no literal *thing* made spiritual. Thus, when hearing that the goal of grace is to have "the Lord Jesus Christ" swallowing up our faith's mind, we may

---

320 2 Thessalonians 1:11,12
321 Zechariah 4:6
322 John 3:6
323 Ephesians 4:23
324 Romans 12:2
325 Hebrews 9:14
326 Luke 24:39

think higher than the words that are spoken, because if by "spirit," then "Jesus Christ" is but a term denoting an end, and we may learn this end by comparing the phrases of certain verses: the first, "The Lord Jesus Christ our Saviour";[327] the second, "The commandment of God our Saviour";[328] the third, "The doctrine of God our Saviour."[329]

8. Herein the Bible may make sense. It does not make sense to imagine some *man* as coming into you, for you to then be considered *just* for some thing. There is no substance behind this thought, but rather a false sense of religious security that can "not make him that did the service perfect, as pertaining to the conscience."[330]

9. When breaking down the Bible's language to comprehend that language's context, we learn that "Christ," or "Jesus Christ," is but a term denoting the living God's new covenant commandment, or the living God's doctrine. Grace's role, then, is in fulfilling the living God's pleasure, which pleasure is in having "Christ," or His wisdom's commandment or doctrine, placed within the heart and mind of the conversation's conscience.

10. Grace is only for the spirit of the conversation's mind. We prove this fact by how it says, "The grace of our Lord Jesus Christ be with your spirit,"[331] and, "The grace of our Lord Jesus Christ be with your spirit."[332]

11. Having now a better understanding of language, to hear that grace flows from out of "Christ" is to hear that grace flows out from *heaven's* new covenant doctrine. Grace is for the spirit of our faith's mind, and if received and applied through the living God's doctrine, then it is not hard to see what grace is for, even like as it says, "The child grew, and waxed strong in spirit, filled with wisdom: and the grace

---

327 Titus 1:4
328 Titus 1:3
329 Titus 2:10
330 Hebrews 9:9
331 Philemon 1:25
332 Galatians 6:18

of God was upon him,"[333] and, "Grow in grace, and in the knowledge of our Lord and Saviour Jesus Christ."[334]

12. To be justified by grace is to be doctrinally cleansed by the refreshing influence of the living God's words upon the conversation's heart. Grace is the living God's rejuvenating influence, and this rejuvenating influence is nothing but knowledge and wisdom added to the personal faith's spiritual understanding.

13. Grace is recorded as being the gift or assisting force of the living God's righteousness. When justified, the conversation is experiencing the living God's righteousness, meaning that creation from His spirit, occurring within our faith's spirit by that spirit, is justifying, or cleansing, or sanctifying, the spirit of our faith's mind.

14. In order for us to claim the promised "newness of spirit,"[335] "Jesus Christ," or the living God's present law and commandment of creation, must be experimented with by faith. Should the conversation faithfully exercise faith on that commandment, it will pick up wisdom and knowledge of *heaven's* intention, which wisdom and knowledge, when further applied and experimented with, adds grace to the inward parts, justifying those inward parts, or transforming the conversation's spiritual understanding into the living God's religious character.

15. Grace is the regenerating influence of the living God's doctrine. When receiving, learning of and proving that doctrine, knowledge of that doctrine's desire will dawn upon the mind. This realization is what opens up grace's door to us, allowing the wisdom obtained through proving the living God's science to become the gift of that science's kindness.

16. Our conversation is indeed justified by grace, that is, cleansed and refined by the wisdom acquired through exercising faith on *heaven's* will. We can therefore have all the faith in the world on whatever we would have faith on, but if that faith is not backed by a personal labor to pick up, learn of, and live the living God's words, that *faith* will not

---

333   Luke 2:40
334   2 Peter 3:18
335   Romans 7:6

lead into grace's realm, where mental rejuvenation for philosophical justification takes place.

17. It is then fair to say that justification occurs through an experimental faith on the Bible's present devotional will and science. Without exercising faith on *heaven's* will, there is no opportunity for grace, but if faithful to the living God's will, grace abounds for justification, making it even more true to say that, without grace, justification fails.

5

Knowledge

1. Justification occurs by one means, and, according to the Bible, that means is through knowledge. We learn this fact from how it says, "By his knowledge shall my righteous servant justify many."[336]

2. This verse is in reference to him that "hath given himself for us an offering and a sacrifice to God for a sweetsmelling savour."[337] Not the man himself, not the physical or literal frame of the man, is given for justification, but, according to the prophet, the knowledge of the man is given for justifying. This then causes us to examine Paul's statement, for he makes it sound as though the man himself is that sacrifice for justification, and this is clearly false to assume.

3. So who is right? Is Isaiah right to say that the knowledge of the living God's chief messenger justifies? Or is Paul right in his statement that the man has given himself a sacrifice for justification? Doubtless Isaiah is correct, leaving it that Paul's statement, without force, must also support Isaiah's, whose statement is also backed by a proverb that says, "Through knowledge shall the just be delivered."[338]

---

336   Isaiah 53:11
337   Ephesians 5:2
338   Proverbs 11:9

4. When examining just what took place on the cross, we will actually learn that the transaction occurring on the cross was not natural, but, being spiritual, was doctrinal. Paul explains to us that the body suspended between heaven and earth should not be viewed as a human body, but rather as a religious philosophy. He forwards this thought by saying, "Having abolished in his flesh the enmity, even the law of commandments contained in ordinances."[339]

5. Herein we cannot forgot how it says, "He that is hanged is accursed of God."[340] According to Paul, what is hanged should be thought of as Moses' religious philosophy of *righteousness* by the religious law, doctrine, tradition, and ordinance.

6. The *body* of that man nailed to the cross represents the spirit of Moses' religion, which religion demands that "righteousness come by the law." To see that body crucified is to see the philosophy of *righteousness, beauty, piety, virtue*, and *favor* by the religious law, crucified. Seeing this philosophy crucified, it is that another philosophy is magnified for replacing what is crucified, which is why it says, "He said, Father, into thy hands I commend my spirit: and having said thus, he gave up the ghost."[341]

7. The transaction occurring is a transaction of *ghosts*. These *ghosts* are minds of philosophical doctrines of devotion. The first *ghost* given up is the *ghost* of Moses' religion, which, according to the Bible, is an "unholy" *ghost*. It is an "unholy" *ghost* because it fails to incorporate the doctrine of the living God's "holy" *ghost*. If, then, through Him abolishing the spirit of Moses' religion from *heaven's* religious character, we learn that "the strength of sin is the law."[342] The philosophy of the religious law, being categorized as "sin," is an "unholy" doctrine, leaving it that the conversation without the philosophy of the religious law is a "holy" conversation.

8. The entire point behind his chief apostle suffering the cross was to expose the difference between the "holy" and the "unholy"

---

339 Ephesians 2:15
340 Deuteronomy 21:23
341 Galatians 2:21
342 1 Corinthians 15:56

conversation. The "unholy" conversation was crucified to the tree, illustrating that the heart and soul of that religious philosophy is abolished from the living God's religious character. But when hearing that, before this "unholy" *ghost* was given up, the living God's man secured the spirit of his conversation to the living God, we are hearing of the fact that a conversation was kept and preserved by the living God, and if preserved by Him, then it has, within it, an acceptable "holy" *ghost*.

9. What makes the philosophy of the religious law so "unholy" is the fact that it does not allow its observer to retain knowledge through an experimental faith. "Without faith it is impossible to please him,"[343] and seeing as how "the law is not of faith,"[344] to handle the philosophy of the religious law is to advance a manner of devotion without faith's course of learning, meaning that the conversation receives no knowledge to justify its mind, keeping the conversation away from the living God's benevolent will and wisdom.

10. So, no, the living God's man did not offer his human or natural flesh to be the literal cause or foundation of *justification*, but rather, according to the Bible's wisdom, the doctrine or science of his conversation's conscience. This is why he says, "It is the spirit that quickeneth; the flesh profiteth nothing: the words that I speak unto you, they are spirit, and they are life,"[345] and, "That which is born of the Spirit is spirit."[346]

11. The use of the man's body is strictly figurative. That body represents the philosophy of the religious law, and nothing more. The crucifixion of that body means the crucifixion of the philosophy of the religious law, which is why it says, "Christ hath redeemed us from the curse of the law, being made a curse for us: for it is written, Cursed is every one that hangeth on a tree."[347]

12. Paul's doctrine is certain and correct, falling into perfect harmony with what is written in the Proverbs and in the book of Isaiah.

---

343   Hebrews 11:6
344   Galatians 3:12
345   John 6:63
346   John 3:6
347   Galatians 3:13

What was sacrificed was the knowledge of a minister's spiritual conversation, and if our conversation would know the justification of that man's conversation, we do well to let our natural reliance upon Moses' train of thought suffer a crucifixion also, which is why it says, "Christ is become of no effect unto you, whosoever of you are justified by the law; ye are fallen from grace."[348]

13. The philosophy nailed to the cross actually contradicts that philosophy secured to the living God, which secured doctrine preaches creation not "through the law, but through the righteousness of faith."[349] "Christ," or the doctrine of *heaven's* kindness upon the conversation's conscience, because it needs an experimental faith to activate it, cannot be known to the conversation enslaved by traditional religious thought and feeling. "Christ" is given "to redeem them that were under the law,"[350] and if yet subject to the philosophy of the religious law, then we cancel the redemption intended by *heaven's* science.

14. Justification is redemption. According to the living God's wisdom, the conversation is to be redeemed or justified from what that crucified body represents. This redemption occurs only in the spirit of the mind, because the war is not flesh-based, but is inward, within the mind of the personal faith. This is why our conversation is "to be strengthened with might by his Spirit in the inner man."[351] This is the pattern of that man's example that suffered the cross, and if we should follow it, our conversation must also suffer a certain *death* to know a certain *resurrection*.

15. What is to suffer resurrection is the spirit of our faith's mind, which is why it says, "Be renewed in the spirit of your mind,"[352] and, "Like as Christ was raised up from the dead by the glory of the Father, even so we also should walk in newness of life."[353]

16. The goal is newness of *life* or of conversation. Naturally, we all are born under the religious law of some religious denomination, and

---

348   Galatians 5:4
349   Romans 4:13
350   Galatians 4:5
351   Ephesians 3:16
352   Ephesians 4:23
353   Romans 6:4

are willingly enslaved by the cogitations of theological philosophers. *Heaven's* goal is the resurrection of our faith›s *body* from traditional religious theories to a more personal experience with creation's present doctrine. This is why our conversation is counseled, "Put off concerning the former conversation the old man...and be renewed in the spirit of your mind; and that ye put on the new man, which after God is created in righteousness and true holiness."[354]

17. Our conversation, according to Paul's statement, is naturally "unholy." Why is it naturally "unholy"? It is "unholy" because it naturally handles the formerly abolished religious philosophy. This abolished religious philosophy teaches that "you are justified by the law,"[355] yet with His chief messenger suffering the cross and confirming that "the strength of sin is the law,"[356] it is that all *justification* coming from the religious law is false, making justification through the knowledge of *heaven's* science a true fact, and every conversation justified by knowledge a "holy" conversation.

18. Therefore "Christ is become of no effect unto you, whosoever of you are justified by the law; ye are fallen from grace,"[357] or are fallen from the knowledge of salvation's present will and effect. To take *justification* by the religious law alters the definition of justification, making it seem as though if there is no belief in the handwritten ritual, baptism, or doctrine, that one is unclean before *God*. But according to the Bible's spiritual understanding, the conversation ruled by the ritual, the doctrine, or the baptism, is actually unclean, and is in need of repenting of such a service in order to claim the intended mental and spiritual renewing.

19. Service to the religious law kills any hope of receiving grace. Why? Because service to the religious law conquers and destroys the mental faculties, grace is solely for the spirit of the mind. When handling the religious law, we are actually handling what prevents the free exercise of faith for knowledge to live by. Our proving that knowledge

---

354   Ephesians 4:22-24
355   Galatians 5:4
356   1 Corinthians 15:56
357   Galatians 5:4

acquired by faith is what actually unseals grace to our conversation's conscience. Grace makes the knowledge we retain easy to receive for mental and spiritual regeneration. If dedicated to the religious law, our mind, being determined to do what is handwritten for a *reward*, is taken away by what is handwritten, keeping it from retaining truly redemptive knowledge.

20. The goal is the mind's redemption from a false philosophical standard. Have we never once thought about what is to suffer redemption, or what we are to be redeemed from? Our mind is to be redeemed from what the living God sees is injurious. "Having abolished in his flesh the enmity, even the law of commandments contained in ordinances,"[358] confirming that "the strength of sin is the law,"[359] it is that redemption and deliverance is to be from what is abolished, even from the philosophy of the religious law.

21. When justified, the conversation's conscience is cleansed and removed from what the living God presently categorizes as "sin," which "sin" is the philosophy of the religious law. Our redemption is forwarded by grace, and grace is only activated by knowledge of salvation's science, which knowledge is to redeem and deliver the conversation's mind from practicing what is nailed to the tree.

22. We ought to therefore remember that no body presently hangs on the cross, but rather a religious philosophy is nailed to it. The *body* that should be there is no longer there, but is in the living God's direct presence. Our responsibility is not to that practice nailed to the cross, but to that preserved mind ascended into the living God's heavenly Sanctuary.

23. The doctrine of this *body* is our conversation's mediator for grace, meaning that, without crucifying our *earth-born* religious *body*, we cannot experience the intended creation within our faith's mind. It is then our present privilege to know creation through the mind of that ascended *body* for knowledge to live by.

---

358   Ephesians 2:15
359   1 Corinthians 15:56

6

Justification

1. The definition of justification is redemption. It is common to perceive the weight of justification through tradition's spiritual paradigm, that, so long as one believes on *Jesus* in a special way, one is justified to receive the promises that come with accepting *Jesus* as an all in all *sacrifice* and *substitute*. Traditional religion would have its supporter believe that the literal flesh of a man holds the key to *justification*, but when observing redemption's course through the Bible's lens, we learn that this deduction is but a false and illogical assumption.

2. Why is it a false and illogical assumption to believe that justification is through the sacrificed flesh of a man? One answer is that, seeing as how the system of sacrificing animals was not pleasing to the living God, what good would the sacrificed flesh of a human being be? Even at that time when the sacrifice of an animal was believed to be a *divine* prerequisite for *righteousness*, *beauty*, and *pardon*, the living God yet said, "I desired mercy, and not sacrifice; and the knowledge of God more than burnt offerings."[360]

3. Paul also rationalizes this fact in many of his discourses. He proves the unnecessary nature of the belief on sacrificed flesh for

---

360   Hosea 6:6

justification by mentioning that "the law having a shadow of good things to come, and not the very image of the things, can never with those sacrifices which they offered year by year continually make the comers thereunto perfect. For then would they not have ceased to be offered? because that the worshippers once purged should have had no more conscience of sins. But in those sacrifices there is a remembrance again made of sins every year."[361]

4. Paul's argument is that the belief on sacrificed flesh should have proved itself to be a valid theory of redemption if the doers of the practice remained without the knowledge of their error within their conscience. But because so many repeated their errors, and because there was a dedicated day to handle religious errors once every year, the flaw in the system of sacrifices and ordinances is that they did not intelligently or thoroughly move their doer away from their wrong, because, failing to heal the inward person, they ultimately cannot intelligently or thoroughly move their doer away from religious error.

5. The living God is not, in a real way, within that former manner of sacrifice. The sacrifice, in and of itself, being written as a *divine* sentence for *pardon* and *favor*, must be believed on as being a divine sentence for atonement to *God*. To do the service, one must believe that they do the service in the sight of *God*, and that as *God* sees, and that as *God* smells the burning sacrifice, that they are then "good" before him. That one must then turn away from the day's events to strengthen their own inward parts by the faith that *God* sees, smells, and has pardoned. Yet, the probability that that one will do again what needed a sacrifice is very high, because there is no true sense of wrong for correction in the sacrificial system, or in the system of ordinances.

6. This is Paul's logic, and it is correct. So now, with knowledge of that rationale, and also knowing that the Bible's spiritual understanding did not care for gifts and sacrifices "which stood only in meats and drinks, and divers washings, and carnal ordinances, imposed,"[362] "how much more shall the blood of Christ, who through the eternal

---

361 Hebrews 10:1-3
362 Hebrews 9:10

Spirit offered himself without spot to God, purge your conscience from dead works to serve the living God?"[363]

7. How is it that the blood of this man may purge the conversation's conscience? The saying is figurative, in that what was figuratively sacrificed opens up the person to receive what that former age of religion could not, namely, the hope of a perfect personal religion that is "perfect, as pertaining to the conscience."[364]

8. We have to remember that, when speaking about what should rise and revive, the living God's chief messenger "spake of the temple of his body."[365] The body nailed to the cross figuratively represents one religious conversation internally holding two religious philosophies. Within that one *body* is the philosophy that "you are justified by the law"[366] and the philosophy that "by the works of the law shall no flesh be justified."[367]

9. When crucified, one *ghost*, or one religious philosophy must pass away, and the other must continue within the *body*. And this indeed happened. "Having abolished in his flesh the enmity, even the law of commandments contained in ordinances,"[368] it is witnessed that "the strength of sin is the law,"[369] and that His "Christ hath redeemed us from the curse of the law,"[370] teaching us that justification is no longer to be thought of as occurring "through the law, but through the righteousness of faith."[371]

10. With the *ghost* of the philosophy of the religious law sacrificed and abolished from the living God's religious character, that preserved temple of His chief apostle's conversation is magnified as being the mediator for *heaven's* new covenant promise. Herein justification is

---

363 Hebrews 9:14
364 Hebrews 9:9
365 John 2:21
366 Galatians 5:4
367 Galatians 2:16
368 Ephesians 2:15
369 1 Corinthians 15:56
370 Galatians 3:13
371 Romans 4:13

proved as proceeding not from the literal flesh of a man, but through the spiritual understanding of a slain minister.

11. Justification, as opposed to being traditionally flesh-based, is biblically mental and spiritual. The image of a crucified man is only intended to clarify the figurative illustration of that crucifixion. The body of the man is only relevant due to what it represents.

12. That body represents a minister's religious conversation. Within that one conversation are two trains of spiritual thought. We can't forget that this man, while saying, "I am in the Father, and the Father in me,"[372] "made himself of no reputation, and took upon him the form of a servant, and was made in the likeness of men."[373] To be made in the likeness of *men* is to be "made under the law,"[374] therefore within this one conversation sat the principles of righteousness with and without the religious law.

13. How then can we know that this man's likeness to ministers, and not to the living God, prevailed? Said another way, how can we know that the philosophy of the religious law was actually abolished and that it does not yet continue? We find our answer from how it says, "I will raise them up a Prophet from among their brethren, like unto thee, and will put my words in his mouth; and he shall speak unto them all that I shall command him."[375]

14. When the foreshadowed Prophet should fulfill his ministry, he should conduct it according to the words of the living God's science. The foundation of that science, should we examine creation, is an experimental faith on His voice for a regenerating knowledge to live by. To hear, "He commanded, and they were created,"[376] is to hear of creation occurring through none other instrument or medium than the living God's *voice*. The use, then, of the religious law, is a philosophy not found at creation, making it sure that His Prophet, when finally

---

372   John 14:11
373   Philippians 2:7
374   Galatians 4:4
375   Deuteronomy 18:18
376   Psalm 148:5

pronounced, should educate on creation's science to verify the religious character of that science found at the beginning.

15. And this Prophet did just that. When he spoke, he made sure to say such things as, "Have faith in God,"[377] and, "That which is born of the Spirit is spirit,"[378] and, "I know that his commandment is life everlasting,"[379] and, "Sanctify them through thy truth: thy word is truth,"[380] and, "I know him, and keep his saying."[381] When also speaking to *men*, he judged their *nature* by saying such things as, "Full well ye reject the commandment of God, that ye may keep your own tradition,"[382] and, "Cleanse first that which is within the cup and platter, that the outside of them may be clean also."[383]

16. When therefore inquiring about what doctrine was magnified by the passing of this man's body on the cross, we ought to trust that the religious philosophy preaching *cleanliness* by way of flesh-based acts should be that doctrine to pass away, for it contradicts the living God's religious character. This is why Paul could conclude that, "having abolished in his flesh the enmity, even the law of commandments contained in ordinances,"[384] His "Christ hath redeemed us from the curse of the law, being made a curse for us: for it is written, Cursed is every one that hangeth on a tree."[385]

17. Truly, then, justification is a sure thing, and only occurring through the knowledge of that resurrected and magnified *temple*. Herein we learn just what is on the living God's mind, even the sanctification of our conversation's conscience. In order to know this sanctification, the conversation must pick up and handle the philosophy of that mind ascended to Him. It is then no understatement to hear

---

377   Mark 11:22
378   John 3:6
379   John 12:50
380   John 17:17
381   John 8:55
382   Mark 7:9
383   Matthew 23:26
384   Ephesians 2:15
385   Galatians 3:15

and consent to the counsel, "Behold my hands and my feet, that it is I myself: handle me, and see."[386]

18. When therefore "just," the conversation mirrors the conversation of *heaven's* chief minister. This conversation is a mind of devotion chasing newness of spiritual thought and feeling not through the philosophy of the religious law, but by an experimental faith on the doctrine preached through the illustration of him suffering the cross. The "just" conversation is created by no other medium than the active and examined impression of the experience of that illustration upon the mind, making justification a baptism for the inward person and not for the natural form.

---

386 Luke 24:39

7

For Doing So

1. The question of justification by faith is not the issue, but the question of what one is justified by faith in, is. According to the Bible's spiritual understanding, the spirit of the personal religious conversation is the subject of justification. There is then no physical or traditional *thing* that one can do or believe on for *justification*, but so long as the conversation's conscience experiences the doctrine of *heaven's* elect conversation, it will receive the intended justification to claim the status of "just."

2. If "just," the spirit of the conversation's conscience is being "perfected." We learn this fact from how it says, concerning the conversation joined to the conversation of the living God's chief apostle, "Ye are come unto mount Si'on, and unto the city of the living God, the heavenly Jerusalem, and to an innumerable company of angels, to the general assembly and church of the firstborn, which are written in heaven, and to God the Judge of all, and to the spirits of just men made perfect."[387]

3. If applying for justification, one submits their conversation's disposition to *heaven's* disposition for becoming "perfect, as pertaining

---

to the conscience."[388] The spirit of the conversation's mind is justification's concern, therefore if "just," or if in the classroom of the "just," it is that our conversation's mind is transitioning from faith on an abolished religious philosophy to faith on a commandment preserved, magnified, and ascended into the living God's direct presence.

4. And this is why grace is such an important aspect of the Bible's spiritual wisdom. Grace assists the mind in its transition from *earth's* religious character to *heaven's* religious character. Grace's balm makes the knowledge we acquire through faith easily acceptable for a resurrection and reform in spiritual thought and feeling, adding comfort to our faith's mind as we grow accustomed to carrying self without "meats and drinks, and divers washings, and carnal ordinances."[389]

5. The justifying of the mind cannot occur without grace. There is a reason why, when mentioning grace, the apostle would have us know that our faithfulness to self, and to one another, must join to "the grace of life."[390] Justification is a process of bringing the conversation into a new phase of "life" or "being," and when assisted by grace, it is that the conversation, being edified by the knowledge retained by faith, is led safely on its journey to being "conformed to the image of his Son."[391]

6. A new phase of "being" cannot commence unless the mind is handled and convinced. Herein is the reason why there is a call to crucify our natural inclination to rely on the philosophy of the religious law for *knowledge* and confidence of heavenly things. Hereafter we do well to remember that "if ye be led of the Spirit, ye are not under the law."[392]

7. We may know whether or not our conversation belongs to the assembly of the "just." We but need to answer certain questions: "If ye be dead with Christ from the rudiments of the world, why, as though living in the world, are ye subject to ordinances...after the commandments and doctrines of men?"[393] or, "Having begun in the Spirit, are ye

---

388   Hebrews 9:9
389   Hebrews 9:10
390   1 Peter 3:7
391   Romans 8:29
392   Galatians 5:18
393   Colossians 2:20-22

now made perfect by the flesh?"[394] or, "Received ye the Spirit by the works of the law, or by the hearing of faith?"[395] or, "After that ye have known God, or rather are known of God, how turn ye again to the weak and beggarly elements, whereunto ye desire again to be in bondage?"[396]

8. When "just," the conversation is "holy," relying on the living God's voice without any handwritten religious *thing*. If "just," our conversation, like that *body* passed away on the tree, has passed away from the philosophy of the religious law.

9. "The strength of sin is the law,"[397] and if "just," the conversation's conscience recognizes that the philosophy of the religious law is "sin" to *heaven's* will and wisdom. The "just" therefore carry self away from what the living God categorizes as "sin," mentally and spiritually perfecting their personal religion through an experimental faith in His present commandment.

10. When naturally conceived, our conversation is born into "sin's" domain, making the *body* of our faith naturally "sinful." Being born under the religious world's umbrella, all we know are the doctrines of the religious world, and how those doctrines teach, "You are justified by the law."[398] But now, having knowledge that the living God categorizes the spirit and philosophy of the religious world as "sin," the "just" responds to this revelation by crucifying that *body* born from the religious world's philosophy, accepting mental resurrection by the doctrine ascended into the living God's presence.

11. This is exactly what is taught by the illustration of the living God's minister suffering the cross, even the *death* of the conversation's mind for the regeneration of the conversation's mind. Herein is why it says, "If we have been planted together in the likeness of his death, we shall be also in the likeness of his resurrection: knowing this, that our old man is crucified with him, that the body of sin might be destroyed,

---

394   Galatians 3:3
395   Galatians 3:2
396   Galatians 4:9
397   1 Corinthians 15:56
398   Galatians 5:4

that henceforth we should not serve sin. For he that is dead is freed from sin."[399]

12. The goal is to be devotionally liberated from what the living God categorizes as "sin." "Having abolished in his flesh the enmity, even the law of commandments contained in ordinances,"[400] it is that "the strength of sin is the law,"[401] therefore with the philosophy of the religious law revealed as the present definition of "sin," it is that the conversation is to be liberated from the spirit of the religious law, making the conversation "just" for doing so.

13. When "just," the conversation is dead to the philosophy of the religious law. Because the philosophy of the religious law is "sin" to *heaven's* will and wisdom, to be dead to the philosophy of the religious law is to be dead to "sin." To be *dead* to "sin" is to be alive to the living God's righteousness, and if alive to His manner of righteousness, then alive to "abundance of grace and of the gift of righteousness,"[402] fulfilling a labor and conversation in likeness to the living God's religious character.

14. If, then, motivated by what the living God categorizes as "sin," we possess an "unjust" religious conversation. If motivated by handwritten religious prescriptions to execute our *zeal* for *God*, we possess an "unjust" religious conversation. If unable to consciously spiritually function without religious laws, baptisms, rites, traditions, doctrines, concepts, and commandments, we are in possession of an "unjust" religious conversation, seeing as how "if ye be led of the Spirit, ye are not under the law."[403]

15. The living God's wisdom moves the conversation away from depending on what is handwritten, the reason being because the living God's wisdom is more concerned with a living experience above a dictated practice. The "just" conversation therefore only knows how it is counseled, "Be not conformed to this world: but be ye transformed

399　Romans 6:5-7
400　Ephesians 2:15
401　1 Corinthians 15:56
402　Romans 5:17
403　Galatians 5:18

by the renewing of your mind, that ye may prove what is that good, and acceptable, and perfect, will of God."[404]

16. The "just" conversation rebels against the conventional course or manner of *righteousness*. Their rebellion is actually the rebellion illustrated in the vision of creation's chief apostle suffering the cross. This rebellion is against the religious world's standard of *righteousness* and *beauty* by the religious law, and if, in the figure of his body, the living God's man, when dying, abolished the religious world's standard, then he has left us an example to follow, in that our conversation must pass away from the religious world's spiritual philosophy to take up and put on *heaven's* acceptable disposition.

17. To crucify that conversation depending on traditional religious prescriptions for its *righteousness* is to enter into the assembly of the "just." And there is, and will be, an immediate fear of being *naked*, and of not having any *thing* to clothe or repair the conversation we willingly injure. There is no fear; the preserved conversation of the living God's chief apostle is the substitute and repairing experience we are to take knowledge of. Our security for justification is in the experience of that resurrected conversation, to know it.

---

404   Romans 12:2

8

To Be

1. What, then, does it mean to be "just"? We further understand the definition of being "just" by comparing certain verses:

2. The first, "There is a vanity which is done upon the earth; that there be just men, unto whom it happeneth according to the work of the wicked; again, there be wicked men, to whom it happeneth according to the work of the righteous: I said that this also is vanity."[405]

3. The second, "For all this I considered in my heart even to declare all this, that the righteous, and the wise, and their works, are in the hand of God: no man knoweth either love or hatred by all that is before them."[406]

4. The third, "Who is a wise man and endued with knowledge among you? let him shew out of a good conversation his works with meekness of wisdom."[407]

5. The fourth, "Who is wise, and he shall understand these things? prudent, and he shall know them? for the ways of the LORD are

---

405   Ecclesiastes 8:14
406   Ecclesiastes 9:1
407   James 3:13

right, and the just shall walk in them: but the transgressors shall fall therein."⁴⁰⁸

6. According to these verses, the "just" are categorized with the "righteous," the "prudent," and the "wise." To be "just" is to be "wise," "prudent," and "righteous" towards the living God's knowledge. To be "just" is to therefore be spotlessly knowledgeable about the living God's wisdom and intention. And why should it matter that the "just" is knowledgeable about *heaven's* course of learning? The answer is simple: "Through knowledge shall the just be delivered."⁴⁰⁹

7. When "just," the conversation, growing fond of "the knowledge of his will in all wisdom and spiritual understanding,"⁴¹⁰ knows and is careful for the intention behind living God's spiritual wisdom. The Bible associates the "just" with the "wise," making them synonymous. The "just" are "wise" and "righteous" because they do *heaven's* knowledge, which knowledge is the living God's righteousness, which righteousness is the decreed deliverance. This is why it says, "Through knowledge shall the just be delivered."⁴¹¹

8. The "just" are "just" due to their experience in the knowledge of the intended righteousness. This is why it says, "He that doeth righteousness is righteous, even as he is righteous,"⁴¹² and, "If ye know that he is righteous, ye know that every one that doeth righteousness is born of him."⁴¹³

9. What then, if doing righteousness equates to the decreed deliverance for becoming "just," does it mean to do righteousness? If "this is the will of God, even your sanctification,"⁴¹⁴ then to do righteousness is to apply the conversation's thoughts and feelings to what increases its experience in that sanctification. Therefore "having abolished in his flesh the enmity, even the law of commandments contained in

408   Hosea 14:9
409   Proverbs 11:9
410   Colossians 1:9
411   Proverbs 11:9
412   1 John 3:7
413   1 John 2:29
414   1 Thessalonians 1:3

ordinances,"[415] we know what to abstain from in order to observe that sanctification. Thus, since "the strength of sin is the law,"[416] "now we are delivered from the law, that being dead wherein we were held; that we should serve in newness of spirit, and not in the oldness of the letter."[417]

10. In order to do righteousness, the conversation must not do what that crucified body of the living God's chief apostle represents. That crucified body, figuratively representing the philosophy of the religious law, reveals the annihilation of the saying, "You are justified by the law."[418] Being, then, "delivered from the law, that being dead wherein we were held; that we should serve in newness of spirit, and not in the oldness of the letter";[419] our conversation puts off that *body* depending on handwritten religious laws and doctrines for its *justification*, putting on a new *body* created in the living God's knowledge, which knowledge is the living God's praise, justness, or righteousness.

11. The annihilation of the religious law, as Paul says, opens us up to observe a better and more fulfilling experience. So long as our conversation rests in the philosophy of the religious law, it is *dead*. The illustration of the living God's *man* suffering and regenerating from the death of the cross explains the regeneration our personal spiritual understanding must experience. Our conversation's conscience is to then be delivered from the religious philosophy that dying body represents. This deliverance leads to the intended sanctification, redeeming the conversation's mind to claim the status of "just."

12. To do righteousness is to do just what the example of His chief apostle suffering the cross teaches. What is taught by this act is as Paul says: "Put off concerning the former conversation the old man...and be renewed in the spirit of your mind; and that ye put on the new man, which after God is created in righteousness and true holiness."[420]

---

415 Ephesians 2:15
416 1 Corinthians 15:56
417 Romans 7:6
418 Galatians 5:4
419 Romans 7:6
420 Ephesians 4:22-24

13. To do righteousness is to thoughtfully learn how to put on that new *mind* of spiritual understanding. The first step of righteousness is to kill that mind relying on what that dead body on the cross figuratively represents. The next step of righteousness is to, now being free from spiritual slavery, feel and experience the Bible's words to refresh the mind's spiritual understanding. The last step of righteousness is to prove the Bible's words by the knowledge we acquire through steps one and two, allowing that knowledge to deliver our spiritual understanding from a false religious experience.

14. This is the living God's righteousness; this is what is called, "The *kingdom* of *heaven.*" This "kingdom" is but the domain, rule, reign, or government of *heaven.* The living God's righteousness is the rule of His science within the conversation's conscience. In order for this rule to take place, the conversation must *die* to the rule naturally inhabiting its mind, which rule demands that "righteousness come by the law."[421]

15. With His minister's *body* suffering and regenerating from the cross, we know that "by the works of the law shall no flesh be justified,"[422] teaching us the eternal fact that His "Christ hath redeemed us from the curse of the law."[423] With that body on the cross representing the philosophy of the religious law, when that body is dead, so too is the philosophy of the religious law to the personal religion. With our faith's *body* now *dead* to that philosophy, our mind may now capture the living God's vision for justification, that it is through personally knowing His *voice*, even like as it says, "By his knowledge shall my righteous servant justify many."[424]

16. Herein the Bible has correctly defined justification for us. This is why, when His chief messenger spoke on *heaven's* manner of justification, he said, "Except your righteousness shall exceed the righteousness of the scribes and Pharisees, ye shall in no case enter into the kingdom of heaven."[425]

---

421 Galatians 2:21
422 Galatians 2:16
423 Galatians 3:13
424 Isaiah 53:11
425 Matthew 5:20

17. What is the *righteousness* of the scribes and Pharisees? At another time, he told them their *righteousness*, saying, "Full well ye reject the commandment of God, that ye may keep your own tradition."[426] Yet he also told them his righteousness, saying, "I know him, and keep his saying."[427]

18. Two different religious perspectives are here revealed: the first is that *righteousness* is defined through doing handwritten religious commandments and traditions; the second is that righteousness is through knowing and keeping the living God's saying. These two religious perspectives are completely opposite, where one would have the doer believe that the judgment of ancient and modern priests and ministers is the only the route to a *beautiful* and *favorable* acceptance before *God*, and where the other would have the doer understand that the knowledge retained and exercised from learning of and proving the Bible's words freshly creates and regenerates the conversation's conscience for a pleasing service.

19. According to the Bible's spiritual understanding, righteousness is defined as the rejuvenation and refreshing of the conversation's conscience through knowing and growing familiar with that present spiritual understanding. A false *righteousness* is applying the conversation to a handwritten routine for supposed divine *favor*. Such a *righteousness* is not the living God's righteousness, who, desiring to resurrect the mind from that crucified religious routine, counsels, "Be not conformed to this world: but be ye transformed by the renewing of your mind, that ye may prove what is that good, and acceptable, and perfect, will of God."[428]

20. The course of the religious world is to seek *righteousness* through handwritten religious laws, traditions, and ceremonies. This *righteousness* is fraudulent because it, in addition to drowning the heart in pride, and cultivating within the person an insensitive, self-serving, complacent self-righteous spirit, adds a false sense of security to the thoughts and feelings. And the living God's chief apostle was not shy

---

426   Mark 7:9
427   John 8:55
428   Romans 12:2

about stating this fact, saying such things as, "Ye Pharisees make clean the outside of the cup and the platter; but your inward part is full of ravening and wickedness."[429]

21. With the body of this man representing the philosophy of the religious law, when that body takes its last breath, so too does the philosophy of the religious law. Hereafter the culture of the inward person should receive attention. Hereafter creation not "through the law, but through the righteousness of faith,"[430] should take place. Hereafter the "just" are discerned by their willingness to be "written not with ink, but with the Spirit of the living God,"[431] which is why it says, "If ye be led of the Spirit, ye are not under the law."[432]

22. To be "just," then, is to be mentally and spiritually liberated from the philosophy of the religious law to "be filled with the knowledge of his will in all wisdom and spiritual understanding."[433] Paul therefore clearly articulates the statement of the "just," saying, "The law of the Spirit of life in Christ Jesus hath made me free from the law of sin and death."[434]

---

429 Luke 11:39
430 Romans 4:13
431 2 Corinthians 3:3
432 Galatians 5:18
433 Colossians 1:9
434 Romans 8:2

9

Justification's Key

1. The goal of salvation's science is to create the conversation, and not the natural person or the human being, "righteous." Due to a failure to examine language and context, it is generally taught and believed that the person or the human being is to be *just* or *righteous*. If salvation's science is for making the person "perfect, as pertaining to the conscience,"[435] then it is evident that the conversation's conscience, and not the human being, is the subject of salvation's science.

2. If summing up *heaven's* intention, it would be fair to say that the living God's intention is to "purge your conscience from dead works to serve the living God."[436] The issue at hand is mentally and spiritually purging the conscience from *dead* "works." How may we know what these "dead works" are? It's simple: "having abolished in his flesh the enmity, even the law of commandments contained in ordinances,"[437] His "Christ hath redeemed us from the curse of the law,"[438] meaning that "the sting of death is sin; and the strength of sin is the law."[439]

---

435   Hebrews 9:9
436   Hebrews 9:14
437   Ephesians 2:15
438   Galatians 3:13
439   1 Corinthians 15:56

3. "Death" equals "sin." "Sin" equals the philosophy of the religious law." The philosophy of the religious law equals "death." To commit "sin" is to practice the philosophy of the religious law. To execute "dead works" is to then commit "sin," "and the strength of sin is the law."[440]

4. "Dead works" are labors of "sin," and with it presently understood that "the strength of sin is the law,"[441] when executing the law of "sin" and "death," the conversation is executing handwritten religious rules or standards "through philosophy and vain deceit, after the tradition of men."[442] The "just" are considered to be "righteous" because they are wise to what "sin" and "death" is, and being wise to what is crucified and passed away, they set their affection on the law that the living God has set in "sin" and "death's" place, which law is the commandment of salvation's benevolent science.

5. The conversation's conscience is salvation's subject. The mind, and not firstly the human being, is to be "righteous." If, then, "all unrighteousness is sin,"[443] and if "the strength of sin is the law,"[444] then doing the philosophy of the religious law makes the conversation "unrighteous." We may then know that, if possessing a conversation without the philosophy of the religious law, our conversation is "righteous," and if "righteous," "just."

6. *Heaven's* intention is to have sincere worshippers of its will and wisdom. The only way to do so is through pruning and purging the conversation's conscience. To properly prune and purge the mind, it must pass through a certain course of learning, which is why knowledge is justification's key, even like as it says, "By his knowledge shall my righteous servant justify many."[445]

7. Herein the Bible corrects traditional religious theories referencing the subject of justification. To the Bible's mind, justification is through knowledge. Seeing as how "when wisdom entereth into thine

---

440   1 Corinthians 15:56
441   1 Corinthians 15:56
442   Colossians 2:8
443   1 John 5:17
444   1 Corinthians 15:56
445   Isaiah 53:11

heart, and knowledge is pleasant unto thy soul; discretion shall preserve thee, understanding shall keep thee";[446] the definition of justification is revealed to be the cleansing of the conversation's conscience for knowledge to live by.

8. Knowledge to guide and direct the personal and devotional *body* is justification's intention. To justify the conscience is to therefore sanctify the conscience, making that mind of devotion more relatable to the living God's religious character. And this is the point of salvation's science, for the conversation "to be strengthened with might by his Spirit in the inner man"[447] for being "conformed to the image of his Son."[448]

9. The image of His chief apostle is no physical or natural image. To take on this minister's *image* is for the conversation's conscience to be mentally transformed into his religious character. What then is this minister's *image*? He tells us by saying, "I know him, and keep his saying."[449]

10. There is a difference between this man's religious nature and the nature of the religious world. This man's nature states, "I know him, and keep his saying";[450] the religious world's nature states, "You are justified by the law."[451] Is it therefore right to associate this man's religious character with the religious world's character? Let him answer for us. He says, "I pray not for the world,"[452] and, "I am not of the world."[453]

11. Our conversation is to take on the image or likeness of this man's religious character. This minister did not practice the routine of priests and ministers, whose routine was to fulfill the saying, "This people draw near me with their mouth, and with their lips do honour

446 Proverbs 2:10,11
447 Ephesians 3:16
448 Romans 8:29
449 John 8:55
450 John 8:55
451 Galatians 5:4
452 John 17:9
453 John 17:16

me, but have removed their heart far from me, and their fear toward me is taught by the precept of men."[454]

12. If dawning this man's *image*, our conversation has become *dead* to taking righteousness from what is handwritten by theologians to say, "I have suffered the loss of all things, and do count them but dung, that I may win Christ, and be found in him, not having mine own righteousness, which is of the law, but that which is through the faith of Christ, the righteousness which is of God by faith: that I may know him, and the power of his resurrection, and the fellowship of his sufferings, being made conformable unto his death."[455]

13. The key, then, to a "just" or "righteous" conversation, is as Isaiah and Paul say. If conformed to the *image* of *heaven's* chief apostle, the *body* of our conversation reflects that chief apostle's spiritual understanding. That spiritual understanding is the knowledge of the living God's righteousness, that His intention is to sanctify our conversation's conscience that that mind, from learning of and proving that righteousness, may, both personally and devotionally, possess a kind wisdom governing our thoughts, feelings, actions, and behaviors.

14. But to possess a "just" or "righteous" conversation, the conversation's conscience must *die* to what His chief apostle died to. We understand what he died to through him figuratively "having abolished in his flesh the enmity, even the law of commandments contained in ordinances."[456] This is why it is important to know that the knowledge of this minister's conversation was sent and given "to redeem them that were under the law."[457]

15. When therefore a patient of salvation's science, the conversation's conscience is undergoing a process of mental and spiritual redemption from the philosophy of the religious law, which philosophy is the law of "sin" and of "death." When "just," the conversation is "righteous" because it lives according to the knowledge it acquires by exercising faith on the words of salvation's science. Our conversation

---

454   Isaiah 29:13
455   Philippians 3:8-10
456   Ephesians 2:14
457   Galatians 4:5

is therefore "just" and "righteous" when it ultimately accepts that His "Christ hath redeemed us from the curse of the law."[458]

16. It basically comes down to how we will govern our faith's mind and *body*. With His minister suffering the cross, two manners of devotion are revealed to us: the first is that *justification* occurs through doing handwritten deeds, laws, and commandments; the second that justification occurs through no religious law or doctrine, but through knowledge acquired by actively exercising faith on the Bible's words. The second manner is the correct one, seeing as how "through knowledge shall the just be delivered."[459]

17. Our conversation's conscience is to be delivered from the first mentioned manner of devotion. This deliverance from *justification* through handwritten religious deeds, laws, and commandments is the point or end of salvation's science.

18. As the mind proves the illustration of His chief messenger suffering and regenerating from the cross, that mind is to experience a refreshing in its spiritual understanding to awaken it to *heaven's* righteousness. This awakening is an enlightenment moving the conversation to act by the knowledge it retains above the handwritten coercion of religious deeds and theories. Our conversation is to possess and spiritually genuine conscience, and this is what is it means to be "just."

19. Our ability to consciously function without the spirit of traditional religious deeds and theories is the reason why His "Christ is the end of the law for righteousness."[460] If truly believing on the illustration of His man suffering the cross, the mind believes that, with that body figuratively representing the philosophy of the religious law, it is time for it to suffer the same crucifixion to the religious world's doctrine for becoming familiar with the living God's manner of devotion. And this is absolute fact, which is why Paul clearly states, "God forbid that I should

---

458   Galatians 3:13
459   Proverbs 9:11
460   Romans 10:4

glory, save in the cross of our Lord Jesus Christ, by whom the world is crucified unto me, and I unto the world."[461]

20. Paul possess the mind of the "just." This mind is crucified to the spirit and theology of the religious world, which spirit and philosophy that body nailed to the cross embodies. If therefore correctly celebrating that body's passing on the cross, the conversation demonstrates its thanksgiving by personally crucifying what that body figuratively illustrates.

21. With it is then understood, from him suffering the cross, that "the sting of death is sin; and the strength of sin is the law";[462] the "just" conversation will refrain from entertaining the philosophy of the religious law to personally know the living God's benevolence. Salvation's science is the mental and spiritual regeneration of the conversation's conscience: to execute this science by an experimental faith for knowledge to live by is to possess a "wise," "righteous," and "just" conversation, but to do so through the philosophy of the religious law is to take *justification* through a "dead" service, which service is presently, and for ever categorized as "sin," making the conversation executing it, "unrighteous."

461   Galatians 6:14
462   1 Corinthians 15:56

10

When Justified

1. True justification, according to the Bible's mind, is the process of unlearning the religious world's *spiritual* custom for *righteousness* to learn of and experience the living God's intention for the conversation' s conscience. If "justified," the conversation's mind is undergoing a process of mental and spiritual regeneration from the religious world's *spiritual* operation, and for the purpose of growing familiar with the living God's mind to claim the kindness of that mind's will for the inward person.

2. If, then, *salvation* is "not by works of righteousness which we have done, but according to his mercy he saved us, by the washing of regeneration, and renewing of the Holy Ghost,"[463] then salvation is strictly held or confined to the spirit of the conversation's mind. The mind is to suffer a renewing and regeneration, and this is the definition of justification, which is why it says, "By his knowledge shall my righteous servant justify many."[464]

3. When "justified," the conversation's conscience is cleansed from the religious world's approach to *righteousness*. What transpires is a

---

463   Titus 3:5
464   Isaiah 53:11

refreshing of the conversation's spiritual understanding, which is why it is important to mentally consent to acquiring knowledge of the living God's religious character.

4. The illustration of salvation's chief minister suffering the cross teaches us this fact about justification, which is why Paul writes, "Like as Christ was raised up from the dead by the glory of the Father, even so we also should walk in newness of life. For if we have been planted together in the likeness of his death, we shall be also in the likeness of his resurrection: knowing this, that our old man is crucified with him, that the body of sin might be destroyed, that henceforth we should not serve sin."[465]

5. Having a clear understanding of what the crucifixion figuratively illustrates, Paul preaches the foundation of salvation's science. With that body, when found nailed to the cross, representing a conversation alive to the philosophy of the religious law, when not only passed away, but found regenerated and without the cross, being taken from *earth* and ascended into the living God's heavenly Sanctuary, the regeneration of the conversation's conscience from what that crucified and dead body represents is preached.

6. So if our faith's *body* suffers the same crucifixion as that body, then our faith's *body* is become *dead* to what that crucified body represents, which representation confirms that "the strength of sin is the law."[466] If, then, our conversation is raised with that body, then our faith's *body* has forgotten about that crucified *body* of "sin" to pick up a conversation without "sin." This new conversation possesses a new mind for how to experience *heaven's* righteousness, learning that salvation is not "through the law, but through the righteousness of faith."[467]

7. When learning by faith, the mind experiences loss of self's traditional comprehension for concrete knowledge. When learning by faith, the mind is learning of and proving the new covenant's commandment for wisdom to direct the thoughts, feelings, actions, and behavior. The righteousness of faith is the pleasure that is received through personally

---

465   Romans 6:4-6
466   1 Corinthians 15:56
467   Romans 4:13

handling the Bible's words, which pleasure, both publicly and privately, "is charity out of a pure heart, and of a good conscience, and of faith unfeigned."[468]

8. Salvation's science knows what it is doing. In order to better our person, in order for us to possess genuine and unfailing confidence in the living God, in order for us to possess, for both self and other minds, a charitable conscience, our conversation's conscience must suffer a mental and spiritual refreshing.

9. A false religion encourages *mental* and *spiritual* sovereignty and security through deeds and acts evincing one's *sincere* religious genius. But this is the *righteousness* of the scribes and Pharisees, of whom it says, "All their works they do for to be seen of men,"[469] and, "Full well ye reject the commandment of God, that ye may keep your own tradition."[470]

10. To the religious world, "a shew of wisdom in will worship, and humility, and neglecting of the body; not in any honour to the satisfying of the flesh";[471] reveals the *righteous* and the *just* person. In addition to mindlessly following the handwritten religious judgment of ancient and modern priests and ministers, the person is deemed *righteous* and intimately connected to *God* when commanding the will through religious laws. This is evidently a false manner of devotion, seeing as how "by the deeds of the law there shall no flesh be justified in his sight."[472]

11. To take *justification* through what priests and ministers concoct is to actually violate the living God's doctrine. "Having abolished in his flesh the enmity, even the law of commandments contained in ordinances,"[473] "the strength of sin is the law,"[474] meaning that "the

468   1 Timothy 1:5
469   Matthew 23:5
470   Mark 7:9
471   Colossians 2:23
472   Romans 3:20
473   Ephesians 2:15
474   1 Corinthians 15:56

righteousness of God without the law is manifested,"[475] confirming that "by the works of the law shall no flesh be justified."[476]

12. Justification, then, according to the Bible's spiritual understanding, takes on a different definition from what is preached within the religious world. To take knowledge of the living God's chief minister suffering the cross is to take knowledge of justification's true operation, that it is a process of mentally and spiritually ridding the conversation's conscience of the belief to let "righteousness come by the law."[477]

13. When "justified," the conversation is without the religious world's philosophy of righteousness and of *unrighteousness*. *Righteousness*, to the religious world, is doing what is handwritten for communion with what is *divine*. The *unrighteous* conversation therefore possesses a demeanor, or a spiritual conscience, that will not do what is handwritten, which is why they looked at the living God's chief apostle as a transgressor, saying to him, "Why do thy disciples transgress the tradition of the elders?"[478]

14. Was this man a transgressor? If it says, "He was numbered with the transgressors,"[479] then yes, this minister, to the religious world, was the greatest transgressor that ever lived. But why was he considered to be a transgressor? Why did they say of him, "We found this fellow perverting the nation"?[480] The answer is found in the question, "Why do thy disciples transgress the tradition of the elders?"[481]

15. To the religious world, one is a *transgressor*, or is a *sinner*, when failing to do the religious doctrine, law, or tradition given by theologians. This man was a transgressor because he taught that true creation and true justification didn't come from doing what was handwritten, but what was engraved upon the heart from personally handling the

475 Romans 3:21
476 Galatians 2:16
477 Galatians 2:21
478 Matthew 15:2
479 Isaiah 53:12
480 Luke 23:2
481 Matthew 15:2

living God's words. This is why it says, "We speak, not in the words which man's wisdom teacheth, but which the Holy Ghost teacheth."[482]

16. The "justified" mind does not follow the spiritual standard of the unjustified mind. The "justified" mind lives from what it is taught by the experience it has with the living God's words. The living God's chief apostle was considered to be a *transgressor* because his doctrine taught the liberty of the conversation's conscience for knowledge to direct the thoughts and feelings, causing many conversations to say, "Why is my liberty judged of another man's conscience?"[483]

17. When this famous *transgressor* spoke, he informed his audience that there is a greater Judge than priests and ministers. This man taught the people that there was a greater Law and Doctrine to observe than the many burdensome and irrationally flesh-based laws and commandments of priests and ministers. That greater Law and Doctrine is creation's new covenant commandment, which states, "That which is born of the Spirit is spirit,"[484] and, "Be renewed in the spirit of your mind."[485]

18. Herein the true condition, process, and aim of justification is revealed. To hear that spirit gives birth to spirit is to hear a doctrine questioning the philosophy of priests and ministers, who claim that by physically doing and believing on their handwritten code, *birth* to *God* commences and remains undefiled. Salvation's chief messenger therefore taught a different doctrine, that if in communion with the living God's wisdom, not the body, or the tradition of the body is *justified*, but that the spirit of the mind is "just," showing that "if ye be led of the Spirit, ye are not under the law."[486]

19. No matter what angle the Bible's spiritual understanding is examined at, it leads back to this one point, that His "Christ hath redeemed us from the curse of the law."[487] If therefore faithfully executing that spiritual understanding, the conversation will pass away

---

482   1 Corinthians 2:13
483   1 Corinthians 10:29
484   John 3:6
485   Ephesians 4:23
486   Galatians 5:18
487   Galatians 3:13

from the notion of *birth* through religious theories to accept and experience birth through the spirit of its mind.

20. This mental and spiritual regeneration is the definition of justification. The mind is to be "justified" or "sanctified" from the philosophy of the religious law. The conversation's conscience is to be "redeemed" or "delivered" from the religious world's definition of *justification* and *righteousness*. When "just," the mind is then passing through a process of mental and spiritual purification to retain not the doctrinal or conversational likeness of priests and ministers, but of the living God's religious character, and of His chief apostle, who says, "I know him, and keep his saying."[488]

21. If our conversation only knows "the commandments and doctrines of men,"[489] our conversation is not "justified." If our conversation only knows religious "philosophy and vain deceit, after the tradition of men, after the rudiments of the world,"[490] our conversation is not "justified." If our conversation does not know that the illustration of the living God's chief minister suffering the cross teaches a doctrine "to redeem them that were under the law,"[491] then our conversation is not "justified." If our conversation presently believes that "you are justified by the law,"[492] our conversation does not possess a "justified" mind or conscience.

22. Justification's definition is the mental and spiritual resurrection of the conversation's spiritual understanding. If presently ignorant to the fact that "the strength of sin is the law,"[493] by maintaining a conversation through the philosophy of the religious law, we maintain an observance through "sin," making our conversation a transgressor to the living God's religious character.

23. Justification is the process of transforming the conversation from being a "transgressor" to being "just." The conversation, when handling what that crucified body represents, is a "sinful" or

---

488 John 8:55
489 Colossians 2:22
490 Colossians 2:8
491 Galatians 4:5
492 Galatians 5:4
493 1 Corinthians 15:56

"transgressing" conversation, but when refraining from that abolished religious philosophy to know the living God's religious character, the conversation is on the track of the "just," for it suffers the loss of "sin" for knowledge to regenerate its spiritual understanding.

24. When "justified," the mind is resurrecting from one religious philosophy into the operation of another. Justification is for the inward person, that when knowledgeable of the living God's spiritual wisdom, that inward person may, for providing a clear demonstration of the living God's will for that mind directing the personal and devotional *body*, kindly edify minds that are outside it.

11

Love

1. Justification, then, although being a process of mental and spiritual regeneration from what is presently categorized as "sin," is more than simply being a process of inward rejuvenation on the Bible's doctrine. What matters, according to the Bible's spiritual understanding, is how one's justification is used.

2. The purpose of justification is the sanctification of the conversation's conscience, but what good is a sanctified mind if it only benefits the person? It is good and well to re-educate the conversation's mind on the living God's doctrine, because then the person may know how to care for their personal and spiritual bodies. But if this is the end of justification, why even bother with it? If the goal is to only settle the individual condition, and without considering the devotional condition of other minds, why even bother selfishly aggravating self to become more intelligent on "love's"saying?

3. Justification is the definition of the living God's "love" towards us. When understanding that *heaven's* intention is to "purge your conscience from dead works to serve the living God,"[494] we are seeing the living God's definition of "love," which is why our conversation is

counseled, "Let every one of us please his neighbour for his good to edification,"[495] and, "Love thy neighbour as thyself."[496]

4. How does the living God define "love"? He defines love through mental and spiritual edification. Justification is the definition of the living God's "love" because when "justified," the conversation's conscience is edified. The saying, "By his knowledge shall my righteous servant justify many,"[497] is then but a confession revealing the living God's "love," for through knowledge the mind is trained and edified on how to carry and better govern its self, allowing us to understand that there is no greater truth than that "through knowledge shall the just be delivered."[498]

5. Again, to further refine the definition of "love," that "love" is but defined as mental edification on the living God's doctrine for ideological regeneration, we compare two verses: the first, "Ye yourselves are taught of God to love one another";[499] the second, "Wherefore comfort yourselves together, and edify one another, even as also ye do."[500]

6. To "love" is to "edify." When "loved" of the living God, the spirit of the conversation's mind is passing through an experience of being edified on His religious character, and through that edification is also edified on the condition of the conversation's present *nature*. Herein is why it says, "I will pour water upon him that is thirsty, and floods upon the dry ground: I will pour my spirit upon thy seed, and my blessing upon thine offspring,"[501] and, "I will pour out my spirit unto you, I will make known my words unto you."[502]

7. From observing these two verses in the book of Isaiah and in the book of Proverbs, we learn that when "blessed" of the living God, or when in communion with His Spirit, an outpouring of His words upon the mind occurs. This outpouring of words is the outpouring of

495   Romans 15:2
496   Leviticus 19:18
497   Isaiah 53:11
498   Proverbs 11:9
499   1 Thessalonians 4:9
500   1 Thessalonians 5:11
501   Isaiah 44:3
502   Proverbs 1:23

the knowledge of the living God's doctrine, even like as it says, "My doctrine shall drop as the rain, my speech shall distil as the dew, as the small rain upon the tender herb, and as the showers upon the grass."[503]

8. When "loved" of the living God, an outpouring of the words of His doctrine falls upon the mind. The conversation "loved" of the living God should then be recognized as a conversation that is "blessed" by Him. In being "blessed," the conversation is edified, and in being edified, the conversation is "loved," and when "loved," the conversation is undergoing justification's process.

9. The conversation "justified" by the living God's doctrine, being a conversation "loved" by His spiritual wisdom, is "justified," or undergoes a process of spiritual re-education, to do for other minds what the living God has done for its mind. This is why it says, "Owe no man any thing, but to love one another,"[504] and, "By this shall all men know that ye are my disciples, if ye have love one to another."[505]

10. If disciples of salvation's science, the demonstration of our fellowship with its wisdom and intention is seen through our conversation refreshing others through the course it is refreshed in. When once "justified" and entered into the *world*, our conversation ought to make many minds confess, "We have great joy and consolation in thy love, because the bowels of the saints are refreshed by thee, brother."[506]

11. Justification is the process whereby the conversation's conscience is purified from the religious world's doctrine and *spiritual* operation, but the end of justification is an active ministry edifying the religious world's spirit and assembly. Is this not the task of the "justified"? Isn't it written, "As thou hast sent me into the world, even so have I also sent them into the world"?[507]

12. How was this minister sent into the religious world? He gives us the answer to this question by saying, "For their sakes I sanctify myself,

---

503 Deuteronomy 32:2
504 Romans 13:8
505 John 13:5
506 Philemon 1:7
507 John 17:18

that they also might be sanctified through the truth,"[508] and, "Him, whom the Father hath sanctified, and sent into the world."[509]

13. The living God's chief apostle, before beginning his public ministry, first embraced justification's process of edification. This minister, before giving his personal religious philosophy as an example of *heaven's* acceptable conversation, sanctified that conversation's mind through learning of and doing the living God's new covenant commandment. Herein is why he says, "I know him, and keep his saying."[510]

14. There is a reason why it says of this minister, "Blessed is he that cometh in the name of the Lord."[511] This man was "blessed" because his conversation was edified by the living God's doctrine. He is acknowledged as being "blessed" because the words of the living God's religious character rested with him and came from out of his doctrine, which is no surprise, because when prophesying of him, the living God said, "I will raise them up a Prophet from among their brethren, like unto thee, and will put my words in his mouth."[512]

15. This saying reveals that a Rabbi from out Moses' religious tradition would rise and be doctrinally separate from the ministers of that priesthood's religious philosophy. Herein we may understand that this man should indeed embrace justification's process of purification, seeing as how the words of the living God are not the words of the Jews' priesthood and religious philosophy.

16. This minister, before placing his doctrine in the religious world, truly refreshed his spiritual understanding, resurrecting in thought and feeling from them that said, "We are Moses' disciples."[513] This man was not Moses' disciple, but was a disciple of the living God's Word and Wisdom. This Word and Wisdom taught mental and spiritual liberty from the philosophy of the religious law for a purifying knowledge to personally and devotionally live by, which is why he taught, "That

---

508   John 17:19
509   John 10:36
510   John 8:55
511   Matthew 21:9
512   Deuteronomy 18:18
513   John 9:28

which is born of the Spirit is spirit,"[514] and, "If ye be led of the Spirit, ye are not under the law."[515]

17. The fact that this minister should come from out of the Jews' priesthood reveals that, in order to fulfill the vision pronouncing his conversation, his conversation must quit and regenerate from the philosophy of Jews' religion. And this is no foreign thought, for even Paul made a similar confession, saying, "Ye have heard of my conversation in time past in the Jews' religion...and profited in the Jews' religion above many my equals in mine own nation, being more exceedingly zealous of the traditions of my fathers. But when it pleased God, who separated me from my mother's womb...immediately I conferred not with flesh and blood."[516]

18. The course of the "just" is unchanging. The conversation must, as Paul says, separate from the *womb*, which *womb* is but the natural traditional spiritual understanding that conversation is *born* into.

19. As Paul put off the Jews' religion, so too did the living God's chief apostle. The reason why His chief messenger is noted as being "the beginning, the firstborn from the dead,"[517] and "the firstborn among many brethren,"[518] is because he is the first to perfectly demonstrate the genius behind the living God's manner of justification.

20. Paul only followed this minister's example. This man, before any other minister thought to silence Moses for Abraham's mind of devotion, put off the Jews' religious tradition for salvation's kind science, executing the living God's commandment of sanctification, opening his conversation up to fulfill the revelation of that Prophet that should come and utter the knowledge of the living God's *name*.

21. All who heard this man knew that his doctrine was the living God's manner of "love." Every priest and minister thinking on the illustration of his saying knew that the voice of that Prophet foreshadowed to appear presently echoed in the temples of that age. And they

514 John 3:6
515 Galatians 5:18
516 Galatians 1:13-16
517 Colossians 1:18
518 Romans 8:29

knew that this was that Prophet because his doctrine caused the mind to contemplate the possible imprisonment it suffered under the Jews' religion, which is why they sought to kill him, because he exposed the difference between the religious world's *spiritual* character and the nature of the living God's religious character.

22. As opposed to enslaving the mind by what is handwritten, the conversation's conscience is to be "written not with ink, but with the Spirit of the living God; not in tables of stone, but in fleshy tables of the heart."[519] The inward person is to have the living God's religious character, and the law and science of that religious character, engraved upon it, and if "that which is born of the Spirit is spirit,"[520] then "if ye be led of the Spirit, ye are not under the law."[521]

23. Having his conversation's conscience sanctified on the living God's true character and intention, this minister, now possessing a conversation perfectly reflecting the *image* of the living God's religious character, stepped out into the religious world, to edify it, and according to the manner in which the living God had edified his mind of devotion. If therefore a disciple of his doctrine, our conversation, like Paul's, will follow his faith's character, fulfilling the saying, "Follow after the things which make for peace, and things wherewith one may edify another."[522]

24. Justification's higher education is only preparing the conversation to fulfill the ministry it is born to execute. Every mind is not the same, and every experience is not the same. Justification's purification is for revealing self to the person, that the person may not only learn how to correctly personally and devotionally care for self, but that by learning how to do so, a spirit of genuine empathy may arise within the mind to deliver a charitable service edifying minds like as it was, and still is being, edified.

25. Justification's course and goal is then the greatest demonstration of "love" that we have from the living God. In this one manner of mental and spiritual learning our inward person is healed by knowledge

---

519   2 Corinthians 3:3
520   John 3:6
521   Galatians 5:18
522   Romans 14:19

to learn how to personally and spiritually live acceptably. The conversation passing through this course of reform will undoubtedly begin to feel for other minds without knowledge of it, causing it to act as the living God acts towards it, giving the saying of its experience to others for convincing them of the personal reform they must make in order to know *heaven's* kind "love."

12

Creation's Term

1. So when determining the meaning of "justification," or of being "just" or "justified," to keep the meaning of these terms in the context of the Bible's language helps to better highlight their purpose or intention. When therefore looking to define one who is "just" or "justified," we then do well to look to how it says, "How then can man be justified with God? or how can he be clean that is born of a woman?"[523]

2. When "just," one is clean, orderly, spotless, or clear with or before "God." This notion of being "clear" with or before "God" is mentioned in the saying, "I acknowledge my transgressions: and my sin is ever before me. Against thee, thee only, have I sinned, and done this evil in thy sight: that thou mightest be justified when thou speakest, and be clear when thou judgest."[524]

3. To be "justified" is to be clear or blank; the only issue is in being clear or blank or spotless from what? Justification is a cleansing from some *thing* separating the conversation's conscience from the Bible's language and context. When "just" or "justified," one is clean from some *thing*; what is that *thing*?

---

523   Job 25:4
524   Psalm 51:3,4

4. David and Job help us to understand what one is to be justified from: to Job, one must be justified of a *woman*; to David, one must be justified of "sin" against the living God. This conclusion of what to be justified from is a fair and correct conclusion, because, when taking into account that the living God's chief apostle was "made of a woman, made under the law,"[525] and that, though him suffering the tree, it is taught that "the strength of sin is the law,"[526] with "sin" being the philosophy of the religious law, it is evident that the "just" possess a conversation without the philosophy of the religious law.

5. A *woman*, in the language of the Bible, figuratively illustrates a church, even like as it says, "As the church is subject unto Christ, so let the wives be to their own husbands in every thing,"[527] and, "The names of them were Aho'lah the elder, and Ahol'ibah her sister: and they were mine, and they bare sons and daughters. Thus were their names; Samar'ia is Aho'lah, and Jerusalem Ahol'ibah."[528] To be born of a *woman* is to therefore be born under a religious tradition drawing relevance through the philosophy of the religious law.

6. To be born under a *woman* is, as Paul says, to possess a spiritual conversation formed by a religious tradition under the philosophy of the religious law. Now, to be, as Paul says, made under the law, is to also be "made in the likeness of men."[529] To be made in the likeness of *men*, or to be made *of* ministers, is to pick up the philosophical nature of ministers, which nature is best understood from how it says, "All their works they do for to be seen of men,"[530] and, "Full well ye reject the commandment of God, that ye may keep your own tradition."[531]

7. To be made in the likeness of *men* is to adopt and practice a religious conversation "through philosophy and vain deceit, after the tradition of men."[532] When therefore hearing Job ask the question

---

525   Galatians 4:4
526   1 Corinthians 15:56
527   Ephesians 5:24
528   Ezekiel 23:4
529   Philippians 2:7
530   Matthew 23:5
531   Mark 7:9
532   Colossians 2:8

of cleanliness for a *man* born under a *woman*, he is asking how the likeness of a *man*; how the nature of a minister's religious conscience and conversation; may be "justified" or become spotless to suit the living God's religious character. And David answers the question! That conversation may become "just" when willing to say, "I acknowledge my transgressions: and my sin is ever before me."[533]

8. Again, with the living God "having abolished in his flesh the enmity, even the law of commandments contained in ordinances,"[534] and acknowledging and confirming that "the strength of sin is the law,"[535] the purpose of justification is seen as being a process of inward devotional sanctification "to redeem them that were under the law."[536] When therefore "just," one is clean or clear from the taint of that abolished religious philosophy, opening up the conversation to become perfect in its operation, and "perfect, as pertaining to the conscience."[537]

9. The term "just," if willing to be consistent and correct in the Bible's spiritual understanding, is a term that should not be associated to the human being. What is to suffer justification is not ultimately the human being, but the spirit of the devotional mind, which is why when joined into the class of souls embracing creation's higher learning, we are joined into the class of "the spirits of just men made perfect."[538]

10. The spirit of the mind is the subject of justification. This allows us to know that when "just," the mind is clean and clear of religious error, being without trace of "sin," that is, without relying on the philosophy that "you are justified by the law."[539]

11. So, how can one born of a *woman* be "justified"? It is only through a process of acknowledging and dying to "sin" so that the conversation's conscience may regenerate and reform from "sin." The answer to this question is found in the illustration of the living God's chief minister suffering the cross, who, figuratively crucifying

533   Psalm 51:3
534   Ephesians 2:15
535   1 Corinthians 15:56
536   Galatians 4:5
537   Hebrews 9:9
538   Hebrews 12:23
539   Galatians 5:4

and annihilating the philosophy of the religious law from his personal spiritual understanding, resurrected from that crucified philosophy, carrying that resurrected mind into the living God's direct presence, even like as it says, "Christ is not entered into the holy places made with hands...but into heaven itself, now to appear in the presence of God for us."[540]

12. The correct context of the term "justification," according to the Bible, is as we have been studying. When "just," the conversation's conscience passes through a stage of doctrinal purification to learn how to stay away from what is presently defined as "sin." Because every conversation is born under some *woman*, it is our responsibility to know that, if that conversation should be considered "just," it must revive and reform from theoretical theological assumptions on the Bible's wisdom to know, for a fact, what reality is; the "just" conversation endures a stage of knowing the foundation of the Bible's wisdom.

13. So then we ought to know whether or not the spirit of our conversation's mind is "just"? If our spiritual thoughts and feeling are under the philosophy of the religious law, our conversation is not "just." If our faith's mind cannot exist without explanations "after the commandments and doctrines of men,"[541] our faith's mind is not "justified." If our conversation would mindlessly let "righteousness come by the law,"[542] that conversation has never passed through justification's course, and is yet without acknowledging the point behind the revelation of the living God's man suspended between heaven and earth.

14. The goal is to be clear or clean or spotless from what the living God presently defines as "sin." Isn't this the living God's will for our faith's mind? Isn't this why it says, "And you, that were sometime alienated and enemies in your mind by wicked works, yet now hath he reconciled in the body of his flesh through death, to present you holy and unblameable and unreproveable in his sight: if ye continue in the faith grounded and settled"?[543]

---

540   Hebrews 9:24
541   Colossians 2:22
542   Galatians 2:21
543   Colossians 1:21-23

15. Paul is teaching us that, with the living God "having abolished in his flesh the enmity, even the law of commandments contained in ordinances,"[544] we too ought to think of our natural religious conversation as joined to that dead *body*. Being joined to that dead *body*, we are also gathered into that resurrected *body*. Being one with that resurrected *body*, our conversation has no memory of the *body* it was formerly servant to, and Paul makes this point very clear, saying, "But now we are delivered from the law, that being dead wherein we were held; that we should serve in newness of spirit, and not in the oldness of the letter."[545]

16. The issue at hand, to Paul, is what that body on the cross ultimately represents. That body has within it two religious philosophies, and when seeing the man die, it is as seeing one religious philosophy passing away, but when observing the *man* risen and gathered into the living God's direct presence, we are seeing the magnification of the preserved religious philosophy.

17. Being figuratively reconciled into this man's *body* means being joined into the same manner of *death* and *resurrection*. When suffering with this body in *death*, the mind of our religious conversation is passing away from relying on the religious theories and prescriptions of the religious world's theologians. When resurrecting with this *body*, the mind of our religious conversation is liberated from handwritten *spiritual* theories to take full knowledge of the living God's words for wisdom to live by.

18. Our conversation, embracing this reform in understanding, serves and honors the Bible's wisdom with a new and more conscious mind of devotion. This new mind of devotion is the product of redemption, meaning that it is the product of justification.

19. The goal is to have, within every conversation honoring the Bible' present science, the creation of a new mind of service similar not to the religious world, but to the living God's religious character. The term defining this goal is called "justification," and when the

---

544   Ephesians 2:15
545   Romans 7:6

conversation wholeheartedly defines its mind by this term, that conversation is recognized as being "just."

20. Thus, in order to beautify the mind of our spiritual understanding, we have a present responsibility to shed the *skin* of that false religious practice received from *women*. To do so is to accept the conditions for possessing a "just" mind of devotion, fulfilling the living God's intention behind his law and wisdom of *life*.

13

For A Habitation

1. So, like as our primary enemy is our own self, we ought to pick up the mind that the primary enemy to our faith's mind is that mind of devotion naturally given to us by the religious world. In essence, if looking to advance in the Bible's wisdom, we do well to understand that we are at war with our own spiritual self, and if we should win the battle, we must let that natural spiritual self pass away, even like as it says, "He that loveth his life shall lose it; and he that hateth his life in this world shall keep it unto life eternal."[546]

2. Ever since the living God openly categorized "sin" for us, a counsel appeared, informing us to check the manner of our spiritual understanding, if it is covered in *white* apparel, or if it is dressed in stained and spotted clothing. With it understood that our present warfare is against our natural spiritual understanding, we ought to know that the goal is to be free of that artificial spiritual nature, even like as it says, "He that overcometh, the same shall be clothed in white raiment."[547]

3. This language is figurative. If the mind of our faith is the subject of justification, then it is that our conversation's conscience must dawn

---

546   John 12:25
547   Revelation 3:5

a *white* covering over it. This *white* covering is a religious character "justified" by the living God's wisdom: it is the fulfilling of the saying, "He hath covered me with the robe of righteousness,"[548] which "robe," or which religious character, is "arrayed in fine linen, clean and white: for the fine linen is the righteousness of saints."[549]

4. This *white* garment or "robe" is the symbol of a clean spiritual understanding. Before receiving it, our spiritual understanding stands *naked*, with figs and leaves as an apron barely covering our faith's members. When able to overcome self's natural spiritual understanding, this garment is given to our mind to separate it from the religious world. To have this *white* "robe," or to possess a "just" spiritual understanding, is to then have the mind of devotion without "sin," allowing our journey in the Bible's wisdom to be as undefiled as our sincere obligation to it.

5. This is important to know because, as we would not like our natural body to be seen naked, so too we should take greater care to have our spiritual *body* clothed and in order. To have the spiritual *body* naked is to have our human condition without counsel or guidance, leading to the public revelation of our uneducated, thoughtless, and merciless character. Our natural self acts according to the image of our spiritual self, therefore if lacking a sound spiritual philosophy, the members of our self will physically demonstrate their person through a careless disposition.

6. The end of justification is a mind acting and behaving in edifying ways. The mind edified by the living God is a mind that has experienced much personal or inward sorrow and forgiveness. This experience allows that mind to generate a certain level of empathy for minds at war with their own self and not fully knowing the controversy they are born in to. Such a mind, learning of its frailty to discover its strength, knowing the trouble of self, extends a benevolent spirit to other minds, serving them for regenerating their intelligence to soberly think and feel for who and what they are, and without the influence of secular or sectarian society.

---

548   Isaiah 61:10
549   Revelation 19:8

7. With the end of justification being a sincere demonstration of "love," it is evident that, this mind of demonstration being associated only with that "robe" of the living God's righteousness, if ever without that "robe," we cannot execute the living God's manner of righteousness. It is then incumbent upon every willing mind to endure the process of becoming "just," because if it says, "As thou hast sent me into the world, even so have I also sent them into the world,"[550] we ought to bear a mind revealing our communion with a course of learning above the religious world's spiritual philosophy.

8. And so the intention behind justification is not hard to discern. When Paul says, "That he might redeem us from all iniquity, and purify unto himself a peculiar people, zealous of good works,"[551] and, "We are his workmanship, created in Christ Jesus unto good works, which God hath before ordained that we should walk in them,"[552] it is obvious that justification's science is for a ministry mirroring the mission of the living God throne, even like as it says, "See, saith he, that thou make all things according to the pattern shewed to thee in the mount."[553]

9. If willing to become "just," one is willing to have their conversation's mind become a temple similar to the fashion of the living God's heavenly Temple. Is this false to say? Doesn't it say, "In whom ye also are builded together for an habitation of God through the Spirit"?[554] Isn't it written, "God hath said, I will dwell in them, and walk in them; and I will be their God, and they shall be my people"?[555]

10. Justification is the process of constructing a soul-temple in likeness to the living God's heavenly Sanctuary. The reason why justification is a course of learning causing the mind to refrain from "sin" is because the temple under construction cannot operate by a religious philosophy contrary to that heavenly Temple's religious character. The mission of justification is for the person to do inwardly what Moses did physically, and this man set up a tabernacle in the midst of a wilderness.

---

550   John 17:18
551   Titus 2:14
552   Ephesians 2:10
553   Hebrews 8:5
554   Ephesians 2:22
555   2 Corinthians 6:16

11. Is not our natural spiritual understanding an empty and barren land? If our natural religious conversation were already *just*, then it would not be wrong to believe that "you are justified by the law,"[556] but "if righteousness come by the law, then Christ is dead in vain."[557] Therefore "having abolished in his flesh the enmity, even the law of commandments contained in ordinances,"[558] "the strength of sin is the law,"[559] confirming that the natural religious conversation is indeed a barren and useless spiritual landscape.

12. As Moses built, in the wilderness, a temple in likeness to the living God's Sanctuary, so too it is our responsibility to construct, with that heavenly Sanctuary's present wisdom, a temple in the midst our barren spiritual understanding in likeness to it. Herein is the reason why justification appears to be so inwardly and mentally taxing, because in order to beautify our *building*, our labor needs precious gifts and jewels to forward its construction, even like as it says, "And they came, every one whose heart stirred him up, and every one whom his spirit made willing, and they brought the LORD'S offering to the work of the tabernacle of the congregation, and for all his service, and for the holy garments."[560]

13. There is a reason why it says, "By his knowledge shall my righteous servant justify many."[561] The key to justification is taking knowledge of the Bible's wisdom for knowledge to practically exercise and live by. The knowledge retained by learning of and proving the Bible's wisdom goes to the construction of our soul's temple, and to the construction of that *white* "robe." Every principle learned by exercising faith on salvation's science is an offering given to the building of our faith's temple, making it all the more important to know that one is "just" not "through the law, but through the righteousness of faith."[562]

---

556   Galatians 5:4
557   Galatians 2:21
558   Ephesians 2:15
559   1 Corinthians 15:56
560   Exodus 35:21
561   Isaiah 53:11
562   Romans 4:13

14. By truly examining the purpose of justification, it is inarguably witnessed that our conversation's conscience is to be "built up a spiritual house, an holy priesthood, to offer up spiritual sacrifices, acceptable to God by Jesus Christ."[563] This is truly a revolutionary thought, because who advised the ancient temple in the wilderness? Was it Moses? Was it Aaron? Or was it not Him that said, "There I will meet with thee, and I will commune with thee from above the mercy seat, from between the two cher'ubims which are upon the ark of the testimony, of all things which I will give thee in commandment unto the children of Israel"?[564]

15. What is taught through the science of justification is the construction of a spiritual *body* in likeness to that *body* before the living God's throne, and the construction of a temple in likeness to the living God's heavenly Sanctuary. As that *body* before the living God presently assumes Aaron's office in the heavenly Sanctuary, so the mind of our spiritual *body* is to assume Moses and Aaron's position, becoming the high priest and counselor for the internal and physical members of our heart and body. Justification is then, although beginning within the mind of the spiritual *body*, for the good of the human condition's natural mind.

16. This makes obtaining that *white* "robe" for our faith's members very important. Because, what minister, of that former age, could enter into the tabernacle without suitable raiment and without clean limbs? Isn't it written, "They made coats of fine linen of woven work for Aaron, and for his sons"?[565] And doesn't it say, "When they go into the tabernacle of the congregation, they shall wash with water, that they die not; or when they come near to the altar to minister, to burn offering made by fire unto the LORD"?[566]

17. Justification is only given to purify the spiritual *body* so that it can safely tend to the inward temple under construction. The spiritual *body* is to keep the devotional understanding's temple in order, communing with that temple's purified knowledge from within that

---

563   1 Peter 2:5
564   Exodus 25:22
565   Exodus 39:27
566   Exodus 30:20

temple for principles of government. As the laws of Moses directed the congregation, so the principles of personal and devotional life acquired by the spiritual *body* is to direct the congregation of the natural heart and mind, making the demonstration of that *body's* transformation evident, and the witness of the Temple it mirrors indisputable.

18. So like Moses did not altogether concoct a philosophy out of his own heart, but invented what presumably mirrored the character of the mind he examined, so too our spiritual *body*, for the security of our faith's temple, must only examine the religious character it is born to adopt. Our spiritual mind must, according to the Bible's spiritual understanding, suffer a resurrection in thought and feeling in order to successfully become "just." And again, we do this through taking personal knowledge of that understanding, even like as it says, "Put on the new man, which is renewed in knowledge after the image of him that created him."[567]

19. The product of this doctrinal renewing is the reception of a *white* covering over our conversation's conscience. We need this change of raiment if we should honestly govern the habitation under construction, seeing as how this *building* will be the *place* our faith's mind receives instruction on how to govern and comfort self.

---

567   Colossians 3:10

14

The New Song of
Rest and Refreshing

1. The name of the Father will be engraved within the mind of the believer of "Christ," for he said, "I am come in my Father's name,"[568] and, "I have declared unto them thy name."[569]

2. Scripture says, "The Spirit, which they that believe on him should receive,"[570] for it says, "To them gave he power to become the sons of God, even to them that believe on his name."[571] It is written, "The Spirit of the LORD caused him to rest,"[572] for if we have believed the saying of the living God's "love," then we do enter into His "rest" by His wisdom, and as "the spirit of truth, which proceedeth from the Father,"[573] adds power and refreshing to the inward person, that same Spirit ushers the reformer into reverence for the blessed Sabbath and Memorial of that Spirit's will and intention.

---

568   John 5:43
569   John 17:26
570   John 7:39
571   John 1:12
572   Isaiah 63:14
573   John 15:26

3. If the reformer should believe on "Christ," then the conversation professing his doctrine should not be without the living God's *name* or wisdom. His chief apostle came to tell the religious world that "God is light,"[574] for the Jews did fulfill the saying, "The name of God is blasphemed among the Gentiles through you."[575]

4. Jewish priests and ministers mistreated the living God's *name*. "Her priests have polluted the sanctuary, they have done violence to the law,"[576] it says, for they prospered by "teaching for doctrines the commandments of men."[577] "But when the fullness of the time was come, God sent forth his Son."[578] Thus, "The time is fulfilled, and the kingdom of God is at hand,"[579] he said, "repent ye, and believe the gospel."[580] This is why "we which have believed do enter into rest."[581]

5. "He that is entered into his rest, he also hath ceased from his own works,"[582] for we know that "a man is not justified by the works of the law,"[583] that is, by "meats and drinks, and divers washings, and carnal ordinances,"[584] which are but "meats"[585] of "divers and strange doctrines."[586] To labor after *divine favor* is to strive after a false form of religion. The reformer lives "as seeing him who is invisible"[587] through faith in His wisdom's operation, that they may know "rest" for magnifying that wisdom's *name*, even as it is said, "Hallowed be thy name."[588] If we have entered into "rest" then we know that "the righteous, and the wise, and their works, are in the hand of God,"[589] which is why

---

574   1 John 1:5
575   Romans 2:24
576   Zephaniah 3:4
577   Mark 7:7
578   Galatians 4:4
579   Mark 1:15
580   Mark 1:15
581   Hebrews 4:3
582   Hebrews 4:10
583   Galatians 2:16
584   Hebrews 9:10
585   Hebrews 13:9
586   Hebrews 13:9
587   Hebrews 11:27
588   Matthew 6:9
589   Ecclesiastes 9:1

creation's science is told, "Put my name upon the children of Israel; and I will bless them."[590]

6. This "rest" is born out of the refreshing of the Bible's wisdom, which refreshing is the washing and renovation of the conversation's conscience to "shew forth the praises of him who hath called you out of darkness into his marvelous light."[591] It is by this wisdom that grace is poured upon the mind, even as it says, "There shall be showers of blessing."[592]

7. The living God ordained life "in Christ, when he raised him from the dead, and set him at his own right hand in heavenly places,"[593] allowing it to be fulfilled, "The LORD shall send the rod of thy strength out of Zion,"[594] for it says, "My grace is sufficient for thee: for my strength is made perfect in weakness."[595] Hereafter "the power of Christ,"[596] and, "with all might, according to his glorious power,"[597] is to keep the conversation "strengthened with might by his Spirit in the inner man."[598] The rod of "Christ" is creation's wisdom bearing the material of justification's force, which force is grace, seeing as how out of "Zion, the city of our solemnities,"[599] comes "all spiritual blessings in heavenly places."[600]

8. "We which have believed do enter into rest."[601] The believing reformer is blessed through "Christ," for the saying, "God which worketh in you,"[602] is now understood. For this cause, "he that loveth

590   Numbers 6:27
591   1 Peter 2:9
592   Ezekiel 34:26
593   Ephesians 1:20
594   Psalms 110:2
595   2 Corinthians 12:9
596   2 Corinthians 12:9
597   Colossians 1:11
598   Ephesians 3:16
599   Isaiah 33:20
600   Ephesians 1:3
601   Hebrews 4:3
602   Philippians 2:13

his life shall lose it; and he that hateth his life in this world shall keep it unto life eternal."[603]

9. Should the believer fail to relinquish their cherished notions, preferences, perceptions and ordinances of religion, "Whosoever he be of you that forsaketh not all that he hath, he cannot be my disciple,"[604] says salvation's science. So then, "what profit hath he that worketh in that which he laboureth?"[605] "The flesh profiteth nothing,"[606] which is why creation's course came and passed and revived, to "deliver them who through fear of death";[607] that is, who reverence "the ministration of death"[608] through the philosophy of the religious law; "were all their lifetime subject to bondage."[609] They who are held under the bond of religious laws and traditions are therefore lifted above the *earth* through the living God's present wisdom. By showers of grace the mind finds rest through the knowledge of this wisdom's will, for it promises, "In returning and rest ye shall be saved."[610]

10. Through "rest ye shall be saved,"[611] even as it says, "According to his mercy he saved us."[612] Now, the living God, "according to his abundant mercy hath begotten us,"[613] and we know how He promised David concerning Solomon, "My mercy shall not depart away from him, as I took it from Saul,"[614] and that how it is written, "The Spirit of the LORD departed from Saul."[615]

11. Again, by the hand of Paul, "then had the churches rest,"[616] for to enter into that "rest" is to be sufficiently "edified; and walking in

---

603   John 12:25
604   Luke 14:33
605   Ecclesiastes 3:9
606   John 6:63
607   Hebrews 2:15
608   2 Corinthians 3:7
609   Hebrews 2:15
610   Isaiah 30:15
611   Isaiah 30:15
612   Titus 3:5
613   1 Peter 1:3
614   2 Samuel 7:15
615   1 Samuel 16:14
616   Acts 9:31

the fear of the Lord, and in the comfort of the Holy Ghost."[617] As the heart learns *heaven's* science, creation's consoling wisdom will be given to every reformer with comforting showers of blessing "purifying their hearts by faith."[618] Through *heaven's* wisdom the believer is to know the living God's *face*, for it says, "He shall redeem their soul from deceit and violence."[619] Thus, when the fullness of times does come again, "the spirit may be saved in the day of the Lord"[620] and only "the spirit of your mind,"[621] so how crucial is the present counsel, "Be ye therefore followers of God, as dear children"?[622]

12. The spirit of the mind, that the conversation's conscience may conquer the natural spiritual mind, is to be "saved," "redeemed," or "delivered," seeing as how "flesh and blood cannot inherit the kingdom of God."[623] If there is no power to control the spiritual appetite, no knowledge of *creation* will be obtained, there will be no new breath in the lungs of the mind. The only way to know the living God is through His "rest," and the only way to enter into that "rest" is to "have received, not the spirit of the world, but the spirit which is of God,"[624] that is, "comparing spiritual things with spiritual"[625] "that we might know the things that are freely given to us of God."[626]

13. The believer quits the spiritual sayings of self along with the precepts and suppositions of ministers; which are "the words which man's wisdom teacheth";[627] and turns to that "which the Holy Ghost teacheth."[628] Creation's wisdom advances the living God's mind in *man* as it did in His wisdom's first *child*, even as it says, "The spirit of the LORD shall rest upon him, the spirit of wisdom and understanding,

---

617   Acts 15:9
618   Acts 15:9
619   Psalms 72:14
620   1 Corinthians 5:5
621   Ephesians 4:23
622   Ephesians 5:1
623   1 Corinthians 15:50
624   1 Corinthians 2:12
625   1 Corinthians 2:13
626   1 Corinthians 2:12
627   1 Corinthians 2:13
628   1 Corinthians 2:13

the spirit of counsel and might, the spirit of knowledge and of the fear of the LORD."[629]

14. "Through the power of the Holy Ghost,"[630] the reformer is to be filled with "goodness, filled with all knowledge,"[631] filled with "the spirit of wisdom and revelation";[632] that is, "filled with the knowledge of his will in all wisdom and spiritual understanding";[633] that they may be "able also to admonish one another."[634] As this wisdom edifies us, it is counseled, "Edify one another,"[635] or rather, "Love one another."[636]

15. The purpose of relinquishing the *life* and *meat* of our heart to "Christ," or to the Bible's present spiritual understanding, is so that this doctrine may revive our inward parts for reviving another mind by our faithful testimony of its brilliance. "He laid down his life for us";[637] "herein is love";[638] and as the conversation begins to perceive "the love of God toward us,"[639] it is that it will to do as does its *Master* to it, and even as he still does, and that is to put away the pride and fear of the heart to bring the mind to safety, "rest," and stillness, that it may be said, "That ye also may have fellowship with us,"[640] and, "That your joy may be full."[641]

16. His "rest" is for them that are weary with the spirit within the religious world and are tired of the lack of nourishment portrayed as *nourishment* through blatant efforts to hide the living God from sight. None will know *heaven's* course of learning if they are yet tied to

629   Isaiah 11:2
630   Romans 15:13
631   Romans 15:14
632   Ephesians 1:17
633   Colossians 1:9
634   Romans 15:14
635   1 Thessalonians 5:11
636   1 Thessalonians 4:9
637   1 John 3:16
638   1 John 4:10
639   1 John 4:9
640   1 John 1:3
641   1 John 1:4

their *life*, which *life* is made up of the idols of the natural spiritual diet "received by tradition from your fathers."[642]

17. The creature in "Christ" proclaims, "Henceforth know we no man,"[643] for it is known, "Thou shalt not plant thee a grove of any trees near unto the altar of the LORD thy God, which thou shalt make thee,"[644] "for the tree of the field is man's life."[645] There should be no *man's life*; that is, no conversation should rely on "man's wisdom,"[646] which is "with fleshly wisdom";[647] near anything that has to do with our confidence on the living God's *voice*, because the believer has "an altar, whereof they have no right to eat which serve the tabernacle."[648] "Let the heart be established with grace"[649] than "with diverse and strange doctrines,"[650] "for the kingdom of God is not in meat and drink; but righteousness, and peace, and joy in the Holy Ghost."[651]

18. There is a "kingdom" that the reformer is to enter, for the Father "hath delivered us from the power of darkness, and hath translated us into the kingdom of his dear Son."[652] The living God's chief minister formerly said, "The kingdom of God is at hand";[653] for they lived under the philosophy of Moses; yet once his saying ascended and took its place by the living God, "Come boldly to the throne of grace,"[654] we are counseled.

19. "We which have believed do enter into rest,"[655] for in order to have first believed, it is that "ye have obeyed from the heart that form of doctrine which was delivered you."[656] Of old it was said, "Obey my

---

642 1 Peter 1:18
643 2 Corinthians 5:16
644 Deuteronomy 16:21
645 Deuteronomy 20:19
646 1 Corinthians 2:13
647 2 Corinthians 1:12
648 Hebrews 13:10
649 Hebrews 13:9
650 Hebrews 13:9
651 Romans 14:17
652 Colossians 1:13
653 Mark 1:15
654 Hebrews 4:16
655 Hebrews 4:3
656 Romans 6:17

voice,"[657] but now it is, "Hear ye him,"[658] for we must still remember, "Serve him, and obey his voice,"[659] because this wisdom "hath in these last days spoken unto us by his Son."[660] The old manner of devotion is passed away and yet the commandment remains, "Obey His voice," for He has spoken through the doctrine of His chief apostle "that ye would walk worthy of God, who hath called you unto his kingdom and glory."[661]

20. Before we may claim the Bible's "rest," and the knowledge born of that refreshing, it is that the heart and the ear must be translated to *heaven* from *earth*. From out of the *Place* where creation's science resides falls showers of blessing to *earth* on the penitent conversation, and to receive the *power* of "Christ" to comprehend its *voice*, the *life* of the conversation must be re-educated.

21. The living God does "rain righteousness"[662] by the evidence of our faith on His present commandment, for He says, "Hear, and your soul shall live."[663] It is by personally hearing *heaven's* doctrine that we may believe and advance in knowing *heaven's* will, because it is promised, "I will dwell in them, and walk in them."[664] He therefore says, "As they taught my people to swear by "Ba'al,"[665] and as they train them to say, "We are Moses' disciples,"[666] so too if the conversation would hear the living God's present *voice*, it must hear creation's "new song," that it says, "Thou wast slain, and hast redeemed us...out of every kindred, and tongue, and people, and nation."[667]

22. The reformer is delivered from spiritual bondage to the pure *image* of the living God's religious character by the *name* and "image" of "Christ"; this new song is derived from the new covenant's

---

657   Jeremiah 7:23
658   Matthew 17:5
659   1 Samuel 12:14
660   Hebrews 1:2
661   1 Thessalonians 2:12
662   Hosea 10:12
663   Isaiah 55:3
664   2 Corinthians 6:16
665   Jeremiah 12:16
666   John 9:28
667   Revelation 5:9

commandment, which is a commandment "that loved us, and washed us from our sins in his own blood."[668] The old or former *song* began through Moses' hand, yet the new song proclaims "a lively hope by the resurrection of Jesus Christ from the dead,"[669] wherein recovery is not by the religious bill, but through the spirit of the mind, and wherein the rule is not on *earth* by ministers, but by *him* "that is passed into the heavens,"[670] "who is consecrated for evermore"[671] by "an unchangeable priesthood."[672]

23. Therefore *he* said, "I will put my law in their inward parts, and write it in their hearts,"[673] because "whatsoever is born of God overcometh the world."[674] Herein are two sure things born of the living God: the first being that which was given on the mount, for "from his right hand went a fiery law for them";[675] the second according to how it says, "A law shall proceed from me."[676]

24. A new *child* was to come from the living God's character that was to turn every heart and mind to His throne's spiritual philosophy, that they may keep His philosophy's order. That of old said, "Obey My voice," and that voice was the character within the Ten Commandments, yet, with that doctrine being "weak through the flesh,"[677] He sent His doctrine "in the likeness of sinful flesh"[678] "that the righteousness of the law might be fulfilled in us."[679]

25. That doctrine which was to proceed from His wisdom is "the doctrine of God our Saviour."[680] This is that *voice* which every conversation is to consider if they would know creation's present pleasure. "We

---

668   Revelation 1:5
669   1 Peter 1:3
670   Hebrews 4:14
671   Hebrews 7:28
672   Hebrews 7:24
673   Jeremiah 31:33
674   1 John 5:4
675   Deuteronomy 33:2
676   Isaiah 51:4
677   Romans 8:3
678   Romans 8:3
679   Romans 8:4
680   Titus 2:10

which have believed do enter into rest,"[681] and through this doctrine are "written not with ink, but with the Spirit of the living God; not in tables of stone, but in fleshly tables of the heart."[682]

26. The counsel is the same as that of old, yet if we would correctly hear it, it is that the heart must know and trust that the living God has presently put creation's science "above all principality, and power, and might, and dominion, and every name that is named, not only in this world, but also in that which is to come: and hath put all things under his feet, and gave him to be the head over all things to the church."[683] "It pleased the Father that in him should all fullness dwell,"[684] and *he*; creation's new covenant doctrine; is now the chief priest of "the temple of the tabernacle of the testimony in heaven,"[685] and "is before all things, and by him all things consist."[686]

27. Therefore that experience currently given through the living God's wisdom is under the new covenant's promise and quenches the spirit of the religious world in our faith's thoughts and feelings, which experience is "the faith of Christ, the righteousness which is of God by faith."[687] Hereafter, "by the law of faith,"[688] the conversation is to finally hear and live for *heaven's* manner of redemption in peace and in simplicity, that by "the law of the Spirit of life"[689] "we might live through him."[690]

681 Hebrews 4:3
682 2 Corinthians 3:3
683 Ephesians 1:21,22
684 Colossians 1:19
685 Revelation 15:5
686 Colossians 1:17
687 Philippians 3:9
688 Romans 3:27
689 Romans 8:2
690 1 John 4:9

15

Created in Faithfulness

1. And *they* were both naked and were not ashamed; but after they had eaten of the cursed tree, they then knew of their nakedness and fell to shame and guilt for that nakedness.

2. If the eating of the cursed tree brought shame, then eating from the tree of *life* brought contentment and wholeness. They were not ashamed of their nakedness when they ate from the tree of life, which tree caused them to "live forever,"[691] which when they ate was a living testimony to their faith in the living God's praise, even His righteousness that comforted their faith's naked conscience. The pair created by His wisdom felt no shame in rendering total dependence upon that praise; from obeying His commandment, by faith they were blessed with a pure mind of service, a heart exercised without taint in reference to what His *voice* had said.

3. If it is that the pair was naked, then it is that they were created "naked, and destitute of daily food."[692] They were created contrary to being "warmed and filled,"[693] and were made without "those things

---

691 Genesis 3:22
692 James 2:15
693 James 2:16

which are needful to the body."[694] Yet when Adam was created, they were made "a little lower than the angels"[695] "with glory and honor,"[696] which glory and honor gave them the opportunity to receive the living God's *image*, for it is said, "Perfect through my comeliness, which I had put upon thee."[697]

4. When actively depending on the living God's commandment, *man* was never ashamed of his estate, for he was created "perfect, as pertaining to the conscience,"[698] and the perfectness of this demeanor maintained through faith in how it was said, "To you it shall be for meat."[699] To step outside of this counsel was to consent to the saying, "Thou shalt surely die,"[700] for as long as man would, through a faith that did work by an active and edifying love, be led to eat directly by the living God's *hand*, he would remain perfect in doctrinal thought and feeling.

5. It was only when the woman sought her own *righteousness*, along with the labor of dressing her own nakedness that they did turn away from creation's science. It was not Eve who was commanded but Adam; it says, "The LORD God commanded the man,"[701] and, "I commanded thee,"[702] for He "called unto Adam."[703]

6. The living God instructed His minister, and it was not, when that minister instructed his *woman*, that "God hath said,"[704] as she so said to their foe, but rather Adam had taught her what he retained, and she, being without conviction of heart, bore within herself a mind contrary to what was in her husband. It was not that after the woman ate of the tree that it then says, "And the eyes of them both were open,"[705] but

---

694 James 2:16
695 Hebrews 2:7
696 Hebrews 2:7
697 Ezekiel 16:14
698 Hebrews 9:9
699 Genesis 1:29
700 Genesis 2:17
701 Genesis 2:16
702 Genesis 3:11
703 Genesis 3:9
704 Genesis 3:3
705 Genesis 3:7

rather after her minister ate, the one to whom the covenant was made and the commandment given, that then "they knew that they were naked."[706] Though the *woman* was deceived, it was the *man* to whom all heavenly *things* were appointed, for it was the absence of a living and intelligent faith that caused their demise.

7. Both the man and the woman were once naked and felt neither fear nor shame because of it, yet they both would know of their nakedness to become ashamed of it; they learned of the fact from a different perspective. After a torn conscience entered into existence, the fact of their *uncircumcision*, of their blemished religious character, surfaced, yet while attached to the living God's commandment, the knowledge of their lacking spiritual understanding did not affect them.

8. These two were born "naked of their clothing,"[707] like "as a wilderness";[708] "like a dry land"[709] and "with thirst."[710] They were born as "hungered,"[711] "thirsty,"[712] "a stranger,"[713] "naked,"[714] "sick,"[715] "in prison,"[716] yet it is written, "And were not ashamed."[717] How is this so?

9. It is because they were "not weak in faith,"[718] ignoring the deadness of their *body*, choosing to stumble "not at the promise of God through unbelief."[719] These believed when it said, "See that you remember 'the tree of life, and eat, and live forever,'"[720] for they were created conscious of their nakedness, yet for their spiritual innocence were unaffected, trusting their faith's mind to the living God's religious character.

---

706 Genesis 3:7
707 Job 22:6
708 Hosea 2:3
709 Hosea 2:3
710 Hosea 2:3
711 Matthew 25:37-39
712 Matthew 25:37-39
713 Matthew 25:37-39
714 Matthew 25:37-39
715 Matthew 25:37-39
716 Matthew 25:37-39
717 Genesis 2:25
718 Romans 4:19
719 Romans 4:20
720 Genesis 3:22

10. Living faith on *heaven's* commandment kept their conscience from unnecessary torment. That commandment's righteousness was their clothing, its *life* and labor their diet, and from unwavering faith in what had been told them, they accepted their need for continual substance to remain *alive* in simplicity. It was a childlike obedience to creation's science that allowed the living God's praise to remain as their own, for they were naked and did know of their shame and had no questions concerning their illness, being accepted through the righteousness of their faith, leaving the members of their *body* unconscious to the fact of their ungodliness.

11. They believed the living God's *voice* and had no cause for doubt. They knew that "he spake, and it was done; he commanded, and it stood fast."[721] The power of His living wisdom was contained in every seed of *fruit* in the garden and was multiplied seven times in the *tree* of *life*, for the commandment was, "Of every tree of the garden thou mayest freely eat,"[722] and the commandment backed by faith provoked a perfectness that was personally linked to the living God's heart.

12. As faith was tested, so was the authority of the living God's wisdom. There is power in His commandment, therefore a lack of faith in that commandment is only proof of unbelief in His power to do what that commandment says it will. So said one to the living God's chief apostle at a certain time, "Speak the word only, and my servant shall be healed."[723] This confidence meant a lot to this man because his doctrine counseled the conversation's conscience to notice how it says, "God created,"[724] and, "God saw that it was good."[725]

13. All *things* that were created were "good," therefore all things, being full of *heaven's* order, were made in the perfect and just nature of the living God's religious character. The serpent knew how Eve came by the age's saying, therefore he said, "Hath God said, Ye,"[726] and the

721   Psalms 33:9
722   Genesis 2:16
723   Matthew 8:8
724   Genesis 1:1
725   Genesis 1:18
726   Genesis 3:1

woman responded, "We may,"[727] and, "God hath said."[728] Only to Eve could the test have come, because Adam knew and saw and heard and handled the *voice* of creation. Adam knew the honor and import of his existence and related the fact to Eve, but it could have only been that "the woman saw that the tree was good."[729]

14. The cursed tree was painted in a new light to the *woman*. She had not heard from the living God that she should not die, but rather He commanded his minister, and it was the man who explained to her the precept to honor. As the woman then began to see the cursed tree as an instrument "to make one wise,"[730] her heart was revealed, and as she gave Adam and he ate, his heart was revealed as one also of unreformed appetite and passion, clinging to the destiny of the one known to his heart as, "Bone of my bones, and flesh of my flesh."[731]

15. Because of his intemperance and willful ignorance, the saying committed to the tree was fulfilled. The counsel was sent to that tree of spiritual falsehood, thereby giving that tree the power of *death*; it is therefore said about any word uttered by the living God, "It shall not return unto me void, but it shall accomplish that which I please."[732]

16. "Sin" was not the living God's intention, but rather loyalty expressed by willing edification through faithfulness. As long as *man* remained confident of the power and authority of creation's science, "it was imputed to him for righteousness."[733]

17. There was nothing within the pair that gave them *righteousness*, for their spiritual mind was, upon *birth*, as innocent as our natural spiritual mind is, yet without conscious awareness of "sin." Their conversation was created without any complete information of the living God's will and wisdom, making it perfect in conscience and obedient in nature. Naked and in shame was Adam created, yet he had bestowed on him creation's righteousness through reverent obedience and singleness of

---

727   Genesis 3:2
728   Genesis 3:3
729   Genesis 3:6
730   Genesis 3:6
731   Genesis 2:23
732   Isaiah 55:11
733   Romans 4:22

heart, and "it was not written for his sake alone, that it was imputed to him; but for us also, to whom it shall be imputed, if we believe on him that raised up Jesus our Lord from the dead."[734]

18. "Such an high priest became us, who is holy, harmless, undefiled, separate from sinners, and made higher than the heavens";[735] who has reclaimed for us the first devotional estate of our first parents. As it was that their mental and spiritual condition was conditional, in that it was based upon the consumption of the *tree's meat*, so too it is written, "This is the promise that he hath promised us, even eternal life,"[736] and, "This life is in his Son."[737]

19. "My flesh is meat indeed,"[738] says the living God's chief messenger, "for the excellency of the knowledge of Christ Jesus"[739] is the new *meat* of our faith's diet, and this is that counsel saying, "Wisdom giveth life."[740] By faith on words, the pair in Eden maintained their countenance and constitution, for we know "the tree of the field is man's life,"[741] therefore these in the garden did express what would be the health of *man* in generations to come. By faith they ate of the *tree* of *life* and were blessed with a covering, and so too today we are counseled to *eat* of the doctrine that is termed, "The Word of Life," for us to receive "the righteousness of God which is by faith of Jesus Christ."[742]

20. The pair was naked and was not ashamed when following, by an active faith, *heaven's* diet in order to uphold His commandment and covenant. By faith the mind will receive creation's righteousness from simple obedience to that righteousness' course of learning, for all who are of faith bear the *name* of Abraham, and we do know how the living God's chief minister "took on him the seed of Abraham."[743]

---

734   Romans 4:23
735   Hebrews 7:26
736   1 John 2:25
737   1 John 5:11
738   John 6:55
739   Philippians 3:8
740   Ecclesiastes 7:12
741   Deuteronomy 20:19
742   Romans 3:22
743   Hebrews 2:16

21. The living God's chief apostle labored so that the adoption of his conversation's experience might provide a new and better way for penitent minds to know the living God. This minister dawned the *nature* of ministers while upholding the spirit of Abraham, meaning that he too remained obedient to creation's science not "through the law, through the righteousness of faith,"[744] and while combatting the ignorant members of his natural spiritual nature. Thus, where *Adam* failed, this man's doctrine prevailed. None need remain ashamed of what their faith or inward person may or may not be, for he who does believe "on him that justifieth the ungodly, his faith is counted for righteousness."[745]

22. As it was that a living faith kept Eden's pair in doctrinal order, so too when living faith is joined to a self-relinquishing spirit for edification, every conversation that is a doer of creation's commandment will be created "just." We who have therefore allowed our hearts to be touched by the counsel of *heaven's* patience will then know the *life* that is to be lived.

23. Was it not once said, "The people pressed upon him to hear the word of God"?[746] And did not one among them say, "At thy word I will"?[747] And when he who heard and did obey the counsel, "Let down your nets,"[748] was it not said, "When Simon Peter saw it, he fell down at Jesus' knees"?[749] What is it that Peter saw? He saw the Bible's new covenant wisdom and the new *song* of the faithful, and that counsel being creation by an active and experimental faith, for he heard, "Let down," and said, "At thy word I will," and then it was, "A great multitude of fishes: and their net brake."[750]

24. As living faith in *heaven's* wisdom kept its *firstborn* sinless, so by faith in the same counsel, the saying given to Peter did *birth* that mind which was not yet conceived. In discouragement he said, "We

---

744   Romans 4:13
745   Romans 4:5
746   Luke 5:1
747   Luke 5:5
748   Luke 5:4
749   Luke 5:8
750   Luke 5:6

have toiled all the night,"[751] but this mind was cancelled by faith in the saying, "Let down,"[752] and from believing on the *voice* of the one who spoke, and acting out that confidence, it was that, "A great multitude of fishes...filled both the ships, so that they began to sink."[753] Peter saw the hope that was to be experienced through creation's present commandment and was touched within his own self, for he then knew that "his abundant mercy hath begotten us again unto a lively hope."[754]

---

751   Luke 5:5
752   Luke 5:4
753   Luke 5:6,7
754   1 Peter 1:3

16

The Word Spoken

1. "If we confess our sins, he is faithful and just to forgive us our sins, and to cleanse us from all unrighteousness."[755]

2. It is written, "He that covereth his sins shall not prosper: but whoso confesseth and forsaketh them shall have mercy,"[756] and it is so written that our conversation may know how it says, "Justified freely by his grace through the redemption that is in Christ."[757]

3. "The Son of man is not come to destroy men's lives, but to save them,"[758] for it was that at a certain time he said, "Maid, arise. And her spirit came again, and she arose."[759] Again, it was confessed by one who had heard of him, "Say in a word, and my servant shall be healed,"[760] for that same one of faith was similar to her that lost her only son, for to her son he said, "Young man, I say unto thee, Arise. And he that was dead sat up, and began to speak,"[761] and also of the servant for that one

---

755   1 John 1:9
756   Proverbs 28:13
757   Romans 3:24
758   Luke 9:56
759   Luke 8:54,55
760   Luke 7:7
761   Luke 7:14,15

of faith, "returning to the house, found the servant whole that had been sick."[762] These were "justified" by faith; the ones who had confidence in *him* and the ones of whom their supplication was made; for as he said and it was done as they had hoped, so it was perfected through faith, and by faith, all were made whole.

4. Hear the magnitude of the living God's commandment: "The word is gone out of my mouth in righteousness, and shall not return,"[763] and, "Because he could swear by no greater, he sware by himself."[764]

5. Why is it that many approached the living God's chief apostle as though his religious character was the living God's religious character? Why did many ask of his doctrine what they asked of the living God's, and indeed carried the same faith in their God for what they asked of his doctrine? Many "sought to touch him: for there went virtue out of him, and healed them all,"[765] and I ask, "Why was it so?" Why would a Roman stranger say to him, "Say in a word,"[766] and why should a woman do for him as it is written, "And began to wash his feet with tears, and did wipe them with the hairs of her head"?[767] These things are written that we may know this man's doctrine has the same force of the living God's will and wisdom.

6. It says, "The life was manifested,"[768] even "that eternal life, which was with the Father." The carrier of this *life* said, "Believe me that I am in the Father, and the Father in me,"[769] and he also said, "If a man keep my saying, he shall never taste of death."[770]

7. Is it not written, "He that was dead sat up"?[771] How was he raised? It is written, "And he,"[772] the living God's man, "said."[773]

---

762   Luke 7:10
763   Isaiah 45:23
764   Hebrews 6:13
765   Luke 6:19
766   Luke 7:7
767   Luke 7:38
768   1 John 1:3
769   John 14:11
770   John 8:52
771   Luke 7:15
772   Luke 7:14
773   Luke 7:14

8. His doctrine could do what it did because it had, within it, the living God's creative power, which is why it says, "God, who created all things by Jesus Christ."[774] Many treated this man's doctrine as though it, and not the doctrine of Moses, was "God," for "God was in Christ,"[775] which is no new thought, seeing as how it says of him, "He shall speak unto them all that I shall command him."[776] For this cause, "As the Father hath life in himself; so hath he given to the Son to have life in himself,"[777] which is why it says, "He that hath the Son hath life."[778]

9. Redemption's science moves the heart to think on creation. When therefore thinking on how that science works, we do well to remember how it says, "Thy faith hath made thee whole."[779] Again, we here have creation's uttered revelation, therefore what we have before us is a fact, and the fact of wholeness established "by the law of faith."[780]

10. The living God's chief minister says that it is our living faith on his *voice* that will make our faith's mind whole, and from none other source is it said, therefore from this counsel come power to this precept, making this charge the conversation's hope. Herein is why it says, "These are written, that ye might believe that Jesus is the Christ, the Son of God; and that believing ye might have life through his name."[781] Faith begins with belief on the *name* of creation's science; from this faith we will receive *life* for the *death*, or dead religious service and confidence, we participate in.

11. If we then have personal confidence in the living God's wisdom, we should know the fact of His *life* and power being made available for our devotional transformation. This is why it says, "I have written unto you that believe on the name of the Son of God; that ye may know that ye have eternal life."[782]

---

774   Ephesians 3:9
775   2 Corinthians 5:19
776   Deuteronomy 18:18
777   John 5:26
778   1 John 5:13
779   Luke 8:48
780   Romans 3:27
781   John 20:32
782   1 John 5:13

12. Is it not said, "This is the promise that he hath promised us, even eternal life"?[783] Didn't he say, "I send the promise of my Father upon you"?[784] What promise is it that would manifest and leave them "endured with power from on high"?[785] Is it not written by the same author, "They were all filled with the Holy Ghost"?[786] Is not this *Holy Ghost* that doctrine the living God's man uttered when *he* said, "I will send unto you from the Father, even the Spirit of truth, which proceedeth from the Father"?[787] Is not this Spirit "that holy Spirit of promise,"[788] which the Father "shed on us abundantly through Jesus"?[789]

13. The same *life* within the living God's spiritual understanding exists within His chief minister's doctrine, which doctrine is made "after the power of an endless life,"[790] seeing as how in *him* rests "eternal redemption"[791] "through the eternal Spirit,"[792] which Spirit is "that eternal life, which was with the Father."[793] This minister's commandment has no choice but to create within the doer of it, "for it pleased the Father that in him should all fullness dwell,"[794] and being filled with that fullness, this will is "equal with God."[795] Thus, he or she who refuses *heaven's* commandment "is a liar, and the truth is not in him."[796]

14. This is the reason why it should be understood that *he* who spoke and it was done on *earth* is the *same* that spoke in the beginning. This doctrine the living God's chief minister gave is the same *Spirit* of creation, and it was because Israel should not lose sight of *heaven's name* that this same doctrine ordained a Memorial for "rest."

783　1 John 2:25
784　Luke 24:49
785　Luke 24:49
786　Acts 2:4
787　John 15:26
788　Ephesians 1:13
789　Titus 3:6
790　Hebrews 7:16
791　Hebrews 9:12
792　Hebrews 9:14
793　1 John 1:2
794　Colossians 1:19
795　Philippians 2:6
796　1 John 2:4

15. It was this doctrine that declared, "Know that I am the LORD that doth sanctify you,"[797] and this sanctification justly arranged by *Himself*, for "God blessed the seventh day, and sanctified it."[798] The living God's saying is again here made into a fact because the Sabbath was not simply instituted without a reason, but for the purpose of relieving and purifying the spiritual understanding. The living God made sure that there could be no other period of time to call *"Life's"* Memorial when it was this doctrine that spoke this "break" into existence and sanctified it, hallowing it for eternal remembrance. This is that remembrance for His Adam, who was neither a Jew nor Christian, but it says, "Adam, which was the son of God."[799]

16. "There remaineth therefore a rest to the people of God,"[800] "for we which have believed do enter into rest."[801] Is it not this same doctrine that said, "Hear all weary and full of anxiety, and I will give you rest?"[802] Again, did *he* not confess, "The Son of man is the Sabbath's Governor?"[803] This doctrine spoke this! We ought to then know that if we believe on creation's wisdom, we will receive power to educate our belief, for it is written, "The Holy Ghost, whom God hath given to them that obey him,"[804] for which cause it says, "Hereby we know that he abideth in us, by the Spirit which he hath given us."[805]

17. No conversation should believe that they are right when refusing to search out mental and spiritual health by creation's present commandment. Maybe we don't know how this doctrine says, "Why call ye me, Lord, Lord, and do not the things which I say?"[806] How may we know creation's "rest" if not willing hear, "The churches had rest... in the comfort of the Holy Ghost"?[807] How may we know that there is

797 Exodus 31:13
798 Genesis 2:2
799 Luke 3:38
800 Hebrews 4:9
801 Hebrews 4:3
802 Matthew 11:28-30
803 Luke 6:5
804 Acts 5:32
805 1 John 3:24
806 Luke 6:46
807 Acts 9:31

no other form of sanctification except through this chosen doctrine? And how may we know the power of that justification if we do not remember the Sabbath of that justification's *name*? This is why it says, "Without faith it is impossible to please him: for he that cometh to God must believe that he is."[808]

18. Our conversation is "just" by faith on the *name* of the living God's wisdom, and through faith will be made whole. John writes our faith's mind we will be "cleansed" of all "unrighteousness," and he says so only because this inwardly redeeming wisdom says, "Their sins and their iniquities will I remember no more,"[809] and, "I will receive you."[810] So hear what Paul says, "God hath said."[811]

19. Again, creation's commandant has spoken our justification! It is presently a living fact that if we would consider the living God's definition of "love," to study after that doctrine to fulfill its will, "whatsoever we ask, we know that we have the petitions that we desired of him."[812] It is then a fact that if our conversation is removing from "unrighteousness," it, in the moment of our supplication, is without self-righteousness and unrighteousness, leaving our faith "naked" before His will and wisdom. In being "naked," there now arises an opportunity to have our mind preserved by that wisdom's pleasure or righteousness, "even the righteousness of God which is by faith of Jesus."[813]

20. Our conversation, patiently applying its mind to creation's spiritual understanding, will be cleansed from all unrighteousness. In being cleansed, it will not be left naked, but will be forgiven and then given its pleasure to cover our sickness. Our Father gives His will's penitent believer the privilege of bearing the righteousness of His chief apostle for "remission of sins."[814] God Himself has said that He

---

808   Hebrews 11:6
809   Hebrews 8:12
810   2 Corinthians 6:17
811   2 Corinthians 6:16
812   1 John 5:15
813   Romans 3:22
814   Romans 3:25

will do this, so "wherefore do I take my flesh in my teeth, and put my life in mine hand?"[815]

21. "Whosoever will save his life shall lose it,"[816] it says. "The righteousness of God which is by faith of Jesus unto all and upon all them that believe"[817] is given by an experimental faith, and with this righteousness "the Spirit, which they that believe on him should receive."[818] As the believer acknowledges this doctrine's praise or righteousness, the knowledge of that doctrine's pleasure is then given to purify the soul's temple, for Abel "obtained witness that he was righteous,"[819] "whereof the Holy Ghost also is a witness to us,"[820] that "if ye be led of the Spirit, ye are not under the law,"[821] and that "by the works of the law shall no flesh be justified."[822]

22. The living God has spoken our faith's course; all the believer needs to do is examine that instruction. Our conversation is made "just" or "righteous" by faith in creation's present commandment. Sincere investigation through whatever circumstance "yieldeth the peaceable fruits of righteousness unto them which are exercised thereby."[823] So then, "exercise thyself rather unto godliness,"[824] seeing as how "godliness is profitable unto all things, having promise of the life that now is, and of that which is to come."[825]

23. Said the living God's chief minister, "Whosoever will lose his life for my sake, the same shall save it."[826]

24. To lose the conversation's identity is to gain the conversation's identity, and to gain that identity is to learn how to love, and being in love, to die for *life* to live courageously honoring creation's

---

815   Job 13:14
816   Luke 9:24
817   Romans 3:22
818   John 7:39
819   Hebrews 11:4
820   Hebrews 10:15
821   Galatians 5:18
822   Galatians 2:16
823   Hebrews 12:11
824   1 Timothy 4:8
825   1 Timothy 4:8
826   Luke 9:24

wisdom, that by exercising faith on every one of that wisdom's principles, we may diligently know why it says, "I am in the Father, and the Father in me."[827] This is why salvation's science says, "Wisdom is justified of all her children,"[828] and, "If a man love me, he will keep my words."[829]

827   John 14:10
828   Luke 7:35
829   John 14:23

17

The Life of Righteousness

1. The taint of "sin" within the soul's temple receives, through creation's present commandment, unadulterated health, but who will believe the fact? "To whom is the arm of the LORD revealed?"[830]

2. The spirit of our conversation's mind is recovered through an experimental faith on the Bible's words. "If we believe on him"[831] "that justifieth the ungodly,"[832] even as him that "staggered not at the promise of God through unbelief,"[833] our faith will be "counted for righteousness."[834] But how can we be sure that this is so? How can we be sure that, for us, "sin" is conquered through creation's course of learning? We know because it says, "I will preserve thee, and give thee for a covenant of the people."[835]

3. It says, "My covenant will I not break, nor alter the thing that is gone out of my lips. Once have I sworn by my holiness that I will not lie unto David."[836]

---

830   Isaiah 53:1
831   Romans 4:24
832   Romans 4:5
833   Romans 4:20
834   Romans 4:5
835   Isaiah 49:8
836   Psalms 89:34,35

4. What is it that, to *His Son David*, "God, that cannot lie, promised before the world began"?[837] It is written, "I shall give thee the heathen for thine inheritance,"[838] and, "As he saith in O'see, I will call them my people, which were not my people,"[839] and, "There it shall be said unto them, Ye are the sons of the living God."[840] Therefore "after he had offered one sacrifice for sins for ever, sat down on the right hand of God; from henceforth expecting till his enemies be made his footstool."[841] This is why it says, "David my servant shall be king over them,"[842] and, "I will make a covenant of peace with them."[843]

5. The living God has said these things, therefore they are as "written with a pen of iron, and with the point of a diamond."[844] God has said that He will give His *Son*; or give the spiritual understanding of His religious character; "for a covenant of the people, for a light of the Gentiles,"[845] and He has sworn and will not break the promise that has passed out of His *mouth*.

6. *Heaven's* promises are for us who currently have air in our lungs and *sickness* flowing through our natural and spiritual veins. So will we believe on what can never be broken? Will we believe, over our pitiful inclinations and suppositions to disbelieve faith's higher learning, on a spiritual understanding that cannot tell a lie? "To whom sware he that they should not enter into his rest, but to them that believed not?"[846]

7. The reward for obedience is not without definitive action to relay the natural acceptance of the commandment embraced. Says scripture, "Having confidence in thy obedience I wrote unto thee, knowing that thou wilt also do more than I say."[847] *Heaven* does not doubt our faithfulness, but it is us who maintain unnecessary thoughts about ourselves

---

837   Titus 1:2
838   Psalms 2:8
839   Romans 9:25
840   Hosea 1:10
841   Hebrews 10:12,13
842   Ezekiel 37:24
843   Ezekiel 37:26
844   Jeremiah 17:1
845   Isaiah 42:6
846   Hebrews 3:18
847   Philemon 1:21

in relation to the *image* our perception has of *God*. So who, to learn the living God's kindness, is willing to stop this habit?

8. The living God has spoken creation's counsel, and that doctrine tells of the fact that the "sins" of His wisdom's believer are passed away, for "whosoever believeth in him shall receive remission of sins."[848] What does this mean? As the believer declares this wisdom as their faith's Savior and High Priest, obeying "from the heart that form of doctrine which was delivered"[849] and acquired by an experimental faith, it will be fulfilled, "Immediately her issue of blood stanched."[850]

9. The error and plague of the heart ceases when once open to the reception of the living God's words. "Sin" is to cease that another active agent may take its place, for which cause it is said, "Where sin abounded, grace did much more abound."[851] Thus, as the penitent relinquishes the *meat* of their heart, immediately given to them is "the righteousness of God which is by faith of Jesus Christ,"[852] along with "abundance of grace."[853]

10. Do we not remember how one came to a man of God with a letter that said, "Recover him of his leprosy"?[854] And how that he grew angry at the living God's simplicity; being familiar with false methods of *health* and presumptuous hypocrites of *medicine*; for what was the counsel given him at that time of his wrath? It was said, "If the prophet had bid thee do some great thing, wouldest thou not have done it? how much rather then, when he saith to thee, Wash, and be clean?"[855]

11. And after he obeyed the advice and did wash and was blessed; for "his flesh came again like unto the flesh of a little child, and he was clean";[856] what then was his testimony after faith had come? He said,

---

848   Acts 10:43
849   Romans 6:17
850   Luke 8:44
851   Romans 5:20
852   Romans 3:22
853   Romans 5:17
854   2 Kings 5:3
855   2 Kings 5:13
856   2 Kings 5:14

"Now I know that there is no God in all the earth, but in Israel."[857] By faith, this stranger to the living God's knowledge was made "clean" by depending on the saying of His man to do as it had said, and for us, the His chief minister says, "Arise, go thy way: thy faith hath made thee whole."[858]

12. Surly the words of the man of God were an intercessor between this man and *God*, and in receiving the counsel of the intercessor, "it was imputed unto him for righteousness,"[859] allowing him opportunity to be taken and refreshed for his faith. The lesson is for us.

13. "There is one God, and one mediator between God and men, the man Christ Jesus; who gave himself a ransom for all,"[860] "specially of those that believe."[861] So "seest thou how faith wrought with his works, and by works was faith made perfect?"[862]

14. "Where is boasting then? It is excluded. By what law? of works? Nay: but by the law of faith."[863] "For if Abraham were justified by works, he hath whereof to glory; but not before God."[864]

15. It was the philosophy of religious works and deeds that was to pass away, allowing for the law of faith to act as creation's new mediator "that we might be justified by faith."[865] Abraham received the law of circumcision not before he was justified by faith, but after his faith's mind was edified by faith "he received the sign of circumcision, a seal of the righteousness of the faith which he had yet being uncircumcised."[866] "Therefore if the uncircumcision keep the righteousness of the law";[867] that is, if they keep the righteousness "witnessed by the law and the prophets";[868] "shall not his uncircumcision be counted

---

857   2 Kings 5:15
858   Luke 17:19
859   James 2:23
860   1 Timothy 2:5,6
861   1 Timothy 4:10
862   James 2:22
863   Romans 3:27
864   Romans 4:2
865   Galatians 3:24
866   Romans 4:11
867   Romans 2:26
868   Romans 3:21

for circumcision?"[869] Herein is why "after that faith is come, we are no longer under a schoolmaster."[870]

16. The saying is therefore true, "If Abraham were justified by works, he hath whereof to glory; but not before God,"[871] for the generally natural religious conversation would rather "glory in appearance, and not in heart."[872] The law of circumcision did not "justify" Abraham, and the Jews were not "justified" by that law "which stood only in meats and drinks, and divers washings, and carnal ordinances, imposed on them."[873] Remember, these things satisfied "a shadow of things to come; but the body is of Christ."[874]

17. Faith was ever the living principle that admitted the conversation's mind for *heaven's* health. That *righteousness* of the philosophy of the religious law, that *righteousness* of circumcision, has always employed a certain level of faith supposedly conforming the mind to the righteousness of *God*. But our conversation is promised that creation is not "through the law, but through the righteousness of faith."[875] How is this possible? "The righteousness of God is revealed from faith to faith: as it is written, The just shall live by faith,"[876] that is, "By the law of faith."[877]

18. Salvation's science "justifies," or heals, our inward person. By faith in "his righteousness for the remission of sins that are passed,"[878] we become "the children of God by faith in Christ."[879] The example is set for us to understand that no *thing* done within our own power may remove personal or devotional error. There is no *thing* within us that can purify us, for it is said that His man did "sanctify the people with his

---

869   Romans 2:26
870   Galatians 3:25
871   Romans 4:2
872   2 Corinthians 5:12
873   Hebrews 9:10
874   Colossians 2:17
875   Romans 4:13
876   Romans 1:17
877   Romans 3:27
878   Romans 3:25
879   Galatians 3:26

own blood."[880] There is no *thing* that we may "work" that can leave us "perfect, as pertaining to the conscience,"[881] for only faith on redemption's science can "purge your conscience from dead works to serve the living God."[882]

19. So then what is the work of the believer? It says, "To him that worketh not, but believeth on him that justifieth the ungodly, his faith is counted for righteousness,"[883] and, "Believe on him that raised up Jesus."[884]

20. As faith on creation's *name* begins to conquer the *fear* within the heart of devotion, the knowledge acquired from that faith will inwardly edify for an entrance into *heaven* for "the communion of the Holy Ghost."[885] By faith we are "sealed with that holy Spirit of promise,"[886] for it is that "the love of God is shed abroad in our hearts by the Holy Ghost."[887] Therefore as faith has open intercourse with the conversation's mind, creation's *name* will provide that mind "abundance of grace and of the gift of righteousness"[888] from "the Spirit of grace."[889]

---

880   Hebrews 13:12
881   Hebrews 9:9
882   Hebrews 9:14
883   Romans 4:5
884   Romans 4:24
885   2 Corinthians 13:14
886   Ephesians 1:13
887   Romans 5:5
888   Romans 5:17
889   Hebrews 10:29

18

The Will of The Father

1. It is the will of the Father that all who care to know Him remove their eyes from *earth* into His heavenly Building, or else He would not have said, "Look unto me, and be ye saved."[890] To be "saved" is to be mentally delivered or rescued by His wisdom, or rather, as the apostle once said, "The Lord shall deliver me from every evil work."[891]

2. It is the will of the Father that, through His chief apostle's doctrine, "he might redeem us from all iniquity,"[892] faithfully translating "us into the kingdom of his dear Son."[893] It is for this cause that "our conversation is in heaven,"[894] for His counsel confirms, "Not every one that saith unto me, Lord, Lord, shall enter into the kingdom of heaven; but he that doeth the will of my Father which is in heaven."[895] Entrance into this kingdom is not future. It is yet a living fact that the living God "hath in these last days spoken unto us by his Son, whom he

---

890   Isaiah 45:22
891   2 Timothy 4:18
892   Titus 2:14
893   Colossians 1:13
894   Philippians 3:20
895   Matthew 7:21

hath appointed heir of all things,"[896] and that His wisdom's *kingdom* is yet upheld by "the throne of grace,"[897] even as like it says, "Thy throne, O God."[898]

3. The *kingdom* spoken of is the reign of the living God's wisdom, to have our conversation "translated into the kingdom of his dear Son."[899] The ancient Israelites were established to educate on this reign of faith on the living God's words, which why "the law having a shadow of good things to come, and not the very image of the things"[900] made no conversation "perfect, as pertaining to the conscience."[901] It was *heaven's* intention to exemplify the foundation of hope through vain customs and rites; these did only "serve unto the example and shadow of heavenly things,"[902] "but the heavenly things themselves with better sacrifices than these."[903]

4. The *kingdom* of the Spirit is the kingdom of *heaven's* wisdom, and it is this *kingdom* and *reign* that the reformer is to enter into. Because this is a living fact, the believer is not void of this Spirit or Wisdom's spiritual understanding, for it beings the heart into communion with the living God's will, and seeing as how this wisdom "is set on the right hand of the throne of the Majesty in the heavens,"[904] it is that "our fellowship is with the Father, and with his Son."[905] This is why it today it says of *heaven's* doctrine, "He shall stand and feed in the strength of the LORD, in the majesty of the name of the LORD his God."[906]

5. Fellowship is today within the living God's heavenly Temple. This we understand from how there is no kingdom of *Christ* on earth. This man, for all inquiring of his doctrine, lets the one observing his

---

896   Hebrews 1:2
897   Hebrews 4:16
898   Hebrews 1:8
899   Colossians 1:13
900   Hebrews 10:1
901   Hebrews 9:9
902   Hebrews 8:5
903   Hebrews 9:23
904   Hebrews 8:1
905   1 John 1:3
906   Micah 5:4

doctrine contemplate the sayings, "The kingdom of heaven,"[907] and, "Your reward in heaven,"[908] and, "Your Father which is in heaven,"[909] and, "Thy kingdom come. Thy will be done in earth, as it is in heaven,"[910] and, "Seek ye first the kingdom of God, and his righteousness."[911]

6. There is plainly a will for the reformer to learn of and do, and it is not found on *earth* or within the *earth's* religious institutions. It is for this reason that the apostle counsels, "Set your affection on things above, not on things on the earth."[912] Because it is the Father who exalted His wisdom "and set him at his own right hand in heavenly places,"[913] it is now our responsibility to know that "Christ is not entered into the holy places made with hands, which are the figures of the true; but into heaven itself, now to appear in the presence of God for us."[914]

7. It is the "inheritance in the kingdom of Christ and of God"[915] that every faithful believer should be concerned with. It does not say, "Enter this kingdom by my will," but rather he counsels us on the will of his Father, saying, "He that doeth the will of my Father."[916]

8. The will and purpose is of the living God but the ministry belongs to His wisdom, and as this commandment is currently seated next to the throne of its Father, as mediator between the throne of God and the throne of grace for the throne of our faith's heart, it is that by learning of and doing the living God's will, every conversation that would accept entrance into the *kingdom* of grace will be made whole, both personally and devotionally.

9. It is "the mystery of his will, according to his good pleasure which he hath purposed in himself,"[917] that should consume our every

907 Matthew 5:3
908 Matthew 5:12
909 Matthew 5:16
910 Matthew 6:10
911 Matthew 6:33
912 Colossians 3:2
913 Ephesians 1:20
914 Hebrews 9:24
915 Ephesians 5:5
916 Matthew 7:21
917 Ephesians 1:9

thought. Entrance into this wisdom's dominion over the soul and spirit cannot commence without an education in the knowledge of creation's present will, which is why we are counseled, "Be filled with the knowledge of his will in all wisdom and spiritual understanding."[918]

10. This wisdom confesses that if the one who believes on its *name* would do its will, then that individual would rest in the "riches of the glory of his inheritance in the saints."[919] Again, this counsel says, "If any man will do his will, he shall know the doctrine,"[920] and again, "This is the will of him that sent me, that every one which seeth the Son, and believeth on him, may have everlasting life."[921] What then is the will of the Father?

11. It is written, "Believe on him whom he hath sent,"[922] but for what purpose? It says, "I will give for the life of the world."[923] And what is this "life" of the "world"? It is said, "The life of the flesh is in the blood,"[924] and what is the "blood" of the religious world? It is said, "Meats offered to idols, and from blood, and from things strangled."[925]

12. If the life of the *world* is found in such gross filth as idols and strangled commandments and doctrines, what then needs to be purified by this commandment's *blood*? It is said, "This is that spirit of an'tichrist, whereof ye have heard that it should come; and even now already is it in the world."[926]

13. The life of the religious world is that spirit within "the lusts of our flesh, fulfilling the desires of the flesh and of the mind,"[927] for it is written, "The whole world lieth in wickedness."[928] It is not heaven's will that we remain in the philosophy of the religious world, "for all that is

---

918   Colossians 1:9
919   Ephesians 1:18
920   John 7:17
921   John 6:40
922   John 6:29
923   John 6:51
924   Leviticus 17:11
925   Acts 15:29
926   1 John 4:3
927   Ephesians 2:3
928   1 John 5:19

in the world, the lust of the flesh, and the lust of the eyes, and the pride of life, is not of the Father, but is of the world."[929]

14. Our mental and spiritual recovery from the religious world's manner of devotion is found in the saying, "I will give for the life of the world."[930] This is a gift that is given to the mind tired of their natural personal and spiritual conversation, and it is found in His chief minister's doctrine "to declare his righteousness for the remission of sins."[931] This wisdom's righteousness is an education removing personal and spiritual error from the conversation's conscience, and with this righteousness is newness of *life* for our philosophy, which is why "the Spirit is life."[932]

15. "For anguish of spirit, and for cruel bondage,"[933] the reformer is given the living God's righteousness the moment they strip themselves of the religious world's pride. This is why it says, "No man putteth a piece of a new garment upon an old; if otherwise, then both the new maketh a rent, and the piece that was taken out of the new agreeth not with the old."[934]

16. Why does he say this? He counsels us to not only seek entrance into his doctrines *kingdom*, but to also learn of his Father's kind righteousness. This we are advised to do according to how it says, "He that doeth the will of my Father."[935] It is known of His widsom's living kingdom and ministry, "A sceptre of righteousness is the sceptre of thy kingdom,"[936] and, "Come boldly unto the throne of grace,"[937] for it is written, "Grace and truth came by Jesus Christ."[938] The mediation of faith's higher learning is one of righteousness' work and effect, for it is

---

929   1 John 2:16
930   John 6:51
931   Romans 3:25
932   Romans 8:10
933   Exodus 6:9
934   Luke 5:36
935   Matthew 7:21
936   Hebrews 1:8
937   Hebrews 4:16
938   John 1:17

"the grace that is in Christ"[939] that is to construct our mind into *heaven's image*.

17. It is for this reason that Paul writes, "An apostle of Jesus Christ by the will of God,"[940] and again, "An apostle of Jesus Christ by the commandment of God our Saviour."[941] He or she that would do heaven's will is one that will accomplish *heaven's* commandment, which commandment, when consented to, encourages "charity out of a pure heart, and of a good conscience, and of faith unfeigned."[942] Its will is according to "the name of God and his doctrine,"[943] which, when assimilated into the stream of *life* flowing into the soul temple, produces the confession, "I have suffered loss,"[944] "that I may know him."[945]

18. That doctrine directing the mind to the living God's will says, "Fulfil the law of Christ."[946] It is "the light of the knowledge of the glory of God in the face of Jesus Christ"[947] that is to cause the mind to care for the living God's words, and this belief governed by learning of and doing the wisdom of those words, and this act accomplished "if ye have faith, and doubt not."[948]

19. "This is the will of God, even your sanctification,"[949] but wherein is purification found if there exists no living faith in His words to do just as they say? It is God who says, "I will work, and who shall let it?"[950] "I have made, and I will bear; even I will carry, and will deliver you."[951] Wherefore we are counseled, "Faithful is he that calleth you, who also

939   2 Timothy 2:1
940   2 Timothy 1:1
941   1 Timothy 1:1
942   1 Timothy 1:5
943   1 Timothy 6:1
944   Philippians 3:8
945   Philippians 3:10
946   Galatians 6:2
947   2 Corinthians 4:6
948   Matthew 21:21
949   1 Thessalonians 4:3
950   Isaiah 43:13
951   Isaiah 46:4

will do it,"[952] and, "The Lord is faithful, who shall stablish you, and keep you from evil."[953]

20. Do we believe on this as fact? Before sanctification begins, what is the only work of the believer? It says, "Believe on him whom he hath sent";[954] that is, actively engage the mind on the saying of His *voice*; for He says, "Every one which seeth the Son, and believeth on him."[955] All that studiously believe "on him that justifieth the ungodly, his faith is counted for righteousness,"[956] and of such it will be reported, "This day is salvation come to this house, forsomuch as he also is a son of Abraham."[957]

21. *Heaven's* will is for the purification of every conversation that confesses their allegiance to His chief angel's *name*. Because it is *heaven's* purpose that every believer maintains faith in the power of its ministry's to purify their inward parts, it is expected that every believing soul humble his or her mind to receive knowledge of creation's law for doctrinal regeneration. It is the duty of the reformer to remain confident in "the promise of the Spirit by faith,"[958] for it is said, "The promise of life which is in Christ Jesus,"[959] or rather, "The grace that is in Christ,"[960] which grace is "the salvation which is in Christ."[961]

22. "God hath given to us eternal life, and this life is in his Son,"[962] for it is that by faith in "the word of truth, the gospel of your salvation,"[963] the reformer will "receive abundance of grace and of the gift of righteousness"[964] "to be conformed to the image of his Son."[965] It

952   1 Thessalonians 5:24
953   2 Thessalonians 3:3
954   John 6:29
955   John 6:40
956   Romans 4:5
957   Luke 19:9
958   Galatians 3:14
959   2 Timothy 1:1
960   2 Timothy 2:1
961   2 Timothy 2:10
962   1 John 5:11
963   Ephesians 1:13
964   Romans 5:17
965   Romans 8:29

is the intention of the Bible's present wisdom that after we have been convinced to offer faith in the testimony of devotional recovery, that "in the fulness of the blessings of the gospel of Christ,"[966] this understanding would "make you perfect in every good work to do his will, working in you that which is wellpleasing in his sight, through Christ."[967]

23. He or she that will do *heaven's* counsel will be edified. When once the soul knows the counsel of its recovery, it is transferred into the *kingdom* of *life* to receive instruction "of the life that now is, and of that which is to come."[968] It is by hearing this counsel; that is, "The gospel preached,"[969] or, "The word preached"[970] that says, "Jesus Christ of the seed of David was raised from the dead"[971] "and declared the Son of God with power, according to the spirit of holiness,"[972] and is "gone into heaven, and is on the right hand of God"[973] "after the order of Melchis'edec";[974] that the conversation will confess, "O wretched man that I am!"[975] Yet, it is intended that the reformer "have as an anchor of the soul, both sure and steadfast,"[976] even "the righteousness of God which is by faith of Jesus Christ unto all and upon all them that believe."[977]

24. The conversation faithfully doing *heaven's* will is "just" to receive the benefits of its wisdom's mediation. If any conversation would enter this wisdom's *kingdom* to receive mental and devotional regeneration, it should study after and do the will of creation's present science.

966　Romans 15:29
967　Hebrews 13:21
968　1 Timothy 4:8
969　Hebrews 4:2
970　Hebrews 4:2
971　2 Timothy 2:8
972　Romans 1:4
973　1 Peter 3:22
974　Hebrews 7:21
975　Romans 7:25
976　Hebrews 6:19
977　Romans 3:22

25. Since its will is, "Handle me, and see,"[978] the conversation doing so, and while depending on it to execute the health that it decrees, "God dwelleth in him, and he in God."[979] No living soul will hear, "I never knew you,"[980] unless they "resist the truth,"[981] becoming "reprobate concerning the faith."[982] "He that hath the Son hath life,"[983] and if "the Spirit is life,"[984] "was Paul crucified for you? or were ye baptized in the name of Paul?"[985] None should be "led away with the error of the wicked"[986] to "heap to themselves teachers, having itching ears,"[987] for what is the counsel? "The anointing which ye have received of him abideth in you, and ye need not that any man teach you."[988]

26. Is this a lie? Does His man not plainly say, "If any man do the will of my Father,"[989] and, "If any man would will to do His will"?[990] Would God speak and have no power follow? Would He ordain and occasion no thoughtful provision? He has said, "I will abundantly bless her provision,"[991] and, "I am come that they might have life, and that they might have it more abundantly."[992] Thus, herein is the faithful work of the sorrowing soul: "Arise, go thy way."[993]

27. Them that had heard this charge, "as they went, they were cleansed,"[994] but what "cleansed" them? This man spoke the counsel, but it could have been that "the word preached did not profit them, not

978   Luke 24:39
979   1 John 4:15
980   Matthew 7:24
981   2 Timothy 3:8
982   2 Timothy 3:8
983   1 John 5:12
984   Romans 8:10
985   1 Corinthians 1:13
986   2 Peter 3:17
987   2 Timothy 4:3
988   1 John 2:27
989   John 7:17
990   John 7:17
991   Psalms 132:15
992   John 10:10
993   Luke 17:19
994   Luke 17:14

being mixed with faith in them they heard it."[995] As these men heard the word, they were "not faithless, but believing."[996] From exercising faith in what the commandment had said, the living God's righteousness conquered their illness, making them available to receive the power of God for restoration.

28. This example is for us. If a *man* or *woman* would enter into the only *Place* where refreshing and redemption occur, it is to be done by studiously investigating and proving the living God's *name* and doctrine.

29. What is the counsel? "Whosoever shall not receive the kingdom of God as a little child shall in no wise enter therein."[997] "Whosoever therefore shall humble himself as this little child, the same is greatest in the kingdom of heaven."[998]

30. A little child will go to their father and say, "My head, my head,"[999] yet the one too "adult," the one too prideful to receive alleviation, would rather unnecessarily die in his or her condition. Wherefore "be not therefore ashamed of the testimony of our Lord...but be thou partakers of the afflictions of the gospel according to the power of God."[1000] "Unto you it is given in the behalf of Christ, not only to believe on him, but also to suffer for his sake,"[1001] "that believing ye might have life through his name."[1002]

31. The Bible counsels the reformer to do *heaven's* will; this is why that will says, "I ascend unto my Father, and your Father; and to my God, and your God."[1003] This will's wisdom is on the throne of salvation's *kingdom* with the Father within His *kingdom*, and it is their intention that many would be "justified"; or mentally and spiritually cleansed

---

995   Hebrews 4:2
996   John 20:27
997   Luke 18:17
998   Matthew 18:4
999   2 Kings 4:19
1000   2 Timothy 1:8
1001   Colossians 1:29
1002   John 20:31
1003   John 20:17

and sanctified; by creation's course to come into personal contact with His religious character.

32. Therefore "let your conversation be as it be cometh the gospel of Christ"[1004] and "live soberly, righteously, and godly, in this present world."[1005] It is *heaven's* will that living faith is exercised to pronounce every mind as being healthy, for then it is evident that by humiliation the soul longs to join into fellowship with its governing commandment. They who would enter the "kingdom" of grace do enter through that righteousness which is only by faith, and upon entrance are blessed with the knowledge of its wisdom to maintain the sobriety of their eyes.

1004   Philippians 1:27
1005   Titus 2:12

19

A Profitable Hope By Faith

1. The counsel for the reformer is, "Live according to God in the spirit,"[1006] seeing as how "he hath said, I will never leave thee, nor forsake thee."[1007]

2. Our Father says, "I will not leave thee, until I have done that which I have spoken to thee of,"[1008] for it is written, "From all your filthiness, and from all your idols, will I cleanse you,"[1009] and, "I will forgive their iniquity, and I will remember their sin no more."[1010] But who will believe this fact? Who will remember that it says, "I have spoken it, I have purposed it, and will not repent, neither will I turn back from it"?[1011]

3. There is hope for the conversation developing their mind and faith in creation's doctrine, and this is why "God sent forth his Son, made of a woman, made under the law, to redeem."[1012] His chief apos-

---

1006 1 Peter 4:6
1007 Hebrews 13:5
1008 Genesis 28:15
1009 Ezekiel 36:25
1010 Jeremiah 31:34
1011 Jeremiah 4:28
1012 Galatians 4:5

tle's conversation is that great sin offering that "hath given himself for us an offering and a sacrifice to God."[1013] Therefore "awake thou that sleepest, and arise from the dead";[1014] that is, "being dead in your sins and the uncircumcision of your flesh";[1015] "dead in trespasses and sins;"[1016] "and Christ shall give thee light."[1017] The active believer on salvation's science may be perfect in devotional thought and feeling when cooperating with *heaven's* law, for it says, "Be ye therefore perfect,"[1018] wherefore "God commendeth his love toward us"[1019] when saying, "My grace is sufficient for thee: for my strength is made perfect in weakness."[1020]

4. The *light* of His grace is the law of His creative benevolence, and since "the law is light,"[1021] our assignment is in learning of and executing the law of that benevolence. The same power that brought all things into existence is that same power that will re-create the conversation's conscience into the likeness of the person of that power's voice.

5. That wisdom bringing all things into existence says, "Know that the Son of man hath power upon earth to forgive sins,"[1022] therefore should the professor remain a thief, holding tightly to whatever stops personal and devotional growth and development? It is written, "Thou shalt not steal,"[1023] yet who will steal back their inward person's *confusion* when it has been buried with His man to never again arise? If it is that the virtue of *heaven's* commandment is believed on, then "if we be dead with Christ, we believe that we shall also live with him."[1024] "He that is dead is freed from sin,"[1025] "for this cause was the gospel

1013 Ephesians 5:2
1014 Ephesians 5:14
1015 Colossians 2:13
1016 Ephesians 2:1
1017 Ephesians 5:14
1018 Matthew 5:48
1019 Romans 5:8
1020 2 Corinthians 12:9
1021 Proverbs 6:23
1022 Luke 5:24
1023 Exodus 20:15
1024 Romans 6:8
1025 Romans 6:7

preached to them that are dead";[1026] that is, "dead in sins";[1027] that the believing conversation should "live according to God in the spirit."[1028]

6. Grace awakens the conversation to the living God's kindness, for "where sin abounded, grace did much more abound."[1029] Creation's present grace contains His chief apostle's *name*; which *name* is "the fullness of the godhead bodily";[1030] and is given by faith on the promise of that grace's intention, for He said, "I will also save you from all your uncleannesses."[1031] Therefore it is said, "According to his mercy he saved us,"[1032] that is, "His abundant mercy,"[1033] or rather, "abundance of peace so long as the moon endureth,"[1034] and this being "abundance of grace and of the gift of righteousness."[1035]

7. If the conversation would adopt the living God's religious character then it needs a certain gift or aid, which "gift" is revealed in showers of blessing over the mind, even showers of grace, which "gift" also brought all *things* to be and "effectually worketh also in you that believe."[1036]

8. It is for this cause that as the counsel enters into the *ear*, "Their sins and their iniquities will I remember no more,"[1037] it is the duty of the hearer to confess, "Lord, to whom shall we go?"[1038] "Whom have I in heaven but thee? and there is none upon earth that I desire beside thee."[1039]

9. The conversation of the living God's chief minister is the complete offering for religious error against the living God's mind, for

---

1026 1 Peter 4:6
1027 Ephesians 2:5
1028 1 Peter 4:6
1029 Romans 5:20
1030 Colossians 2:9
1031 Ezekiel 36:29
1032 Titus 3:5
1033 1 Peter 1:3
1034 Psalms 72:7
1035 Romans 5:17
1036 1 Thessalonians 2:13
1037 Hebrews 8:12
1038 John 6:68
1039 Psalms 73:25

it is said, "Ye are complete in him,"[1040] and, "God will redeem my soul from the power of the grave."[1041] The conversation and its conscience is to be "redeemed" and no thing else, for it is purposed "that the spirit may be saved in the day of the Lord Jesus."[1042] The conversation is to be directly fed by the living God's words through faith on His chief *son's name*, to the end our conversation knows "that we should serve in newness of spirit."[1043]

10. Paul, on one occasion, was put on trial for strange allegations. At this time he said, "Men and brethren, I have lived in good conscience before God until this day,"[1044] and after one was commanded to strike him for these words, he said, "Commandest me to be smitten contrary to the law?"[1045] Why did Paul associate cleanliness of mind with Moses' religious philosophy?

11. That law of types and shadows brings light to the fact of the present doctrinal dispensation. Within "the dispensation of the grace of God"[1046] it is counseled, "Be filled with all the fullness of God,"[1047] or rather, "Be filled with the Spirit."[1048] Through the Levit'ical priesthood, the people were given a routine to open their hearts to the knowledge of that fullness.

12. It is written that if the soul of an Israelite "sin through ignorance,"[1049] "and if he have erred, and not observed all these commandments, which the LORD hath spoken unto Moses,"[1050] "if his sin, which he hath sinned, come to his knowledge: then he shall bring his offering";[1051] "the priest shall make an atonement for him, and it

---

1040　Colossians 2:10
1041　Psalms 49:15
1042　1 Corinthians 5:5
1043　Romans 7:6
1044　Acts 23:1
1045　Acts 23:3
1046　Ephesians 3:2
1047　Ephesians 3:19
1048　Ephesians 5:18
1049　Leviticus 4:27
1050　Numbers 15:22
1051　Leviticus 4:28

shall be forgiven him."[1052] Again, if a conversation trespass through ignorance, "The priest shall make an atonement for him concerning his ignorance wherein he erred and wist it not, and it shall be forgiven him."[1053]

13. The apostle confessed a pure mind before God because he knew of himself, "I obtained mercy, because I did it in ignorance."[1054] Paul was well educated in the law of Moses, for he was "taught according to the perfect manner of the law of the fathers,"[1055] that is, he "profited in the Jews' religion."[1056] Such a conversation contained "the form of knowledge and of the truth in the law,"[1057] that is, in "the book of the law."[1058] It is this law that, when heard and correctly obeyed, reveals from the believer's actions "the work of the law written in their hearts."[1059]

14. The "work" of the law "that is of the heart, in the spirit,"[1060] is "the righteousness of the law."[1061] Such righteousness admits, "God hath sent forth the Spirit of his Son into your hearts,"[1062] therefore the keeping of the honor within salvation's law is fulfilled in the saying, "We through the Spirit wait for the hope of righteousness by faith."[1063] This is why it says, "The law was our schoolmaster to bring us unto Christ, that we might be justified by faith."[1064]

15. Paul confessed a good conscience by faith and joined such a doctrine to the religion of Moses because it was known, "After that faith is come, we are no longer under a schoolmaster."[1065] That doctrine pointing the people to righteousness by faith on salvation's law became

1052 Leviticus 4:26
1053 Leviticus 5:18
1054 1 Timothy 1:13
1055 Acts 22:3
1056 Galatians 1:14
1057 Romans 2:20
1058 Galatians 3:10
1059 Romans 2:15
1060 Romans 2:29
1061 Romans 2:26
1062 Galatians 4:6
1063 Galatians 5:5
1064 Galatians 3:24
1065 Galatians 3:25

"a stone of stumbling, and a rock of offence."[1066] Because "the law is not of faith,"[1067] but was rather accomplished through "carnal ordinances, imposed on them,"[1068] it was that every operation of priest and convicted sinner was to point the people to that "more perfect tabernacle, not made with hands."[1069] This allows us to know that, today "we have such an high priest, who is set on the right hand of the Majesty in the heavens"[1070] who "became us, who is holy, harmless, undefined, separate from sinners, and made higher than the heavens."[1071]

16. As the sinner once brought an offering to make the conversation clean, so now it is that the reformer, after personally accepting the weight, meaning, and intention of *heaven's* offering, is to enter into creation's classroom with the words, "Draw nigh unto my soul, and redeem it,"[1072] for it is written, "He shall redeem their soul from deceit and violence."[1073] Recovery of the conversation's conscience has always been the living God's mission, and by actively engaging with His wisdom, it is that, by our faith on that counsel's will, that wisdom can now do what man has so pitifully been trying to do for himself, namely, achieve a good conscience before the living God.

17. As the conversation accepts *heaven's* will and joins by faith into its arms through the course of its mediation, it will confess, "We also joy in God through our Lord Jesus Christ, by whom we have now received the atonement."[1074] Hereafter, through *heaven's* counsel, the saying is fulfilled, "The priest shall make an atonement for his sin that he hath committed, and it shall be forgiven him."[1075]

18. Our sacrifice for religious error is accomplished. Our atonement and reconciliation to *heaven's* throne is a living fact. By faith on

---

1066   1 Peter 2:8
1067   Galatians 3:12
1068   Hebrews 9:10
1069   Hebrews 9:11
1070   Hebrews 8:1
1071   Hebrews 7:27
1072   Psalms 69:18
1073   Psalms 72:14
1074   Romans 5:11
1075   Leviticus 4:35

His Prophet's understanding, the believer is "circumcised with the circumcision made without hands"[1076] as soon as they willingly turn to that "more perfect tabernacle, not made with hands."[1077]

19. The living God has given our conversation creation's course to teach and to convict, to pronounce and to dress, to direct and to comfort, and it is to be experienced for the purpose of mental and spiritual health. He has spoken and ordained the process concerning our personal faith's redemption; who will hear Him? He has fulfilled the reconciliation of the penitent and heartbroken to His throne, their errors in devotional thought and deed covered the moment their mind accepts the invitation, yet who will hear, "Let him that is athirst come"?[1078]

20. Know creation's doctrine. Embrace the law of its will that it may freely execute its *name*, ever progressing in a living experience by an experimental faith. There is no need to overthink faith's simplicity, for "because he believed in his God,"[1079] Daniel was saved from the mouth of lions.

1076   Colossians 2:11
1077   Hebrews 9:11
1078   Revelation 22:17
1079   Daniel 6:23

20

An Ancient Lesson On Faith

1. Jeremiah once wrote, "Thus saith the LORD to me; Make thee bonds and yokes, and put them upon thy neck, and send them to the king of E'dom, and to the king of Moab, and to the king of the Am'monites, and to the king of Ty'rus, and to the king of Zi'don, by the hand of the messengers which come to Jerusalem."[1080]

2. "Command them to say unto their masters, Thus saith the LORD of hosts, the God of Israel...now have I given all these lands into the hand of Nebuchadnez'zar the king of Babylon, my servant... all nations shall serve him, and his son, and his son's son...And it shall come to pass, that the nation and kingdom which will not serve the same Nebuchadnez'zar the king of Babylon, and that will not put their neck under the yoke of the king of Babylon, that nation will I punish, saith the LORD, with the sword, and with the famine, and with the pestilence, until I have consumed them by his hand."[1081] "But the nations that bring their neck under the yoke of the king of Babylon, and serve

1080 Jeremiah 27:2,3
1081 Jeremiah 27:4-8

him, those will I let remain still in their own land, saith the LORD; and they shall till it, and dwell therein."[1082]

3. It was counseled, "Be not afraid of the king of Babylon, of whom ye are afraid; be not afraid of him, saith the LORD: for I am with you to save you, and to deliver you from his hand."[1083]

4. And again, they were counseled, "Serve the king of Babylon, and live,"[1084] but what was the disposition of the people towards this advice? It is written, "As for the word that thou hast spoken unto us in the name of the LORD, we will not hearken unto thee."[1085] Thus, for disobeying this charge, "in the ninth year of Zedeki'ah king of Judah, in the tenth month, came Nebuchadnez'zar king of Babylon and all his army against Jerusalem, and they besieged it. And in the eleventh year of Zedeki'ah, in the fourth month, the ninth day of the month, the city was broken up."[1086]

5. "They took the king, and brought him up to the king of Babylon to Rib'lah; and they gave judgment upon him."[1087] "The rest of the people that were left in the city, and the fugitives that fell away to the king of Babylon, with the remnant of the multitude, did Neb'uzar-a'dan the captain of the guard carry away."[1088] This same guard "brake down the walls of Jerusalem round about"[1089] "and he burnt the house of the LORD, and the king's house, and all the houses of Jerusalem."[1090]

6. "Whatsoever things were written aforetime were written for our learning,"[1091] and it is that as the living God counseled His people of old to rest under the rule of His appointed king, so too has He commanded "that every tongue should confess that Jesus Christ is Lord, to the glory of the Father."[1092]

1082   Jeremiah 27:11
1083   Jeremiah 42:11
1084   Jeremiah 27:17
1085   Jeremiah 44:16
1086   Jeremiah 39:1,2
1087   2 Kings 25:6
1088   2 Kings 25:11
1089   2 Kings 25:10
1090   2 Kings 25:9
1091   Romans 15:4
1092   Philippians 2:11

7. It was God who did promise that "he would raise up Christ to sit on his throne,"[1093] for which cause it says, "This is my beloved Son: hear him."[1094] "Therefore being by the right hand of God exalted, and having received of the Father the promise of the Holy Ghost, he hath shed forth this"[1095] "to them that obey him."[1096]

8. It was only by obeying *heaven's* counsel that them of old could rest secure, but the people rejected His voice, leaving Him to declare against them, "I will watch over them for evil, and not for good."[1097] It was because of fear that none heard *heaven's* advice, for it says that king Zedeki'ah said, "I am afraid,"[1098] but the prophet advised him to exercise faith in the living God, saying, "It shall be well unto thee, and thy soul shall live."[1099]

9. It is in the same sense that salvation's science says, "Keep my commandments, and live; and my law as the apple of thine eye,"[1100] and, "Let thine heart retain my words: keep my commandments, and live."[1101]

10. It is our responsibility to know the living God's present *voice*. He says, "Give me thine heart, and let thine eyes observe my ways,"[1102] for it is "the doctrine of God our Saviour";[1103] which doctrine is "the word of faith"[1104] "and of the knowledge of the Son of God";[1105] that is to be heard and made the diet of the reformer. We then do well to know that when taking hold of this wisdom, and of every detail explaining the recovery of the conversation through it, the heart will feel for the living

1093 Acts 2:30
1094 Mark 9:7
1095 Acts 2:33
1096 Acts 5:32
1097 Jeremiah 44:27
1098 Jeremiah 38:19
1099 Jeremiah 38:20
1100 Proverbs 7:2
1101 Proverbs 4:4
1102 Proverbs 23:26
1103 Titus 2:10
1104 Romans 10:8
1105 Ephesians 4:13

God, and to the *body* of our faith will be given an education executed in the temple of the soul.

11. The Jews of old rejected the living God's counsel. It was fear that took their heart into the route of stubbornness, and for us today, the saying is no different: "Grieve not the holy Spirit of God."[1106]

12. It is written, "They hated knowledge, and did not choose the fear of the LORD,"[1107] but if we would learn anything from them, it should be to faithfully learn of and prove "the law of Christ."[1108] It is only by hearing and doing *heaven's* doctrine; or as He says, "The word of my patience";[1109] that we may come to know that "fear hath torment."[1110] It is by faith on *heaven's* intention that love will be made a living virtue, and as His doctrine is heard and received, so it will be "that Christ may dwell in your hearts by faith."[1111]

13. *Heaven* wisdom says, "Keep my commandments,"[1112] letting us known that to this doctrine belongs "the ordinances of justice,"[1113] that is, the precepts of how "God would justify the heathen through faith."[1114] "That we might be justified by the faith of Christ,"[1115] it was confirmed in Abraham, "I will bless them that bless thee,"[1116] to the end that all who would take on Abraham's *nature* should have one who "took on him the seed of Abraham."[1117]

14. This seed and *nature* is "the faith of Abraham";[1118] "the righteousness which is by faith";[1119] that "the righteousness of God which is by faith of Jesus Christ"[1120] would fall on the faithful conversation "for

---

1106 Ephesians 4:30
1107 Proverbs 1:29
1108 Galatians 6:2
1109 Revelation 3:10
1110 1 John 4:18
1111 Ephesians 3:17
1112 John 14:15
1113 Isaiah 58:2
1114 Galatians 3:8
1115 Galatians 2:16
1116 Genesis 12:3
1117 Hebrews 2:16
1118 Romans 4:13
1119 Hebrews 11:7
1120 Romans 3:22

the remission of sins that are past."[1121] By faithfully experimenting with the Bible's present spiritual understanding, the doer will be placed into that understanding's classroom or *kingdom* for receiving "abundance of grace and of the gift of righteousness"[1122] to purify their mind and to edify one another, for they now have "an advocate with the Father,"[1123] even an interceding commandment that "ever liveth to make intercession for them."[1124]

15. As "the first covenant had also ordinances of divine service, and a worldly sanctuary,"[1125] so too the present covenant has a heavenly Sanctuary with *ordinances* for *heaven's* will and wisdom. "Our conversation is in heaven"[1126] "where Christ sitteth on the right hand of God,"[1127] for therein rests every promise of the *Godhead* to their wisdom's doer.

16. Our present counsel is "to be conformed to the image of his Son."[1128] The living God "made peace through the blood of his cross"[1129] "to reconcile all things to himself";[1130] it is intended that our conversation's conscience "should be holy and without blame before him in love,"[1131] and "that we might be made the righteousness of God in him."[1132] The saying of *heaven's* righteousness is concealed within the Bible's present spiritual understanding. When obeying this wisdom, it will be fulfilled, "I will dwell in them, and walk in them; and I will be their God, and they shall be my people."[1133]

17. His words "not being mixed with faith"[1134] will profit no one. The Jews of old refused to obey *heaven's* advice and felt the penalty. "Those

---

1121 Romans 3:25
1122 Romans 5:17
1123 1 John 2:1
1124 Hebrews 7:25
1125 Hebrews 9:1
1126 Philippians 3:20
1127 Colossians 3:1
1128 Romans 8:29
1129 Colossians 1:20
1130 Colossians 1:20
1131 Ephesians 1:4
1132 2 Corinthians 5:21
1133 2 Corinthians 6:16
1134 Hebrews 4:2

mine enemies, which would not that I should reign over them,"[1135] says *heaven's* doctrine, "God shall send them strong delusion...because they received not the love of the truth, that they might be saved."[1136] The conversation refusing to humble its heart and to quiet its mind so that creation's counsel may subdue, heal, and elevate its inward person, will "stumble, and fall, and be broken, and be snared, and be taken"[1137] "away with the error of the wicked."[1138]

18. God said that He would give all things into the hand of Nebuchadnez'zar the king of Babylon, and then told His people, "Seek the peace of the city whither I have caused you to be carried away...that ye may be increased there."[1139]

19. At this time, we should know that "the Father loveth the Son, and hath given all things into his hand";[1140] "of the increase of his government and peace there shall be no end."[1141] Therefore "see that ye refuse not him that speaketh";[1142] "that speaketh from heaven";[1143] even that mediating wisdom "passed into the heavens, Jesus the Son of God."[1144]

20. The "just" is born when personally accepting *heaven's* new covenant wisdom as their conversation's Savior. By faithfully learning of and proving *heaven's* commandment, the conversation enters into creation's classroom to become perfect. "Listen and 'thy soul shall live,'"[1145] said the prophet to the king of Judah, and the same counsel is for every one that cares to feel for *heaven's* present intention. If indeed the heart is surrendered to the living God's science, the saying will be

---

1135   Luke 19:27
1136   2 Thessalonians 2:10-12
1137   Isaiah 8:15
1138   2 Peter 3:17
1139   Jeremiah 29:6,7
1140   John 3:35
1141   Isaiah 9:7
1142   Hebrews 12:25
1143   Hebrews 12:25
1144   Hebrews 4:14
1145   Jeremiah 38:20

fulfilled, "I am come that they might have life, and that they might have it more abundantly."[1146]

21. All of these things relating to the health of our faith's mind is fulfilled by the living God and confirmed in His spiritual understanding. All things for mental and spiritual health are by and flow through *heaven's* wisdom. The eye of our faith should patiently wait on this wisdom's benefit, for it is written, "On mine arm shall they trust,"[1147] therefore it is said, "God hath sent forth the Spirit of his Son into your hearts."[1148]

22. "The Spirit is life,"[1149] and "if any man have not the Spirit of Christ, he is none of his."[1150] It is the power of the Mind behind *heaven's* commandment that is to fill the reformer's inward parts, for it says, "Be filled with the Spirit,"[1151] or rather, "Be filled with all the fullness of God,"[1152] which fullness is contained "in the fullness of the blessing of the gospel of Christ."[1153] So we see that to receive the full power of God there must be compliance with the word spoken by Him, for without faithfully observing His words, there can be no benefit.

23. If the Jews of old had obeyed their commandment, blessing would have followed them. As the king of Babylon was blessed to rule the earth, so too the living God presently says of His doctrine, "Thy throne, O God, is for ever and ever."[1154] Refusing to actively believe on creation's new covenant doctrine will keep the heart separated from *heaven's* gifts, which shower is as medicine assisting our conversation's transformation into the likeness of *heaven's religious character*. The commandment was rejected of old, and it resulted in destruction; refusing creation's law, and refusing to acknowledge that commandment by an experimental faith, will do the same to the heart of our faith.

1146   John 10:10
1147   Isaiah 51:5
1148   Galatians 4:6
1149   Romans 8:10
1150   Romans 8:9
1151   Ephesians 5:18
1152   Ephesians 3:19
1153   Romans 15:29
1154   Hebrews 1:8

21

By The River Jordan

1. "John did baptize in the wilderness, and preach the baptism of repentance for the remission of sins. And there went out unto him all the land of Judae'a, and they of Jerusalem, and were all baptized of him in the river of Jordan, confessing their sins."[1155]

2. John preached purification by repentance for the cessation of sin in the inward parts, and he did this by bringing the attention of his hearers to Jordan. Many came from him pure in heart and mind, reconciled to the living God by faith, most desirous of that understanding concerning "the fellowship of the mystery."[1156] And he revealed this doctrine of his LORD by the way of Jordan, but how and why?

3. Traveling back to Jordan, we read: "When ye see the ark of the covenant of the LORD your God, and the priests the Levites bearing it, then ye shall remove from your place, and go after it."[1157] "It shall come to pass, as soon as the soles of the feet of the priests that bear the ark of the LORD, the Lord of all the earth, shall rest in the waters of Jordan, that the waters of Jordan shall be cut off from the waters that come

---

1155   Mark 1:4,5
1156   Ephesians 3:9
1157   Joshua 3:3

down from above; and they shall stand upon an heap."[1158] "Hereby ye shall know that the living God is among you."[1159]

4. The LORD once told Moses, "Make thee an ark of wood";[1160] "overlay it with pure gold, within and without shalt thou overlay it."[1161] The ark was to be of wood, for it is written, "The tree of the field is man's life,"[1162] and since it is that "all have sinned, and come short of the glory of God,"[1163] the wood was to be overlaid with gold, or as it says concerning gold, "Take the spoil of gold...the store and glory,"[1164] for it was in figure overlaid with glory or with righteousness. Within that chest of wood covered with gold were to rest the tables of the covenant, as it is written, "Put into the ark the testimony which I shall give thee,"[1165] and, "There was nothing in the ark save the two tables which Moses put there."[1166] As John did preach and edify many of his hearers in Jordan, he spoke on the work of One through flesh wearing the righteousness of His God and being filled with the testimony of His character, even as it is written, "He will magnify the law,"[1167] and, "I bring near my righteousness."[1168]

5. "The priests that bare the ark of the LORD's covenant stood firm on dry ground in the midst of Jordan,"[1169] for it was that "when it passed over Jordan, the waters of Jordan were cut off."[1170]

6. He who should appear before men, who beforehand bore the heart of the LORD's divine similitude, was to be "found in fashion as a man."[1171] Christ labored on His Father's earth as His LORD's represen-

1158 Joshua 3:13
1159 Joshua 3:10
1160 Deuteronomy 10:1
1161 Exodus 25:11
1162 Deuteronomy 20:19
1163 Romans 3:23
1164 Nahum 2:9
1165 Exodus 25:16
1166 2 Chronicles 5:10
1167 Isaiah 42:21
1168 Isaiah 46:13
1169 Joshua 3:17
1170 Joshua 4:7
1171 Philippians 2:8

tative, "being the brightness of his glory, and the express image of his person."[1172] This Christ wore the righteousness of His Father by faith on His Spirit's will while in fully sinful human flesh. While covering humanity's organs with divinity's wisdom and power, this Man housed within His inward parts "that eternal life, which was with the Father,"[1173] for it is written, "God anointed Jesus of Nazareth with the Holy Ghost and with power."[1174] Herein it is fulfilled, "God was in Christ."[1175] Christ, as that revelation of the Father's manner of love, bore the testimony of His LORD's name within His spirit, which is why He teaches, "That which is born of the Spirit is spirit."[1176]

7. John pointed his hearers to that terrible wonder of God from their past history. "'The LORD is great and very terrible,'[1177] said John, "'he shall baptize you with the Holy Ghost, and with fire';[1178] therefore remember how it is said, 'I will give to Jerusalem one that bringeth good tidings.'"[1179] Christ "came and preached peace,"[1180] that is, "Preached the gospel,"[1181] and John called the attention of those looking for the Christ to remember Jordan, confessing, "This is the word which by the gospel is preached unto you."[1182]

8. The Ark of the Covenant was to create a way for the Israelites to pass through the waters. As "the feet of the priests that bare the ark were dipped in the brim of the water,"[1183] the waters "stood and rose up upon an heap";[1184] "all the Israelites passed over on dry ground."[1185] God's Man; whose learning came from that Building above the earth;

1172 Hebrews 1:3
1173 1 John 1:2
1174 Acts 10:38
1175 2 Corinthians 5:10
1176 John 3:6
1177 Joel 2:11
1178 Matthew 3:11
1179 Isaiah 41:27
1180 Ephesians 2:17
1181 Luke 20:1
1182 1 Peter 1:2
1183 Joshua 3:15
1184 Joshua 3:16
1185 Joshua 3:17

conquered the constitution of human flesh and the sickness within it by that wisdom contained within His spirit; as it says, "Let the word of Christ dwell in you richly in all wisdom";[1186] that His experience should be shared with whoever would care to overcome their own self even as He Himself overcame. Through the righteousness which is only by faith on His approach to godliness, they who would take hold on this Man's name will pass through waters onto dry ground, for the Spirit has promised, "When thou passest through the waters, I will be with thee."[1187] But what do the waters represent for us? It is written, "Terrors take hold on him as waters,"[1188] and, "Snares are found about thee, and sudden fear troubleth thee; or darkness, that thou canst not see; and abundance of waters cover thee."[1189] Therefore it was fulfilled in Him, "The people which sat in darkness saw great light; and to them which sat in the region and shadow of death light is sprung up."[1190]

9. Again it is known, "Dead things are formed under the waters,"[1191] therefore it is written, "Jesus went unto them, walking on the sea."[1192] It was ordained that Christ, "by the grace of God should taste death for every man,"[1193] "that through death he might destroy him that had the power of death"[1194] "and deliver them who through fear of death were all their lifetime subject to bondage."[1195] Our High Priest desires to liberate every willing and humble spirit from self's "bondage of corruption"[1196] and from "the spirit of bondage again to fear"[1197] the religious world, therefore it is written, "He shall redeem their soul from deceit and violence."[1198]

1186 Colossians 3:16
1187 Isaiah 43:2
1188 Job 27:20
1189 Job 22:10,11
1190 Matthew 4:16
1191 Job 26:5
1192 Matthew 14:25
1193 Hebrews 2:9
1194 Hebrews 2:14
1195 Hebrews 2:15
1196 Romans 8:21
1197 Romans 8:15
1198 Psalms 72:14

10. This Christ conquered mental and spiritual death for us, and He let us know that He would by walking on water. They who would believe on the virtue of His name "are made nigh by the blood of Christ,"[1199] that is, are brought to God through faith in the assurance of "the blood of his cross."[1200] If death exists within and under the waters, and if His Man is above the waters that keep confusion, then the counsel is true, "Seek those things which are above, where Christ sitteth on the right hand of God."[1201] Truly "our conversation is in heaven"[1202] "where neither moth nor rust doth corrupt, and where thieves do not break through nor steal."[1203] Therefore, "Look upon Zion...not one of the stakes thereof shall ever be removed,"[1204] says the LORD, "neither shall any of the cords thereof be broken."[1205] "Look unto me, and be ye saved."[1206] If the believer should exercise a living faith on their salvation's Captain, they too will walk on the same water as their Lord of this transformation, for what is written? "When Peter was come down out of the ship, he walked on the water, to go to Jesus."[1207]

11. The eye of faith allowed Peter to walk on water, "but when he saw the wind boisterous, he was afraid; and beginning to sink, he cried, saying, Lord, save me."[1208] What then was the counsel given to Peter? "O thou of little faith,"[1209] He said. It took faith to believe that an ark of wood and covered with gold should produce any effect on nature when carried by men. It was present faith that caused God to do "that which is against nature,"[1210] for the waters did "stand upon an heap,"[1211]

1199 Ephesians 2:13
1200 Colossians 1:20
1201 Colossians 3:1
1202 Philippians 3:20
1203 Matthew 6:20
1204 Isaiah 33:20
1205 Isaiah 33:20
1206 Isaiah 45:22
1207 Matthew 14:29
1208 Matthew 14:30
1209 Matthew 14:31
1210 Romans 1:26
1211 Joshua 3:13

and "every thing was finished that the LORD commanded."[1212] As soon as Joshua had finished rehearsing the Spirit's words, "the people removed from their tents, to pass over Jordan"[1213] "not faithless, but believing."[1214]

12. The LORD reports of His host, "Ye have not kept my ways, but have been partial in the law,"[1215] therefore John said, "Make straight the way of the Lord."[1216] The way of God is accomplished when one continues on "as seeing him who is invisible."[1217] The one who rests in His every word by faith on the end to appear by that saying, to them will be given power to advance in what seems utterly far from accomplishment. Due to their faithfulness, the Israelites were told upon passing over Jordan, "Circumcise <u>again</u> the children of Israel the second time."[1218] As these placed faith into the hand of God and were again recognized as His, so too when faith is placed on Him that will also conquer the waters of the soul and the terrors of the mind, the believer will then be "circumcised with the circumcision made without hands."[1219] At this, John counseled his hearers, "Behold the Lamb of God."[1220] In Jordan there was to be a second circumcision more perfect than the first. This is why John counseled, "God is able of these stones to raise up children unto Abraham."[1221]

13. Why did John not say of their God, "And raise up children unto Himself?" It is because Christ "took on him the seed of Abraham,"[1222] which seed is that seed "made like unto his brethren,"[1223] for of His own brethren He said, "Whosoever shall do the will of God, the same

---

1212 Joshua 4:10
1213 Joshua 3:14
1214 John 20:27
1215 Malachi 2:9
1216 John 1:23
1217 Hebrews 11:27
1218 Joshua 5:2
1219 Colossians 2:11
1220 John 1:29
1221 Matthew 3:9
1222 Hebrews 2:16
1223 Hebrews 2:16,17

is my brother."[1224] It is for this reason that the Spirit says, "Thou, Israel, art my servant, Jacob whom I have chosen, the seed of Abraham my friend."[1225] The Israel of God are formed after the name and character of Abraham, which virtue Christ also took on, wherefore the Spirit says, "Look unto Abraham your father,"[1226] for He meant that all should "walk in the steps of that faith,"[1227] for "faith was reckoned to Abraham for righteousness,"[1228] and after that faith was exercised, "he received the sign of circumcision."[1229] The Israelites at Jordan commanded the attention of God by their faith in His counsel, as did Abraham please God from believing His promise, for Christ declared, "O faithless and perverse generation,"[1230] to the end it would be known, "Thy faith hath saved thee."[1231]

14. John pointed his hearers to a second circumcision as it was depicted of old. He said, "If the blood of bulls and of goats, and the ashes of an heifer sprinkling the unclean, sanctifieth to the purifying of the flesh: how much more shall the blood of Christ...purge your conscience from dead works to serve the living God?"[1232] John took the people to the way of Jordan and taught how faith on the Spirit's course would pronounce justification, and from that sanctification a circumcision by "the Spirit of the living God; not on tables of stone, but in fleshly tables of the heart."[1233] From yielding implicit faith on the fact that the LORD "hath reconciled us to himself by Jesus Christ,"[1234] taking hold of every precious promise of hope given for the stability of the spirit and preservation of the will, the believer will know the LORD

1224 Mark 3:35
1225 Isaiah 41:8
1226 Isaiah 51:2
1227 Romans 4:12
1228 Romans 4:9
1229 Romans 4:11
1230 Matthew 17:17
1231 Luke 7:50
1232 Hebrews 9:13,14
1233 2 Corinthians 3:3
1234 2 Corinthians 5:18

of this kindness, fulfilling the saying, "I will dwell in them, and walk in them."[1235]

15. Them of old who were again circumcised heard the word, "This day have I rolled away the reproach of Egypt from off you."[1236] After that angel "descended from heaven, and came and rolled back the stone from the door,"[1237] it was that a new hope entered into the atmosphere of the religious world for every spirit therein, and it was then reinforced, "I will not leave you comfortless."[1238] It was said of old, "He will comfort all her waste places,"[1239] and now it is fulfilled, "In Christ Jesus ye who sometimes were far off are made nigh by the blood of Christ."[1240] Christ takes those ordinances that are "against us, which were contrary to us"[1241] "after the commandments and doctrines of men,"[1242] and in their place has permitted faith as the means to have us "quickened together with him."[1243] Thus, it is said, "Whosoever believeth that Jesus is the Christ is born of God,"[1244] for it is by faith on the doctrine of God that the spirit will achieve His righteousness by the gift of righteousness, to the end the soul would be purified by His Spirit, as it says, "Ye have purified your souls in obeying the truth through the Spirit."[1245]

16. In both instances; that of Abraham and that of Israel led by Joshua; trust in the word of God provided circumcision through a faith that pronounced once righteous. John had carried his audiences to this pillar of their history to announce that faith would birth an experience apart from that commonly known, which is why to those who heard John, Christ said, "Except your righteousness shall exceed the righteousness of the scribes and Pharisees, ye shall in no case enter

---

1235 2 Corinthians 6:16
1236 Joshua 5:9
1237 Matthew 28:2
1238 John 14:18
1239 Isaiah 51:3
1240 Ephesians 2:13
1241 Colossians 2:14
1242 Colossians 2:22
1243 Colossians 2:13
1244 1 John 5:1
1245 1 Peter 1:22

into the kingdom of heaven."[1246] Thus, faith "on him that justifieth the ungodly"[1247] educates on this point: "God imputeth righteousness without works."[1248]

17. John was pointing hearts to an instance of faith exercised by their own people, which faith they had forgotten through "Jewish fables, and commandments of men, that turn from the truth."[1249] John announced: "Behold the Lamb of God who is to bear away our errors against our LORD and Father that we may more perfectly serve Him, even that Spirit who will operate through the members of the flesh while covered and filled with a divine law that we cannot perceive but by faith. 'What he hath seen and heard that he testifieth.'[1250] 'He that hath received his testimony hath set to his seal that God is true.'"[1251]

18. The Ark in the midst of the waters caused the waters to part, allowing the people to safely pass through. Christ appeared as the living oracle of the Spirit "who gave himself for our sins,"[1252] to the end we might, "by the faith of him,"[1253] safely pass into that heavenly Place of recovery "according to the will of God."[1254]

19. Our Priest would have every believer keep His name at the center of their terrors as that Captain over the ship of their liberty from the island of personal and religious bondage. He has gained our victory over this death in His own soul and body for us, but who will believe the fact? An unstable heart is no more felt by personal and ignorant fear when in Christ's law, but who will experience this fact to obtain this testimony? John purified in the way of Jordan to call all to re-establish the LORD's benevolence within their spirit by an experimental religion on heaven's pure will. Christ said, "If ye were Abraham's children,

1246 Matthew 5:20
1247 Romans 4:5
1248 Romans 4:6
1249 Titus 1:14
1250 John 3:32
1251 John 3:33
1252 Galatians 1:4
1253 Ephesians 3:12
1254 Galatians 1:4

ye would do the works of Abraham,"¹²⁵⁵ for the work of Abraham is to be accomplished now. The seed of Abraham know, "Believe on him whom he hath sent";¹²⁵⁶ "believe on the name of his Son Jesus Christ";¹²⁵⁷ for "he that believeth on the Son of God hath the witness in himself."¹²⁵⁸ Having His witness for the Father's good kindness towards man's inward person, the believer has life, and that life is blessed of His Spirit, therefore "through the Spirit wait for the hope of righteousness by faith,"¹²⁵⁹ because "the Spirit is life."¹²⁶⁰

20. John desired all to know that the faith of Abraham would reign in the priesthood of the Spirit's Christ. No longer would the weak order of men prevail among God's host, for the religious experience was to enter into the direct presence of the LORD and His Son by faith alone. In Jordan we find ourselves confronted with a testing judgment, which when obeyed resulted in blessing, and the lesson is for us. If the heart would obey the Spirit's counsel for the ransom and regeneration of the soul and spirit; a saying that confronts the carnal human sensibilities and challenge the perverse human rationale; our Father will finish the work. Obedience will engrave the promise within the conscience, "It is God which worketh,"¹²⁶¹ for experience from obedience will move the heart to confess, "I also labour, striving according to his working, which worketh in me mightily."¹²⁶²

21. The Christian becomes a co-worker with God, cooperating with His Spirit to perfect His name in them, and that perfecting "to the praise of the glory of his grace."¹²⁶³ God has secured "a new and living way, which he hath consecrated for us"¹²⁶⁴ to draw nearer to His throne "by the blood of Jesus"¹²⁶⁵ "with a true heart in full assurance

---

1255 John 8:39
1256 John 6:29
1257 1 John 3:23
1258 1 John 5:10
1259 Galatians 5:5
1260 Romans 8:10
1261 Philippians 2:13
1262 Colossians 1:29
1263 Ephesians 1:6
1264 Hebrews 10:20
1265 Hebrews 10:19

of faith."[1266] Thus, for every inquiry, and for the accomplishment of His benevolent will, "ye are come unto mount Si'on, and unto the city of the living God"[1267] which holds "the general assembly and church of the firstborn."[1268] In this heavenly Building, Christ is "the mediator of the new covenant"[1269] bearing "an unchangeable priesthood"[1270] as that King of the LORD's righteousness upon grace's throne. Thus, when the sorrowful soul cries, "Rid me, and deliver me out of great waters,"[1271] the Lord of this science will hear and say, "'I will,'[1272] but what about you?"

22. "Peace, be still,"[1273] says our Priest, for "the wind and the sea obey him."[1274] Christ demolished spiritual confusion and then gave life for those errors that were "against us, which was contrary to us,"[1275] for He and His Father said in council, "The wind was contrary unto them,"[1276] that is, the "wind of doctrine, by the slight of men."[1277] John knew that "where the Spirit of the Lord is, there is liberty,"[1278] therefore he "bare witness unto the truth"[1279] of the Spirit's intention and said, "Behold the Lamb of God!"[1280]

23. Says this Lamb, "John came unto you in the way of righteousness,"[1281] for all were taught by him in the manner of righteousness through faith by the way of Jordan. The end of faithfulness is a spirit that actuated our Priest to be "made in the likeness of men,"[1282]

<hr>

1266 Hebrews 10:22
1267 Hebrews 12:22
1268 Hebrews 12:23
1269 Hebrews 12:24
1270 Hebrews 7:24
1271 Psalms 144:7
1272 Mark 1:41
1273 Mark 4:39
1274 Mark 4:41
1275 Colossians 2:14
1276 Mark 6:42
1277 Ephesians 4:14
1278 2 Corinthians 3:17
1279 John 5:32
1280 John 1:36
1281 Matthew 21:33
1282 Philippians 2:8

to the end that His character would be reproduced not simply within us, but by revelation of His name through us, that those within our sphere would be touched and benefitted from observing His work in our person, "that now at this time your abundance may be a supply for their want."[1283] John came in the way of righteousness, that is, he taught many to cultivate faith by diligently exercising the members of the heart and mind through "the righteousness of faith,"[1284] for there would be a doctrine from God's Spirit to obey, and that word preached being "the gospel of the kingdom of God."[1285] It is this law of God's Spirit that, when accepted and acted out by faith, and when diligently divided in the presence of the Godhead, will bring the soul into complete harmony with His will and laws of government.

1283   2 Corinthians 2:8
1284   Romans 4:13
1285   Romans 4:13

22

The Character of Rebellion

1. "The serpent said unto the woman, Ye shall not surely die"; but they were told, "Of the tree of the knowledge of good and evil, thou shalt not eat of it: for in the day that thou eatest thereof thou shalt surely die."[1286]

2. The counsel was: "I have given you every herb bearing seed, which is upon the face of all the earth, and every tree, in the which is the fruit of a tree yielding seed; to you it shall be for meat."[1287] "But of the tree of the knowledge of good and evil, thou shalt not eat of it: for in the day that thou eatest thereof thou shalt surely die."[1288]

3. The commandment was a decree of *life* and *death*, and anything against this message should have caused the heart to grow faint and weary. There was a promise given to Adam in this commandment, and the promise was *death*. Because the Creator had spoken this counsel, immediately His promise would fill the violator of it, yet the charge spoken against His commandment was by a serpent "which the LORD God had made";[1289] leaving no power in the creation but rather in the Creator; yet Eve obeyed the creation above the Creator.

1286   Genesis 2:17
1287   Genesis 1:29
1288   Genesis 2:17
1289   Genesis 3:1

4. God had anointed the fruit of the tree with a *death* as soon as He had pronounced the consequence for indulging in it, for, before this time, "He spake, and it was done,"[1290] yet Eve honored the voice of creation above that Creator giving *power* to His endeavor.

5. Eve is our lesson. The conversation not willing to diligently honor the living God's voice, carefully studying after the pattern of His impression to honor His decreed will, will remain within the voice of *God's creation* holding dear to that philosophy He did initiate, but which He has placed no current power of authority in.

6. The words of God comes first, and seeing as how He has made all things, His voice is not given to all things, but all things rather derive their form from His voice and at His command are swept away at His choosing, as it says, "Thou, Lord, in the beginning hast laid the foundation of the earth; and the heavens are the works of thine hands: they shall perish; but thou remainest,"[1291] and, "That which decayeth and waxeth old is ready to vanish away."[1292] Eve did not believe the living God's commandment, and did only care to have a voice consent to her own thoughts to justify her own beliefs to have a way to perform her own actions. Nevertheless, despite her inclination, the Creator's words stood firm.

7. The conversation not willing to be governed by the living God's wisdom will be left to govern the *body* of its faith's alone. The conversation that would observe tradition over a personal experience, or that would obtain *power* from numbers of *bodies*, placing emotion as the drive of their overall devotion, will, unless that conversation's mind is surrendered to His science, pass away in the vanity of such an experience. The conversation desiring to be its own savior will be given the right to be its own savior at the expense of self-violation, for when self is continually violated, the heart becomes numb to its correction, and the seed of delusion is all that may be given until that *person* is laid in the *grave*.

1290   Psalms 33:9
1291   Hebrews 1:10
1292   Hebrews 8:13

8. The Bible's words are living. These words are "quick, and powerful,"[1293] in that they are "a discerner of the thoughts and intents of the heart,"[1294] and those who would reject *heaven's* influence for such a labor occurring in them "hath never forgiveness, but is in danger of eternal damnation."[1295] In essence, to reject the mental and spiritual correction given from learning of and proving the Bible's words is to situate our faith's mind in a place where it will degenerate into the superstition we believe on and trust.

9. To disregard a thorough investigation of the Bible's present counsel, and the means to obtain its prize, and the process of continual regeneration to maintain reconciliation with that source of mental and inward health, is to deny *life* and *health* to the conversation's conscience, and to reject the authority of the living God's mind over that conscience. Herein it is well to remember how it is said, "Ye were not redeemed with corruptible things, as silver and gold, from your vain conversation received by tradition."[1296]

10. A *curse* against the conversation's conscience is, like as of old, presently pronounced against the mind not willing to personally study creation's science. There is an appointed *death* for the conversation failing to concern its self with the waymarks leading to the current *place* of His voice.

11. His commandment's chief apostle once instructed his disciples to go and to secure a place for feasting. Of his instructions, it is said, "His disciples went forth, and came into the city, and found as he had said."[1297]

12. Why was it done as he had said? Why did the very things told to the disciples come to pass as spoken? How could every event he spoke of beforehand line up with the events that took place when they were physically established afterward? The answer is found in the saying, "He commanded, and they were created."[1298]

1293 Hebrews 4:12
1294 Hebrews 4:12
1295 Mark 3:29
1296 1 Peter 1:18
1297 Mark 14:16
1298 Psalms 148:5

13. The living God's religious character was pronounced to *men*; the counsel to be obeyed by *men* came from the philosophy of His chief minister, who spoke the entire plan behind *heaven's* will. How then can one say, "I am of Christ," when failing to honor and examine his saying with a pure heart? How may the conversation claim obedience to that saying while remaining subject to what His own voice has annihilated? How can one maintain trust without subjecting the heart to a trial by faith? How can one claim the Bible's religion, yet by *dead* services uplift what turns His commandment's mind away?

14. Eve had placed faith in that which God had made and not in what He had spoken, for that which He had created had a persuasive voice, but it did not have *power* within itself to override the word first spoken by Him.

15. The voice proceeding out of the creature that was created touched the *flesh*, or the *body* of the conversation, and nothing else. That which God had made, which He Himself had deemed "good" within itself was "good" in and of itself, but no matter how good that *thing* of God was, it was not to be held higher than the Creator of it.

16. The thing made did not originate from its self. The substance of *God* within the serpent did work to cause the essence of *life* to exude from it, but the creature had its own *diet* to abide by. This is why it says, "To every beast...wherein there is life, I have given every green herb for meat."[1299]

17. There was *life* within the beast that man was not to come into contact with. This life, upon *man's* regeneration, was not in *man*, for "man became a living soul."[1300] To the *life* of *man* was added a soul with a conscience to will and to provoke. But after their error, "Adam called his wife's name Eve; because she was the mother of all living,"[1301] or rather, because she had blatant intercourse with *life*, which *life* was *death* at the expense of her soul, making her state of mind the womb of the spiritually rebellious.

1299   Genesis 1:30
1300   Genesis 2:7
1301   Genesis 3:20

18. You will not see that the flood of old destroyed the soul of just any *person*, but it says, "To destroy all flesh, wherein is the breath of life."[1302] Was not life ordained "to every beast of the earth, and to every fowl of the air, and to every thing that creepeth upon the earth, wherein there is life"?[1303] For what reason is that *diet* of a lower order found within that group created for a higher purpose?

19. That which contained *life* so mingled with ministers that they became flesh-based. By setting aside the original *diet* given to them by *heaven* for the regulation of their *body*, mind, and spirit, they devised a service according to their own spiritual desire, fulfilling the saying, "They whose judgment was not to drink of the cup have assuredly drunken."[1304]

20. The doctrine of the mother of all living procured a "flood upon the world of the ungodly,"[1305] and the grain of her creed could have been avoided if she, for herself, had contemplated *heaven's* instruction. The conversation possessing Eve's statement of faith is noted by Scripture as the "ungodly," for these are "them that hate the LORD,"[1306] handling what was advised to be put away. Because she failed to let herself become familiar with His commandment, she had no living relationship with creation's wisdom. It was therefore easy to allow her heart to mingle error with truth, seeing as how she had already, at heart, rejected this will as a rule over her faith's mind.

21. There is a category for those who would not have creation's new covenant experience, and it is as said: "Those mine enemies, which would not that I should reign over them,"[1307] and, "Presumptuous are they, selfwilled, they are not afraid to speak evil of dignities."[1308]

22. Eve showed no fear when she spoke against *heaven's* counsel when admitting, "The tree was good."[1309] Who is the minister to declare

---

1302   Genesis 6:17
1303   Genesis 1:30
1304   Jeremiah 49:12
1305   2 Peter 2:5
1306   2 Chronicles 19:2
1307   Luke 19:27
1308   2 Peter 2:10
1309   Genesis 3:6

that *thing* "good" which God Himself has accursed as being not good? Who is *man* to continue in a *thing* cursed and forgotten of the living God? He spoke against the fruit of the tree and left the matter alone, not concerning Himself with what His man could or would do, for He placed simple and unadulterated trust in ministers. Yet Eve did not trust His advice, and her response, "God hath said, Ye shall not eat of it, neither shall ye touch it, lest ye die,"[1310] was full proof of her heart.

23. *Heaven* doesn't compel to do or to not do; it is known, "Is it any pleasure to the Almighty, that thou art righteous? or is it gain to him, that thou makest thy ways perfect?"[1311] and, "Except your righteousness shall exceed the righteousness of the scribes and Pharisees, ye shall in no case enter into the kingdom of heaven."[1312]

24. "God is no respecter of persons,"[1313] "but in every nation he that feareth him, and worketh righteousness, is accepted with him."[1314] That which Eve recited was not of the living God, for "God commanded the man,"[1315] and that which she rehearsed was that which she comprehended from Adam, and that tone of her voice admitting that she was not content with what she had heard from him, nor did believe any *thing* spoken to him. God had simply said, "Thou shalt not eat of it,"[1316] and He left from the matter to declare why, saying, "For in the day that thou eatest thereof thou shalt surely die,"[1317] but all that the woman gathered from Adam was, "God hath said, Ye shall not,"[1318] therefore she quickly obeyed the word given to her.

25. That which took place in the garden repeated itself in the time of Moses, for Moses, in relation to the Israelites, had said of himself, "I stood between the LORD and you...to shew you the word of the

---

1310 Genesis 3:3
1311 Job 22:3
1312 Mathew 5:20
1313 Acts 10:34
1314 Acts 10:35
1315 Genesis 2:16
1316 Genesis 2:17
1317 Genesis 2:17
1318 Genesis 3:3

LORD."[1319] Adam took up the work of Moses and made known to the woman the Creator's words, but she would not receive them. Instead of allowing the consequences for disobedience to reach her heart, instead of listening to Adam recite the *power* within His voice to awaken fear for *eating* what was accursed, Eve kept hidden, in her heart, the fact that she could not *eat*, and in not being able to recognize what was being said, she then concluded, "I cannot eat, I cannot touch."

26. In not being able to touch, she concluded, "Everything here spoken is foolishness," and in concluding the commandment foolish, she already believed, within "her heart, I am, and there is none beside me."[1320] Hence, it was easy to receive the saying, "God doth know that in the day ye eat thereof, then your eyes shall be opened, and ye shall be as gods,"[1321] for the woman had the foundation of rebellion within her religious character due to her failing to exercise that wisdom appearing only by an experimental faith.

27. Eve grew tired of obtaining righteousness from humble obedience. This is exposed from how, when "the woman saw that the tree was good for food, and that it was pleasant to the eyes, and a tree to be desired to make one wise, she took of the fruit thereof, and did eat."[1322]

28. The righteousness of *man* had been freely given because of his compliance with the living God's voice. So long as Adam obeyed the commandment, he was upheld by creation's righteousness, but the woman refused to let creation's law permeate into the temple of her soul, for it only reached her *flesh* and no father.

29. Eve would not blatantly disregard the *man* of her God, for although Adam spoke to her, she knew the voice was of God, but there was in her a misapprehension of that voice, causing a breach in her heart. She therefore, as the Israelites of old, flippantly declared, "All that the Lord has said, I will obey and do."[1323] But when even *creation*

1319 Deuteronomy 5:5
1320 Zephaniah 2:15
1321 Genesis 3:5
1322 Genesis 3:6
1323 Exodus 19:8

agreed with her perceptions and inclinations; which disposition she received without confirmation by the living God's voice, being led by her own heart; she received confidence to slight the only true and present commandment that mattered.

30. Eve heard the saying, but in her mind, she said, "I will not hear or 'obey the voice of the LORD your God.'"[1324] Of old, during the construction of the temple, it was said, "We are separated... in what place therefore ye hear the sound of the trumpet, resort ye thither unto us: our God shall fight for us."[1325] Eve had been separated from her husband, and at the sound of the trumpet; "the sound of a trumpet, and the voice of words";[1326] at the words which should have been as "the sound of the trumpet, the alarm of war";[1327] the heart of the woman was still.

31. What war did the woman encounter? It is said, "They have made void thy law."[1328]

32.Eve met a *creation* of *God* and failed to discern the character of the Creator from His creation. That which God has spoken becomes law unless nullified by His own voice, and should the creation of God disagree with its Architect? Because she spent no time cultivating her faith's mind, and no time encouraging and establishing a culture for her spirit through spiritual obedience, she didn't know the living God's religious character from His *creation's*, and so the snare within her heart could easily take her away from loyalty.

33. "My heart maketh a noise in me; I cannot hold my peace, because thou hast heard, O my soul,"[1329] said Jeremiah when discerning the sound of *heaven's* commandment. Because that word had reached into his soul, his heart could feel what needed to be felt in order for him to strengthen himself and those of God. Eve brought no thing of God into her soul, therefore her heart made no noise when creation openly denied the counsel of its Creator.

1324   Jeremiah 42:13
1325   Nehemiah 4:19,20
1326   Hebrews 12:19
1327   Jeremiah 4:19
1328   Psalms 119:126
1329   Jeremiah 4:19

34. "Shall the work say of him that made it, He made me not? or shall the thing framed say of him that framed it, He had no understanding?"[1330] If Eve had received the counsel, "In what place therefore ye hear the sound of the trumpet, resort ye thither,"[1331] and, "Our God shall fight for us,"[1332] she would not have tried to banter with error.

35. Eve was self-righteous and complacent within her own code of ethics; she did not need God to fight for her. While inwardly rejecting sincere observance to His voice, what was filling the place of humility was strange self-assuredness, and so when the serpent came preaching that the Creator has no understanding, but rather desires to keep His subjects ignorant for worship and for self-glory, it was easy for the woman to say, "I communed with mine own heart,"[1333] and, "I justify myself."[1334]

36. *Heaven's* professed need to be able to discern *God* from the work of His hands. But the record is that "the harp, and the viol, the tabret, and pipe, and wine, are in their feasts: but they regard not the work of the LORD, neither consider the operation of his hands."[1335] "Because they regard not the works of the LORD, nor the operation of his hands, he shall destroy them, and not build them up."[1336]

37. If the one professing the living God cannot discern His commandment, and yet does live as though their mid is within His commandment, they are indeed living out a religion not blessed of His religious character. How can that be said? It says, "He that saith, I know him, and keepeth not his commandments, is a liar."[1337]

38. The lesson established through Eve is to direct the conversation touched by *heaven's* sacrifice to personally know the living God. There is a present commandment and covenant of God, and a current

1330 Isaiah 29:16
1331 Nehemiah 4:20
1332 Nehemiah 4:20
1333 Ecclesiastes 1:16
1334 Job 9:20
1335 Isaiah 5:12
1336 Psalms 28:5
1337 1 John 2:4

house of God, with current *precepts, ordinances, statutes* and *judgments* for the reformers of that present *kingdom* or disposition. "Through the faith of the operation of God,"[1338] the reformer is to "grow in grace, and in the knowledge of our Lord,"[1339] but if His words are slighted, the spirit will thin, inevitably causing the heart to declare unlawful control over the *person*, leaving the experience to *eyes* that are faded through a hardened and delusional heart.

39. They that claim love to God must take their self and learn reform. Eve's condition, although taken from a *son* of God, was naturally grotesque. She didn't care for the Creator to nurture her, for she stopped *heaven's* flow from reaching her soul temple.

40. How can one, after having their heart touched by the living God's wisdom, after hearing, and in that moment believing and receiving that saying of hope and confidence, refuse to continually surrender authority towards that which is already under authority? Eve, in strange innocence, left creation's confidence, forsaking the power of His voice and the value of His kindness. How can one professing His science willingly continue in a form of religion when the time of the reign and power of His counsel yet is?

41. Let the heart stop to contemplate just what the Bible is saying. Give the heart time for cultivating a religion based on personal principle above traditional policy. Eve refused to learn "through patience and comfort of the scriptures,"[1340] counting the word of God vain and subsidiary, and the example is for the Christian, in that they would follow after the Bible's spiritual understanding by an experimental faith, that through His kindness the conversation's inwards would receive that nourishment neither *man* nor self nor tradition can provide.

42. "God shall supply all your need according to his riches in glory by Christ,"[1341] but how? It says, "Ask, and it shall be given you; seek

---

1338 Colossians 2:12
1339 2 Peter 3:18
1340 Romans 15:4
1341 Philippians 4:19

and ye shall find; knock and it shall be opened unto you."[1342] Eve did not care to personally familiarize herself with the living God's spiritual wisdom, for "through idleness of the hands the house droppeth through,"[1343] that is, it was that her hands did "refuse to labour."[1344]

43. Eve, in relation to her Creator, refused to study the *nature* around her. She refused to examine her relation to her environment's knowledge, and how she too was linked to the Creator by it. As soon as she "saw that the tree was good,"[1345] she believed her form of religion could then become a powerful fact, for she longed after some *thing* "to make one wise,"[1346] when she should have heard the counsel declare of itself, "If ye abide in me, and my words abide in you, ye shall ask what ye will, and it shall be done unto you."[1347]

44. The call for a personal religion made no proper impression on the woman. The counsel told to her by *heaven's angel* was, "Incline thine ear unto wisdom, and apply thine heart to understanding";[1348] "O taste and see";[1349] "for every one that asketh receiveth; and he that seeketh findeth; and to him that knocketh it shall be opened."[1350]

45. The work of the garden is the same labor for our conversation presently. Our faith's present work is the cleansing of our inward temple through a living experience with His words, to the end our heart may hear and keep the saying, "Let the word of Christ dwell in you richly in all wisdom."[1351]

46. The soul is to be nourished by *heaven's* wisdom, and the *body* and its members are to be maintained from that knowledge obtained by faith. Eve refused to depend on faith's higher learning, and from his actions, Adam exposes himself to be a liar also, for

1342 Luke 11:9
1343 Ecclesiastes 10:18
1344 Proverbs 21:25
1345 Genesis 3:6
1346 Genesis 3:6
1347 John 15:17
1348 Proverbs 2:2
1349 Psalm 34:8
1350 Luke 11:10
1351 Colossians 3:16

since the commandment was refused entrance into their heart, fear and error magnified itself against simple faith and reason, leaving it that their soul was estranged from God, when by faith they would have come by wisdom to remain content in His will to prolong their *life*, obtaining a cleanliness of mind accepted by an exercising of faith.

23

His Prescribed Diet Of Faith

1. How is it that we may know Eve *died* before both she and her husband tasted the curse? It is written, "When the woman saw that the tree was good for food, and that it was pleasant to the eyes, and a tree to be desired to make one wise, she took of the fruit thereof, and did eat, and gave also unto her husband with her."[1352]

2. Is "death" revealed in this saying? What is "death's" sign? It is written, "He that loveth not his brother abideth in death."[1353]

3. How did Eve display "hate," which "hate" was an express revelation of her inward death, and to Adam should have been a clue that she neither loved him nor their *God*? It is written, "Thou shalt not hate thy brother in thine heart: thou shalt in any wise rebuke thy neighbour, and not suffer sin upon him."[1354]

4. Eve failed on two points. First, she did not rebuke the *serpent*. By refusing to rebuke "that old serpent, called the Devil,"[1355] she was refusing to "speak, and exhort, and rebuke with all authority,"[1356] every *thing* against *heaven*.

1352 Genesis 3:6
1353 1 John 3:14
1354 Leviticus 19:17
1355 Revelation 12:9
1356 Titus 2:15

5. God's character states, "I rebuke and chasten,"[1357] and, "The LORD said unto Satan, The LORD rebuke thee."[1358] The *angels* that ministered to both Adam and Eve advised them, "Resist the devil,"[1359] and, "Your adversary the devil, as a roaring lion, walketh about, seeking whom he may devour: whom resist stedfast in the faith."[1360] The distraction of creation's faith was to keep the pair from wandering into spiritual vanity, yet what was the issue but that Eve halfheartedly listened to its *voice*, therefore she could not rebuke what she had found no reason to rebuke.

6. When the living God's man spoke, many "were astonished at his doctrine: for his word was with power."[1361] The same powerful counsel spoken at that time maintained the same essence that spoke in the garden. When this man came to a fig tree and "found nothing but leaves,"[1362] "Jesus answered and said unto it, No man eat fruit of thee hereafter for ever."[1363] "And in the morning, as they passed by, they saw the fig tree dried up from the roots."[1364] What happened to the tree? It says, "Peter calling to remembrance saith unto him, Master, behold, the fig tree which thou cursedst is withered away."[1365]

7. Again, there is another tree on earth cursed by the same mind and in the same manner as was done before, and that manner by the same power of the same voice. This is why the reformer is counseled, "Remember the former things of old: for I am God...declaring the end from the beginning, and from ancient times the things that are not yet done."[1366] "That which 'goeth forth out of my mouth: it shall not return unto me void,'[1367] says the living God, "but it shall accomplish...and

---

1357   Revelation 3:19
1358   Zechariah 3:2
1359   James 4:7
1360   1 Peter 5:8,9
1361   Luke 4:32
1362   Mark 11:13
1363   Mark 11:14
1364   Mark 11:20
1365   Mark 11:21
1366   Isaiah 46:9,10
1367   Isaiah 55:11

it shall prosper in the thing whereto I sent it."[1368] Eve was taught the faith of the doctrine of the power of the living God's utterance; that its instruction *is*, and does uphold what it pronounces; but the words refused entrance into her heart "not being mixed with faith."[1369]

8. Eve wasn't around to see the power of God, but she saw the results. Eve was not around to see the privilege given to Adam for his obedience to creation's law, but she saw the results. Eve was not there when creation's law was spoken; it says, "God commanded the man."[1370] Eve was not there to hear the curse, "In the day that thou eatest thereof thou shalt surely die."[1371] Eve was born as everything was set; she knew nothing but order and beauty, she felt nothing besides the power of every *faculty* and the joy of spiritual simplicity; yet she had no personal experience with *heaven's* law doctrine to convince her heart to obey that practice; she had to obtain it.

9. It is written, "In his temple doth every one speak of his glory,"[1372] and the same voice rehearsed in the heavenly Temple spoke His glory in the garden. The psalmist also declared, "O LORD, how manifold are thy works! in wisdom hast thou made them all: the earth is full of thy riches,"[1373] and, "His understanding is infinite."[1374] Although she was not present to observe His movements, Eve had all *things* open for her enjoyment of learning; she had the living *voice* of creation without error; yet the evidence did not convince her, and because of this, she could not rebuke the serpent's stance.

10. Eve's test was not Adam's, nor was his test hers, but both were under an investigation of inward integrity and loyalty. From the moment God's voice spoke the curse, causing a division in *nature* and also one between the conscience and the heart, an examination had begun. Eve's faith was to be tested, and for the one who personally

---

1368   Isaiah 55:11
1369   Hebrews 4:2
1370   Genesis 2:16
1371   Genesis 2:17
1372   Psalms 29:9
1373   Psalms 104:24
1374   Psalms 147:5

communed with God before she was created, his heart was to be exposed.

11. Eve failed her first test, in that she gave place to enticement, allowing that spirit to so mingle with the doctrine of her heart, causing her to forget Eden's wisdom. Had she persevered, taking confidence in Eden's commandment, even the little faith she had would have birthed a greater *structure*. She could not rebuke error because she did not believe in the creative power of God to know fact from fiction. Thus, "when the woman saw that the tree was good,"[1375] it was not that at this one particular time the tree had become "good," for in her heart, the curse never existed, therefore what came out of her was only a vision made to inevitably occur.

12. Why would God do this to them? It says, "For this cause, when I could no longer forbear, I sent to know your faith, lest by some means the tempter have tempted you, and our labour be in vain."[1376]

13. The living God took Adam before Eve was created and said to him, "My son, if sinners entice thee, consent thou not."[1377] Did Adam obey? It is written, "And he did eat."[1378]

14. The living God loved His minister and even told him to his *face*. Likewise the *angels* continually confessed to him, "He careth for you."[1379] This counsel made it easy for Adam to hear, "I passed by thee, and looked upon thee, behold, thy time was the time of love; and I spread my skirt over thee, and covered thy nakedness: yea, I sware unto thee, and entered into a covenant with thee, saith the Lord GOD, and thou becamest mine."[1380]

15. The *angels* gave witness to this fact, saying, "The LORD thy God in the midst of thee is mighty; he will save, he will rejoice over thee with joy; he will rest in his love, he will joy over thee with singing."[1381] But this was not sufficient for *heaven's* mind, for it knew

---

1375 Genesis 3:6
1376 1 Thessalonians 3:5
1377 Proverbs 1:10
1378 Genesis 3:6
1379 1 Peter 5:7
1380 Ezekiel 16:8
1381 Zephaniah 3:17

the "love wherewith he loved us,"[1382] but it is of that mind to chasten for the purpose of purifying ambition, hope, unity, faith, devotion, and assurance. "I will make thy lewdness to cease from thee,"[1383] He said to Adam, "and will consume thy filthiness out of thee,"[1384] "that thou shalt not lift up thine eyes unto them."[1385]

16. "Eve cannot be a sinner," thought Adam. "It is remarkable! She is not dead after the manner we believed! Even though she disregarded the commandment, she is before my *face* with no apparent difference in *her.*"

17. But wait! Was Eve different? Can innocent *eyes*, beholding what is defiled, know that what they see is defiled? These two had never once seen *death*, but the one who should have discerned "death" was Adam, for he was told, "If sinners entice thee, consent thou not."[1386]

18. The second point that Eve failed on was therefore suffering "sin" on Adam's conscience, and this how we know that she was a "sinner" now *dead*, and that the words of God were true. "Whosoever hateth his brother is a murderer,"[1387] and it is counseled not to hate, which hate is exemplified when suffering "sin" on another's inward parts. For this cause it is said, "Thou shalt not kill,"[1388] and, "Whosoever is angry with his brother without a cause shall be in danger of the judgment."[1389]

19. Eve despised the commandment of God, therefore she despised the commandment keeper, and the only way to convert Adam to her point of view was to find something "against him concerning the law of his God."[1390] Eve was a murderer. She was not only a *murderer* but was covetous, in that she saw the tree was great to make one *wise*, therefore she held "inordinate affection, evil concupiscence, and covetous-

1382 Ephesians 2:4
1383 Ezekiel 23:27
1384 Ezekiel 22:15
1385 Ezekiel 23:27
1386 Proverbs 1:10
1387 1 John 3:15
1388 Exodus 20:13
1389 Matthew 5:22
1390 Daniel 6:5

ness, which is idolatry,"[1391] in her heart towards this *tree*. This is why it is said, "Have no other gods before me,"[1392] for when the record of the conversation states, "A deceived heart hath turned him aside, that he cannot deliver his soul, nor say, Is there not a lie in my right hand?"[1393] the heart will admit a doctrine preaching violation of self along with *heaven's* precepts. The result of her disobedience is therefore the birth of the first murder and form of hatred.

20. To the confused Adam, Eve was living proof that God's voice was weak, for she had not literally perished. She was living proof that *heaven's* authority could be questioned. She looked the same, she sounded the same, she had no apparent shame of what she had done, and she stood before Adam with breath in her lungs while *covered* by the same innocent *light*. It was the fact that she suffered Adam's conscience to choose between her and his God that should have awoken him to her false condition.

21. Eve stood before Adam as a "sinner" *dead* in and by "sin," and the entire scene caused Adam to trust in his heart above his reason. It was only after Adam had eaten that "they knew that they were naked,"[1394] for the covenant was with Adam and not Eve, but *death* was limited to neither.

22. Their record is for our faith's enlightenment, that we might be "full of goodness, filled with all knowledge, able also to admonish one another."[1395] "Open rebuke is better than secret love,"[1396] for by open confession the hidden parts of the heart are made known and do receive health. We are then to commune with one another "that there should be no schism in the body; but that the members should have the same care one for another."[1397]

23. Eve cared for neither God nor her *husband*, and this is plainly seen by the fact that she would cause Adam to err against the

---

1391 Colossians 3:5
1392 Exodus 20:3
1393 Isaiah 44:20
1394 Genesis 3:7
1395 Romans 15:14
1396 Proverbs 27:5
1397 1 Corinthians 12:25

commandment he kept and knew to be right. This is how Adam should have known that she was *dead*. He should have known that no right mind would dare speak "lies in hypocrisy; having their conscience seared."[1398]

24. "How could Eve terrorize my heart and mind, unless hers too was contaminated?" Adam should have thought. "How could she consume my spirit with the saying, 'You will not die?'"

25. Within her innocent frame rested everything foreign to *heaven's* culture, therefore Adam should have remembered how he was told, "There must be also heresies among you, that they which are approved may be made manifest among you."[1399] Eve's condition is here presented as one effectually determined to "bring in damnable heresies, even denying the Lord that bought,"[1400] and this is exactly what she did.

26. Eve was purchased from Adam, yet she never let her heart accept the reality of her being, nor her duty to reverence both God and her *husband*. "What is the Almighty, that we should serve him? and what profit should we have, if we pray unto him?"[1401] she said in her heart, making it easy to give "also unto her husband with her."[1402]

27. "No murderer hath eternal life abiding in him,"[1403] and this fact established through that tree which they were to "eat, and live for ever."[1404] Eve immediately lost her pure *life* upon consumption of what was cursed, and the result of her diet outwardly put her inward commentary on display.

28. By faith in the power of salvation's commandment to cleanse our soul's temple, and to uphold us in our developing *heaven's* acceptable religious character, "we might receive the promise of the Spirit through faith,"[1405] and "this is the promise that he hath promised us,

---

1398   1 Timothy 4:2
1399   1 Corinthians 11:19
1400   2 Peter 2:1
1401   Job 21:15
1402   Genesis 3:6
1403   1 John 3:15
1404   Genesis 3:22
1405   Galatians 3:14

even eternal life."[1406] And this "eternal life" is specific. The living God's man "received of the Father the promise of the Holy Ghost"[1407] for our faith to not only become "perfect, as pertaining to the conscience,"[1408] but that we may "minister the same one to another,"[1409] "having compassion one of another,"[1410] "as bound with them,"[1411] that is, joined in one mind to conquer the same "body of the sins of the flesh."[1412]

29. This is *heaven* appointed *love*, even as it says, "All that believed were together, and had all things common."[1413] Thus, the counsel is, "Give to him that needeth,"[1414] and, "Give to him that asketh thee, and from him that would borrow of thee turn not thou away."[1415] Why? It says, "For Christ pleased not himself."[1416] The living God's chief minister "gave himself for our sins, that he might deliver us";[1417] that is, rescue or deliver our conversation's conscience; by "his own body on the tree, that we, being dead to sins, should live unto righteousness: by whose stripes ye were healed."[1418] Our faith's mind is healed by experiencing the saying of this man's conversation, therefore through his example we should "be able to comfort them which are in any trouble, by the comfort wherewith we ourselves are comforted of God."[1419]

30. "Whom the Lord loveth he chasteneth,"[1420] and "Lo, all these things worketh God oftentimes with man, to bring back his soul from the pit."[1421] "That he may withdraw man from his purpose, and hide

---

1406   1 John 2:25
1407   Acts 2:33
1408   Hebrews 9:9
1409   1 Peter 4:10
1410   1 Peter 3:8
1411   Hebrews 13:3
1412   Colossians 2:11
1413   Acts 3:44
1414   Ephesians 4:28
1415   Matthew 5:42
1416   Romans 15:3
1417   Galatians 1:4
1418   1 Peter 2:24
1419   2 Corinthians 1:4
1420   Hebrews 12:6
1421   Job 33:29,30

pride from man,"[1422] He suffered *man* with a test in the garden, because they were neither fully pure nor complete in their *birth* by *heaven's* standard. As Adam rose from the ground and looked creation's law in its face, "Jesus beholding him loved him, and said unto him, One thing thou lackest."[1423]

31. *Man* needed, on their own, to arrive at the conclusion, "There is one God; and there is none other but he: and to love him with all the heart, and with all the understanding, and with all the soul, and with all the strength, and to love his neighbour as himself, is more than all whole burnt offerings and sacrifices."[1424]

32. Adam did not have this mind because God could not, nor would He ever, create it in him. Unadulterated love is the foundation of obedience. The living Gods words can only work in a heart generated out of free love, and Adam was not created with a certified function to "obey"; we see this in their open willingness to disobey.

33. From the beginning, man has ever had the choice to experiment with humility to procure blessing, but God will not create in man the feature of a subjected willpower. The beauty of free and innocent love, at the risk of pain and disappointment, is a perfect symbol of faith that works by love to the purifying of the soul's temple: *heaven* will only accept this form of love.

34. The heart fearful to learn how to trust in the Bible's spiritual understanding will never be firmly built. Adam and Eve were not complete creations. *Heaven* needed to understand these two by their faithfulness, for it was only by remaining faithful to that counsel given them that they would be considered perfect, righteous, or whole. Herein is a fact, that the believer of salvation's science is not perfect until they put off their own *righteousness* and put on and accept *heaven's*.

35. The believer is given "his righteousness for the remission of sins that are past,"[1425] that is, creation's promise for what is accom-

---

1422   Job 33:17
1423   Mark 10:21
1424   Mark 12:32,33
1425   Romans 3:25

plished, ended, over, done, and forgotten by His man suffering the tree. The righteousness, or the commandment of His chief apostle brings the reformer to know and remember, "I will forgive their iniquity, and I will remember their sin no more."[1426] Herein they know that "the mercy of the LORD is from everlasting to everlasting upon them that fear him, and his righteousness unto children's children; to such as keep his covenant, and to those that remember his commandments to do them."[1427]

36. *Man* may have been created in spiritual simplicity, and his stature deemed "good" by his Creator, yet the perfection of *man*, even in a "sinless" state, was not truly accepted as perfection before the living God. *Man* did not achieve the perfect standard of God from *birth*, for if he did, then there need not have been an examination of faith. It is then not enough to hear and believe, but its says, "Come now, and let us reason together."[1428]

37. It is written, "Ask me of things to come concerning my sons, and concerning the work of my hands command ye me."[1429] Yet what is the counsel concerning our response to this prayer? It says, "They said, We will not hearken."[1430] "They have chosen their own ways, and their souls delighted in their abominations,"[1431] it is written, when all that needs to be done is as it is said, "Have faith in God."[1432] But have faith in what of God? It says, "That is, the word of faith, which we preach."[1433]

38. "Now all these things happened unto them for ensamples: and they are written for our admonition, upon whom the ends of the world are come."[1434] Through Adam and Eve, we do learn faith's law, that justification is not through any prescribed religious instrument, but

---

1426   Jeremiah 31:34
1427   Psalms 103:17,18
1428   Isaiah 1:18
1429   Isaiah 45:11
1430   Jeremiah 6:17
1431   Isaiah 66:3
1432   Mark 11:23
1433   Romans 10:8
1434   1 Corinthians 10:11

through an experimental faith on the living God's voice. The issue at hand is then intemperance in spiritual *things*, therefore "put a knife to thy throat, if thou be a man given to appetite."[1435]

39. A self-sufficient heart sees no need to cast its *righteousness* aside, seeing as though it need not feel anything, for it has felt all things and knows all things. If *man*, in the beginningm was found incomplete without faithfulness demonstrated by a reasonable love, how much more are we today "unrighteous" when refusing to allow creation's doctrine to penetrate our the heart of our faith's conscience?

40. At the root of love for God should be an intellectual desire for the living God's commandment, seeing as how "the end of the commandment is charity out of a pure heart, and of a good conscience, and of faith unfeigned."[1436] There is *life* in *heaven's* precepts, and when patiently studied, they will awaken a desire to stand by those principles of wisdom they teach. Eve lost sight of the fact that she was not created to be lazy, but was to rather educate herself on the living God's character by applying the members of her faculties to spiritual enlightenment. The creation is a revelation of the Creator's *name* and *power*, and in that name is the mystery of His faith's promise, which faith, when studied, leads to "one spirit, with one mind striving"[1437] to have "the same love, being of one accord, of one mind."[1438]

41. Eve was *dead* as soon as she ate from that tree, and it is fair to say that she was *dead* even before that time. Eating does not begin physically, but rather mentally. The fruit tasted no different from any other tree, nor did it look or feel any different, but it was her imagination that first conquered the landscape of her faith, and her disobedience proved her ruin.

42. Hereafter "GOD saw the wickedness of man,"[1439] "that every imagination of the thoughts of his heart was only evil continually."[1440]

1435 Proverbs 23:2
1436 1 Timothy 1:5
1437 Philippians 1:27
1438 Philippians 2:2
1439 Genesis 6:5
1440 Genesis 6:5

Yet, "God having provided some better thing for us,"[1441] "sent his Son to be the propitiation for our sins";[1442] that is, for our conversation's religious error; "that we might live through him."[1443]

43. It is an ever-present fact that we are "sinners," that is, that we possess a personal religion naturally contrary to the living God's religious character. But there is a greater fact, that God "justifieth the ungodly,"[1444] to the end the reformer may be given "the righteousness of God which is by faith of Jesus Christ."[1445]

44. The pair may have erred in the garden, *earth's* progenitors may have opened the gates of *death*, but God never left Himself without a witness in their error. He stood true to His character and revealed the depth of the knowledge of the conversation's redemption, for "the LORD God made coats of skins, and clothed them."[1446]

45. Blessed hope! Creation's doctrine was advanced after *man's* fall from *heaven's* manner of learning, and its words were, "But put ye on the Lord Jesus Christ, and make not provision for the flesh, to fulfill the lusts thereof."[1447] That word, "But," signifies that there is another *thing* we can put on, and that other *thing* is the government of a flesh-based conversation.

46. Indeed, "according to the power that worketh in us,"[1448] we will remove our mind from Eve's doctrine and will be joined to the Mother of our confidence in *heaven*, and to that commandment promising, "I 'will be a Father unto you, and ye shall be my sons and daughters.'"[1449]

47. There is, in Eden's garden, The Law of Righteousness by Faith, The Law of Charity and True Benevolence, The Law of *heaven's* Ten Commandments, and The Law of the personal religion's Diet. These things would have been added to Eve from simple obedience to

---

1441 Hebrews 11:40
1442 1 John 4:10
1443 1 John 4:9
1444 Romans 4:5
1445 Romans 3:22
1446 Genesis 3:21
1447 Romans 13:14
1448 Ephesians 3:20
1449 2 Corinthians 6:18

the counsel of her age, yet because she failed to exercise faith on that counsel, the saying was fulfilled, "Follow peace with all men, and holiness...lest any root of bitterness springing up trouble you, and thereby many be defiled."[1450]

_____

1450 Hebrews 12:14,15

24

The Sound Of Justification

1. It is written of the living God's chief apostle, "Who gave himself for our sins"[1451] "that we might by justified by faith."[1452]

2. How is it that we are to be justified? It says, "Justified by faith."[1453] So then in what way may one exemplify this justification? It says, "By thy words thou shalt be justified."[1454]

3. We are to maintain and express *heaven's* justification by our *voice*, that is, by the language of our conversation's demeanor, for it says, "And speaketh the truth in his heart."[1455] Wherein, from such a voice, is one found "just" before God? It says, "Justified by faith,"[1456] that is, "Through faith in his name."[1457] So then it is plain to see that the voice of the reformer exceeds what is audible and is issued by the mind through the *body*, to the end every natural sense may perceive faith's

---

1451   Galatians 1:4
1452   Galatians 2:16
1453   Galatians 2:16
1454   Matthew 12:37
1455   Psalms 15:2
1456   Galatians 2:16
1457   Acts 3:16

virtue, for "he that speaketh truth sheweth forth righteousness."[1458] The evidence of faith is thus seen in that which comes from the conversation's conscience, for it is not said in vain, "Every one that doeth righteousness is born of him."[1459]

4. By our words we are justified, and it is evident that our confession of the living God's science is seen not only by word. It is therefore said, "Let us not love in word, neither in tongue; but in deed and in truth."[1460]

5. What is our tongue? "The tongue," being an organ of our conversation, can be "a fire, a world of iniquity."[1461] To love by the tongue is to love by word; it is to comfort by the members of "the body of sin"[1462] within "the flesh and of the mind."[1463] Upon such a heart touched by such a tongue rests the despair, "Miserable comforters are ye,"[1464] and, "Why do ye persecute me as God, and are not satisfied with my flesh?"[1465]

6. It is said of every one of us, "Alienated and enemies in your mind,"[1466] but what is the record? "When we were enemies, we were reconciled to God by the death of his Son."[1467] For this cause it is an ever present fact, "Who gave himself for our sins"[1468] "that we might by justified by faith."[1469]

7. The conversation allowing creation's new covenant doctrine to touch their soul does as it is said, "They took him even as he was."[1470] Every conversation is justified by faith in the virtue of that doctrine's *name*, and upon acceptance of it, the soul is given into the hands of its

---

1458 Proverbs 12:17
1459 1 John 2:29
1460 1 John 3:18
1461 James 3:6
1462 Romans 6:6
1463 Ephesians 2:3
1464 Job 16:2
1465 Job 19:22
1466 Colossians 1:21
1467 Romans 5:10
1468 Galatians 1:4
1469 Galatians 2:16
1470 Mark 4:36

wisdom for purification that it may work as it works, and in the example of the confidence it provides.

8. To do is to confess or speak, and "whosoever shall confess that Jesus is the Son of God, God dwelleth in him, and he in God."[1471] How is it that we know "God" is in us? It says, "We know that he abideth in us, by the Spirit which he hath given us."[1472] Therefore what completes our confession to receive and maintain justification? It is written, "No man can say that Jesus is the Lord, but by the Holy Ghost."[1473]

9. That which tends to *life* and an honest confession of salvation's service begins where? It says, "Do the will of my Father which is in heaven."[1474] Where is this Father's Spirit? John confessed, "I saw the Spirit descending from heaven."[1475] So where should the *eye* of the reformer rest? It is written, "Our conversation is in heaven,"[1476] and more specifically, "Where Christ sitteth on the right hand of God."[1477]

10. There is a *voice* whose essence is derived from faith, even as it says, "Whosoever shall do the will of my Father which is in heaven."[1478] The living God's will for the reformer is in *heaven*, and it is only there. From diligently searching creation's *Building*, the heart will grow fond of its duty in relation to its personal Savior, for it says, "The lips of the righteous feed many,"[1479] and again, "He distributed to the disciples, and the disciples to them that were set down."[1480]

11. Wherein, then, did salvation's chief messenger provide an example of the work of faith that would justify the doer of the living God's will? It is said, "He arose, and rebuked the wind, and said unto the sea, Peace, be still."[1481]

1471   1 John 4:15
1472   1 John 3:24
1473   1 Corinthians 12:3
1474   Matthew 12:50
1475   John 1:32
1476   Philippians 3:20
1477   Colossians 3:1
1478   Matthew 12:50
1479   Proverbs 10:21
1480   John 6:11
1481   Mark 4:39

12. Where did his courage come from? It was that "the wind ceased, and there was a great calm,"[1482] but from where did this *power* come from to do so? He gives the answer by saying, "Where is your faith?"[1483]

13. Did he command the sea within himself? Did he himself cause the calm by his own power? How are his own words forgotten? Listen: "I do nothing of myself."[1484] "If I honour myself, my honour is nothing: it is my Father that honoureth me."[1485] Herein is our example; herein is the seed or foundation of justification by faith.

14. This man heard the living God's instruction and declared, "I was not rebellious, neither turned away back."[1486] If this was his conversation's inward principle, what principle is this? It is said, "The righteousness which is by faith."[1487]

15. He knew the character of his Father; this man knew the voice and blessedness of his God; therefore he could openly confess, "He that sent me is with me: the Father hath not left me alone; for I do always those things that please him."[1488] No *thing* could terrify this man, for he spent more time sanctifying his God in his heart than allowing any other *thing* to enter into it. He took on the living God's knowledge and maintained a living experience by faith on those words, which is why he says, "Take my yoke upon you, and learn of me."[1489]

16. It is our responsibility to know "the faith"[1490] "of the knowledge of the Son of God."[1491] This man had courage in the living God because he knew how it was said, "He maketh the storm a calm, so that the waves thereof are still,"[1492] for it was also said, "Be still, and know that I am God."[1493] This man was "declared to be the Son of God with

1482 Mark 4:39
1483 Luke 8:25
1484 John 8:28
1485 John 8:54
1486 Isaiah 50:15
1487 Hebrews 11:7
1488 John 8:29
1489 Matthew 11:29
1490 Ephesians 4:13
1491 Ephesians 4:13
1492 Psalms 107:29
1493 Psalms 46:10

power,"[1494] for it is said, "Jesus returned in the power of the Spirit."[1495] The reformer is to rest in "the power of Christ,"[1496] seeing as how "it pleased the Father that in him (in his conversation's saying) should all fullness dwell."[1497]

17. We may now see why there is a call to keep our conversation in *heaven*. "All power is given unto me in heaven and in earth,"[1498] says His man of his doctrine, for we "are complete in him"[1499] who is "the head over all things to the church."[1500] We ought to therefore know that "faith cometh by hearing, and hearing by the word of God."[1501]

18. What is developed first: faith or hearing? The living God's man spoke on faith's course, saying, "He wakeneth morning by morning, he wakeneth mine ear to hear as the learned."[1502] From such daily communion he could then confess, "The Lord GOD will help me,"[1503] and, "He is near that justifieth me."[1504]

19. Indeed this minister "committed himself to him that judgeth righteously,"[1505] and from this "hath given us an understanding, that we may know him."[1506] He did not obtain faith until he learned, day by day, to patiently re-educate the members of his *body*, for it was from personally hearing and carrying out the voice of his Father that faith was added and engraved within his conversation's mind. Thus, in this *flesh* "learned he obedience by the things which he suffered."[1507]

20. Truly this man, observing religious error among his *brethren*, was "touched with the feeling of our infirmities."[1508] This is what it

---

1494   Romans 1:4
1495   Luke 4:14
1496   2 Corinthians 12:9
1497   Colossians 1:19
1498   Matthew 28:18
1499   Colossians 2:10
1500   Ephesians 1:22
1501   Romans 10:17
1502   Isaiah 50:4
1503   Isaiah 50:7
1504   Isaiah 50:8
1505   1 Peter 2:23
1506   1 John 5:20
1507   Hebrews 5:8
1508   Hebrews 4:15

means when it says, "He gave himself for us," for even in those *things* that are so missed and are not counted as worthy of our attention, this man noticed them all and handled them all, for he "was in all points tempted like as we are,"[1509] "that he might be a merciful and faithful high priest."[1510] This is the education the conversation must embrace, even the knowledge that his commandment is, "God is with us."[1511]

21. He being with us means that His wisdom will never be without our faith's attention, or that our conversation will never be without His wisdom's effect. "The sacrifices of God are a broken spirit: a broken and a contrite heart,"[1512] and should the reformer "feel after him, and find him,"[1513] it says, "Ye shall seek me, and find me, when ye shall search for me with all your heart,"[1514] and, "Every one that asketh receiveth; and he that seeketh findeth; and to him that knocketh it shall be opened."[1515]

22. The living God's prophesied Prophet operated through a living faith in his Father's doctrine, and for the reformer, they are to be "risen with him through the faith of the operation of God."[1516] This faith begins by settling the heart to hear and believe salvation's counsel, to the end the mind receives health and comfort to store the precepts of that wisdom within the heart and mind.

23. We "might be justified by the faith of Jesus"[1517] if we would first search wherein we are accounted "just." We "might be filled with the knowledge of his will in all wisdom and spiritual understanding,"[1518] and "through the power of the Holy Ghost,"[1519] if we would "be clothed with humility"[1520] when reviewing His words. "We might be made

---

1509 Hebrews 4:15
1510 Hebrews 2:17
1511 Isaiah 8:10
1512 Psalms 51:17
1513 Acts 17:27
1514 Jeremiah 29:13
1515 Luke 11:10
1516 Colossians 2:12
1517 Galatians 2:16
1518 Colossians 1:9
1519 Romans 15:13
1520 1 Peter 5:5

the righteousness of God in him"[1521] if we would "be subject one to another";[1522] the end of private knowledge is public comfort, which is why he said, "Give, and it shall be given unto you."[1523]

24. How did the living God's man carry his conversation? It is said, "God anointed Jesus of Nazareth with the Holy Ghost and with power: who went about doing good, and healing all that were oppressed of the devil; for God was with him."[1524]

25. The living God's wisdom was with his spiritual understanding; salvation's science was with his faith's thoughts and feelings; so where is God for us? It says, "God is with us."[1525] And if he is "God" with "us" as "God" was with "him," by what words may we then be justified? It is said, "By this shall all men know that ye are my disciples, if ye have love one to another."[1526] *Heaven's* dialect is mental and spiritual unity imprisoned by edification, and as the *life* and actions confess *heaven's* language, all who see such a fragrant soul will know, "God is greater than our heart."[1527]

26. The living God's knowledge is greater than our heart. His wisdom is greater than the binding self-doctrines and audacious *spirits* within us. We are justified by our words, and what should come out from our faith's mind should be what was first inwardly appreciated. They who will take on the promise of salvation's science speak one language, and that language is benevolent unity sanctified by *heaven's* wisdom through faith. This was the reason why he gave his conversation for *us*. From personally learning of his charge, his *yoke* would produce a people to be a witness of that wisdom's *power* from their free self-sacrificing godly affection.

27. It is said, "Whosoever doeth not righteousness is not of God, neither he that loveth not his brother."[1528] The expression of *heaven's*

1521   2 Corinthians 5:21
1522   1 Peter 5:5
1523   Luke 6:38
1524   Acts 10:30
1525   Isaiah 8:10
1526   John 13:35
1527   1 John 3:20
1528   1 John 3:10

righteousness is through *comfort*, as it says, "All may learn, and all may be comforted."[1529] "Comfort" is a term denoting learning, or edifying, and to hear that "God was in Christ,"[1530] is to hear that the living God's wisdom edified His chief apostle, making it well for us to not simply edify our personal religion through learning of and proving the Bible's words, but to also edify one another by what is written on our heart as we experience those words.

28. This is why it is said, "Whoso hath this world's good, and seeth his brother have need, and shutteth up his bowels of compassion from him, how dwelleth the love of God in him?"[1531] This is the faith of the Bible's spiritual understanding that every conversation must know, for its expression gives witness to "the words of our Lord Jesus Christ, and to the doctrine which is according to godliness."[1532]

29. "By thy words thou shalt be justified, and by thy words thou shalt be condemned."[1533] "Many deceivers are entered into the world, who confess not that Jesus Christ is come in the flesh."[1534] "Hereby know ye the Spirit of God: Every spirit that confesseth that Jesus Christ is come in the flesh is of God."[1535]

30. How is it that one may not confess "Christ," but to prove, faithlessly from their conversation, that *heaven's* science has no effect? If "Christ" is in our heart, what becomes the doctrine of the conversation's conscience? It is written, "Put ye on the Lord Jesus Christ, and make not provision for the flesh."[1536]

31. Heaven's righteousness is joined to one work, for it says, "He that doeth righteousness is righteous, even as he is righteous."[1537] If our conversation is of this science, then it will be in, of, and with the living God's religious character to look, sound and think like that character,

---

1529 1 Corinthians 14:31
1530 2 Corinthians 5:19
1531 1 John 3:17
1532 1 Timothy 6:3
1533 Matthew 12:37
1534 2 John 1:7
1535 1 John 4:2
1536 Romans 13:14
1537 1 John 3:7

for it is said, "He that saith he abideth in him ought himself also so to walk, even as he walked."[1538]

32. How did he walk? He says, "I have kept my Father's commandments,"[1539] and, "I do always those things that please him."[1540] He said, "I have given you an example, that ye should do as I have done to you,"[1541] which is why the apostle counsels, "Do those things that are pleasing in his sight."[1542]

33. Our conversation's conscience is justified by an experimental faith in the virtue of the living God's sacrifice, meaning that, our faith's mind is sanctified only through consistently proving the illustration of His man suffering the cross. The sign, then, of true discipleship to that illustration's science is known in the conversation born of the revealed character contained in the statement of that illustration. The philosophy of the mind submitted to that doctrine therefore becomes, "Not seeking mine own profit, but the profit of many,"[1543] for the heart has encountered salvation's unadulterated science, fulfilling the saying, "The name of our Lord Jesus Christ may be glorified in you."[1544]

34. Hear what pleases *heaven*: "I in them, and thou in me, that they may be made perfect in one; and that the world may know that thou hast sent me, and hast loved them, as thou hast loved me."[1545]

35. How long must this prayer go unheard and unfulfilled? How long must confusion and dissension ruin *earth*? The living God's will is situated within His heavenly Sanctuary that we may have faith and peace on *earth*; the individual soul must know their "high priest, who is set on the right hand of the throne of the Majesty in the heavens."[1546] Our faith's mind must depend on its *High Priest* as the living God's Prophet depended on His words; our conversation must have the same

1538 1 John 2:6
1539 John 15:10
1540 John 8:29
1541 John 13:15
1542 1 John 3:22
1543 2 Corinthians 10:33
1544 2 Thessalonians 1:12
1545 John 17:23
1546 Hebrews 8:1

relationship with this man's doctrine that he had with the living God's religious character.

36. Creation's chief minister "died for all, that they which live should not henceforth live unto themselves, but unto him which died for them, and rose again."[1547] Such a confession is according to *heaven's* will, who intends for the reformer "to be conformed to the image of his Son,"[1548] to the end every conversation may know that His man's spiritual philosophy is a prerequisite to have His throne's precepts written and engraved on the heart of the mind.

37. The reformer's education is knowledge of the living God's new covenant will and wisdom; anything less is of no concern. A practical religion will, both spiritually and intellectually, develop a practical faith, causing an effect on the appetite to uplift the person morally. Such an experience by faith will be blessed, for it is promised, "Thy presses shall burst out with new wine,"[1549] and "Blessing shall be upon the head of him that selleth it."[1550]

38. The apostle pleads, "Let brotherly love continue."[1551] Why? Because the speech of "every tree is known by his own fruit,"[1552] and without the sign of discipleship it will be fulfilled, "They went out from us,"[1553] and, "If they had been of us, they would no doubt have continued with us: but they went out, that they might be made manifest that they were not all of us."[1554] As the conversation is to be in *heaven*, so again Paul counsels, "Let your conversation be without covetousness,"[1555] for it is covetousness, or greed, that stops the movement of self-effacing kindheartedness.

39. Our conversation, through an experimental faith on creation's new covenant illustration, is to be joined to the *nature* of the living

---

1547   2 Corinthians 5:15
1548   Romans 8:29
1549   Proverbs 3:10
1550   Proverbs 11:26
1551   Hebrews 13:1
1552   Luke 6:44
1553   1 John 2:19
1554   1 John 2:19
1555   Hebrews 13:5

God's man on this *earth*. "That the righteousness of the law might be fulfilled in us,"[1556] it is advised, "Speak the mystery of Christ,"[1557] for "the law of Christ"[1558] working in the reformer confesses, "As we have therefore opportunity, let us do good unto all men,"[1559] and, "In the spirit of meekness; considering thyself";[1560] "do good and to communicate forget not";[1561] "comfort yourselves together, and edify one another";[1562] "and the Lord make you to increase and abound in love one toward another, and toward all men."[1563]

40. It says, "Go home to thy friends, and tell them how great things the Lord hath done for thee, and hath had compassion on thee."[1564] "Now the end of the commandment is charity out of a pure heart, and of a good conscience, and of faith unfeigned,"[1565] "to the end he may stablish your hearts unblameable in holiness before God."[1566]

41. "That we should be holy and without blame before him in love,"[1567] the living God's man gave us the privilege of possession his mind of devotion that we should "through the Spirit wait for the hope of righteousness by faith."[1568] "Therefore being justified by faith, we have peace with God through our Lord Jesus Christ,"[1569] for "according to the truth of the gospel,"[1570] "we might be justified by the faith of Christ, and not by the works."[1571]

1556 Romans 8:4
1557 Colossians 4:3
1558 Galatians 6:2
1559 Galatians 6:10
1560 Galatians 6:1
1561 Hebrews 13:16
1562 1 Thessalonians 5:11
1563 1 Thessalonians 3:12
1564 Mark 5:19
1565 1 Timothy 1:5
1566 1 Thessalonians 3:13
1567 Ephesians 1:4
1568 Galatians 5:5
1569 Romans 5:1
1570 Galatians 2:14
1571 Galatians 2:16

25

As In The Days Of Noah

1. It says, "It is not for you to know the times or the seasons, which the Father hath put in his own power."[1572] "Of that day and hour knoweth no man, no, not the angels of heaven, but my Father only. But as the days of No'e were, so shall also the coming of the Son of man be."[1573]

2. We will know that *Christ* draws nearer to our age, and that our faith's probation is nearing its end, when that spirit passing through Noah's age fully repeats. What sign may we then look for to know that the times of Noah are come to a full, and that *heaven's* flood is inevitably apparent? It is written, "God looked upon the earth, and, behold, it was corrupt,"[1574] and, "And God said unto Noah, The end of all flesh is come before me; for the earth is filled with violence through them."[1575]

3. What violence had then been committed that will soon be reproduced in full? It is said, "They have made void thy law,"[1576] and, "The

---

1572   Acts 1:7
1573   Matthew 24:36,37
1574   Genesis 6:12
1575   Genesis 6:13
1576   Psalms 119:126

earth also is defiled under the inhabitants thereof; because they have transgressed the laws, changed the ordinance, broken the everlasting covenant."[1577] Then will the seed of Noah announce, "It is time for thee, LORD, to work,"[1578] and, "Come out of her, my people, that ye be not partakers of her sins, and that ye receive not of her plagues."[1579]

4. "The flood upon the world of the ungodly"[1580] will at this time be revealed from "the vials of the wrath of God upon the earth,"[1581] "the seven last plagues,"[1582] for it says, "Pour out thy wrath upon the heathen that have not known thee, and upon the kingdoms that have not called upon thy name."[1583] When the living God's full Doctrine is openly and nationally violated, it will then be fulfilled, "I will pour out my wrath upon them like water,"[1584] leading to the event, "In flaming fire taking vengeance on them that know not God, and that obey not the gospel of our Lord."[1585]

5. The knowledge of God is revealed from only one source, and that is from "the excellency of the knowledge of Christ,"[1586] which is "the gospel of the grace of God"[1587] emphasizing "the word of the truth of the gospel."[1588] By "the knowledge of the Son of God,"[1589] the living God's character is revealed, and as the believer comes into contact with that character from believing on His man's doctrine, the reality of His wisdom will be heard and obeyed, and like Noah, the spirit will claim "the righteousness which is by faith."[1590]

1577 Isaiah 24:5
1578 Psalm 119:126
1579 Revelation 18:4
1580 2 Peter 2:5
1581 Revelation 16:1
1582 Revelation 15:1
1583 Psalms 79:6
1584 Hosea 5:10
1585 1 Thessalonians 1:8
1586 Philippians 3:8
1587 Acts 20:24
1588 Colossians 1:5
1589 Ephesians 4:13
1590 Hebrews 11:7

6. The days of Noah were one hundred twenty years, and at the end of those days of probation, the then chief religious and political institution of *earth* had filled up her cup of violence. That which was before the flood were the days in which Noah lived, and although he lived in a time of uncensored personal and devotional appetite, those days leave us with a fact for thought, that "Noah was a just man and perfect."[1591]

7. The scenes of *God's wrath* upon the "ungodly" are strange and fearful scenes indeed, even for the Bible's Author. Scripture says of this time, "He shall be wroth as in the valley of Gib'eon, that he may do his work, his strange work; and bring to pass his act, his strange act."[1592] For this cause it says, "Have I any pleasure at all that the wicked should die? saith the Lord GOD: and not that he should return from his ways, and live?"[1593]

8. The living God says, "All souls are mine,"[1594] but how is this so? It is written of His man, "Who gave himself for our sins,"[1595] and, "Who gave himself a ransom for all."[1596] This is why scripture would have its honest student remember, "Ye are not your own,"[1597] and, "Ye are bought with a price."[1598]

9. Every conversation was purchased "with the precious blood of Christ."[1599] It is because every conversation literally belongs to the living God's science that He would "have all men to be saved, and to come unto the knowledge of the truth."[1600] Yet who will this knowledge save or ransom from *death* to bring up into the manners of *heaven*? It is written, "We trust in the living God, who is the Saviour of all men, specially of those that believe."[1601]

1591 Genesis 6:9
1592 Isaiah 28:21
1593 Ezekiel 18:23
1594 Ezekiel 18:4
1595 Galatians 1:4
1596 1 Timothy 2:6
1597 1 Corinthians 6:19
1598 1 Corinthians 6:20
1599 1 Peter 1:19
1600 1 Timothy 2:4
1601 1 Timothy 4:10

10. To them that actively believe on the living God's science, these will personally know the fact behind His intention to escape *wrath*, for it says, "To whom sware he that they should not enter into his rest, but to them that believed not?"[1602] Them that will know consent to His knowledge will not know His name, and if they do not know His name, then they are indeed "ungodly" and open to all things *contrary* to His religious character. Yet to whom is the gospel preached? It says, "For this cause was the gospel preached also to them that are dead,"[1603] that is, "dead in trespasses and sins."[1604]

11. His saying of reconciliation is the unbreakable link between our and His throne, which counsel will transform the nature of the religious character willingly consecrating its self to that saying's intention. If indeed the days of Noah were filled with unparalleled violence against the heart and conscience by the *inhabitants* of *earth*, it must also be remembered that during this time another doctrine was flourishing that caused one to escape *God's* fury, for He said to him, seeing as how "Noah was a just man and perfect in his generations,"[1605] "Thee have I seen righteous before me in this generation."[1606]

12. To be "just" is to be "perfect" in conversation, and to be "perfect" in conversation is to be known of God as one executing his will and wisdom by faith, for Noah was justified by faith in the doctrine he had been given. Thus he, "being warned of God of things not seen as yet, moved with fear, prepared an ark to the saving of his house; by the which he condemned the world, and became heir of the righteousness which is by faith."[1607]

13. There is a way to escape *wrath*, and only one way: it is by faithfully holding and appropriating the virtue of His man's doctrine to the conversation's conscience; "according to the truth of the gospel,"[1608]

1602 Hebrews 3:18
1603 1 Peter 4:6
1604 Ephesians 2:1
1605 Genesis 6:9
1606 Genesis 7:1
1607 Hebrews 11:7
1608 Galatians 2:14

"we might be justified by the faith of Christ."[1609] The living God's man said that as Noah's days were, so shall they be at *his* appearing. Noah's days began with an allotted period constrained to an investigative judgment, that at the end of that time a judgment should fall on them that did not obey *heaven's* counsel. Before the year of this appearing, we then ought to do well by considering how it says, "Fear God, and give glory to him; for the hour of his judgment is come."[1610]

14. As was in the time of Noah, we now alive upon the *earth* share the same essence of that age. The living God's man brought up the days of Noah not that one should connect that time to a flood, but that the eye of faith may rest on the hope and saying of that time, and that wisdom founded upon the ground of justification for a perfection rendering the conversation righteous, for it says, "Therein is the righteousness of God revealed from faith to faith: as it is written, The just shall live by faith."[1611]

15. After Paul says the just are to live by faith, what is his next subject? He says, "For the wrath of God is revealed from heaven against all ungodliness and unrighteousness of men."[1612] Because of a rejection to subscribe to a fundamental education by His wisdom, "ungodliness" will constrain the demeanor, leading to that conversation sealing to it the living God's *wrath*. As we are now living in the *days* that will soon reveal that time of expected violence, *heaven's* professed must hear, "To him that worketh not, but believeth on him that justifieth the ungodly, his faith is counted for righteousness."[1613]

16. The living God's edification is for the recovery of the inward person that outwardly the conversation may be a blessing. David experienced the living God's doctrine, and on his heart longed the inquiry, "Is there not yet any of the house of Saul, that I may shew the kindness of God unto him?"[1614] What was the kindness of God? David expressed it by saying, "I will surely shew thee kindness for Jonathan thy father's

---

1609 Galatians 2:16
1610 Revelation 14:7
1611 Romans 1:17
1612 Romans 1:18
1613 Romans 4:5
1614 2 Samuel 9:3

sake, and will restore thee all the land of Saul thy father; and thou shalt eat bread at my table continually."[1615] "So Mephib'osheth dwelt in Jerusalem: for he did eat continually at the king's table; and was lame on both his feet."[1616]

17. In figure, David represents the dispensation of grace, with Jonathan representing the living God's chief minister, and the son of Jonathan as our representative.

18. Notice the doctrine of God and the aim of that wisdom: that one born lame should eat at the table of the *king* for ever, having their infirmity completely ignored by the king, having their loss of possessions restored to them for the sake of one, and that they may eat of royal bread and share the blessings of the royal throne.

19. This son was lame on both of his feet, he was paralyzed from birth, and yet the king sought to relay the compassion of God in full, and so preaching His counsel and will in the same sentiment. We, who are spiritually crippled from *birth*, may receive free help through faith on the fact of our atonement to *heaven's* throne. As our conversation is "ungodly" by nature, being born to an honest inclination fulfilling "the desires of the flesh and of the mind,"[1617] we are helpless within ourselves to awaken ourselves to conceive pure right from pure wrong. "But after that the kindness and love of God our Saviour toward man appeared,"[1618] we "who sometimes were far off are made nigh by the blood of Christ."[1619] This is why it says, "Come boldly unto the throne of grace."[1620]

20. Noah, in his generation, was righteous, his conversation was perfect and just, and the just, and only those that are just before the living God's commandment, are them that exist in that commandment's intention by faith. What is written? It says, "Believe in the LORD your God, so shall ye be established; believe his prophets, so shall ye prosper."[1621] What is then the present inquiry? It says, "What

---

1615   2 Samuel 9:7
1616   2 Samuel 9:13
1617   Ephesians 2:3
1618   Titus 3:4
1619   Ephesians 2:13
1620   Hebrews 4:16
1621   2 Chronicles 20:20

shall we do, that we might work the works of God?"[1622] And what is the answer? It says, "This is the work of God, that ye believe on him whom he hath sent."[1623]

21. The work is to believe on the living God's spiritual understanding, and belief is not born one-sided or through laziness. *Heaven's* new covenant counsel is to awaken the conscience from its "vain conversation received by tradition,"[1624] "that ye should shew forth the praises of him who hath called you out of darkness into his marvellous light."[1625] If indeed we exist under creation's present jurisdiction, we will know that, like Mephib'osheth, we rest in the reign of the living God's consolation, wherein rests His fullness for our life, and His benevolence for our peace.

22. At this time, the doctrine and example of Noah is to become our own. The ark and *house* of their soul temple is to be devoted to the living God's religious character for the purpose of a perfectly constructed personal religion. It is of God that the believer "be conformed to the image of his Son,"[1626] for the only thing that may deliver the soul in this later day is if "the name of our Lord Jesus Christ may be glorified in you."[1627] By aggravating the soul to hear and to understand salvation's voice, from "obeying the truth through the Spirit,"[1628] salvation's student will grow up in its wisdom to collect, and to properly order, Justification's ordinances that they may faithfully confess, "I serve with my spirit in the gospel of his Son."[1629]

23. John sought to place the ministers of the early Christian church in remembrance of their personal work, saying, "We should believe on

---

1622   John 6:28
1623   John 6:6
1624   1 Peter 1:18
1625   1 Peter 2:9
1626   Romans 8:29
1627   2 Thessalonians 1:12
1628   1 Peter 1:22
1629   Romans 1:9

the name of his Son."[1630] In his time the church announced, "You are justified by the law,"[1631] when in reality "it is God that justifieth."[1632]

24. How is it that God justifies? It says, "God would justify the heathen through faith."[1633] But the church of old began to falsely let "righteousness come by the law,"[1634] when it is "that no man is justified by the law in the sight of God,"[1635] "for, The just shall live by faith."[1636]

25. Noah is called a "just" *man* because as apostasy grew, his faith in the living God's commandment strengthened, and because his faithfulness provoked action, in his generation his devotion to *heaven's* wisdom pronounced him "righteous." "Now it was not written for his sake alone, that it was imputed to him; but for us also, to whom it shall be imputed, if we believe on him that raised up Jesus our Lord from the dead; who was delivered for our offences, and was raised again for our justification."[1637]

26. Said David, "I will shew thee kindness for Jonathan thy father's sake,"[1638] for which cause the apostle wrote, "Your sins are forgiven you for his name's sake."[1639] And considering this, the counsel is yet given, "Be ye kind one to another, tenderhearted, forgiving one another, even as God for Christ's sake hath forgiven you."[1640]

27. Every active believer excels from faith to capture the virtue of salvation's science that they may retain *heaven's* wisdom to patiently educate self to give the compassion first given to *them*. The believing conversation is freely justified or cleansed by faith "through the redemption that is in Christ,"[1641] and by faith are then given "his righteousness

---

1630 1 John 3:23
1631 Galatians 5:4
1632 Romans 8:33
1633 Galatians 3:8
1634 Galatians 2:21
1635 Galatians 3:11
1636 Galatians 3:11
1637 Romans 4:23-25
1638 2 Samuel 9:7
1639 1 John 2:12
1640 Ephesians 4:32
1641 Romans 3:24

for the remission of sins"[1642] "that they might have life, and that they might have it more abundantly."[1643]

28. The end of faith is a living experience. Noah's doctrine was righteousness by its faith on what was promised. In his day, as the religion and spirit of Eve flourished, there was a move away from the living God's doctrine, for it says that the living God did "make coats of skins, and clothed them."[1644] This doctrine once taught by Noah is that which yet is to be heard by us, and has ever been ordained for observation through faith. It is for this reason that the He says, "Perfect through my comeliness,"[1645] "for unto us was the gospel preached, as well as unto them: but the word preached did not profit them, not being mixed with faith in them that heard it."[1646]

29. How was *Noah* "just" and "perfect"? It says, "Perfect though my comeliness."[1647] This was the message that Noah preached, whether by voice or by the demonstration of his living spiritual understanding.

30. In the days of Noah God didn't leave *men* without His doctrine, for that which was rejected by *men* and procured a flood will secure His wrath to our conversation. The same word that was to be upheld by faith at that time, it is the same counsel we too are to actively believe on, yet, "God having provided some better thing for us"[1648] to observe justification's precepts, has ordained for us gifts and precious promises by "that which is through the faith of Christ, the righteousness which is of God by faith."[1649]

31. When every conscience on the face of the earth has made their decision on *heaven's* doctrine and commandments, when every living soul has had the opportunity to consciously make their choice respecting His throne's every precept, then will the end begin before the "ungodly" even recognize it. But before this time of *wrath*, which

---

1642   Romans 3:25
1643   John 10:10
1644   Genesis 3:21
1645   Ezekiel 16:14
1646   Hebrews 4:2
1647   Ezekiel 16:14
1648   Hebrews 11:40
1649   Philippians 3:9

time we now live in, "Acquaint now thyself with him, and be at peace: thereby good shall come unto thee. Receive, I pray thee, the law from his mouth, and lay up his words in thine heart,"[1650] we are counseled.

32. Remember how it is written, "Unto which of the angels said he at any time, Thou art my Son, this day have I begotten thee? And again, I will be to him a Father, and he shall be to me a Son?"[1651] for in reality it is said, "Unto which of the ministers said He at any time, Your *name* is My Son and My High Priest, this day have I begotten it? And again, I will be to your *name* a Father, and it shall be to Me a Minister?"

33. The coming of the Son of man to His temple; "the temple of the tabernacle of the testimony in heaven";[1652] is the coming of the living God's *High Priest* to not only receive *His* kingdom, but also for the sealing up of the members of that *house* through an investigative judgment. It is of God that *men* and *women* would take their faith and set their faces on His spiritual understanding "that is passed into the heavens"[1653] and found "after the second veil, the tabernacle which is called the Holiest of all."[1654]

34. As Noah's day is synonymous with ours, so too is that word and *work* of old preached for a present diet. Noah was justified by faith in the living God's commandment, and so too is the believer justified by faith in "the confidence and the rejoicing of"[1655] "the full assurance of hope."[1656] As Noah obeyed His voice and was rescued from strange events, so too now "the mystery of God should be finished"[1657] in them that have "found grace in the eyes of the LORD."[1658]

1650   Job 22:21,22
1651   Hebrews 1:5
1652   Revelation 15:5
1653   Hebrews 4:14
1654   Hebrews 9:3
1655   Hebrews 3:6
1656   Hebrews 6:11
1657   Revelation 10:7
1658   Genesis 6:8

26

The Spirit Of Justification

1. It is written, "The Father himself loveth you,"[1659] but how and why? It continues: "Because ye have loved me, and have believed that I came out from God."[1660]

2. How is it that one may be loved of God? It says, "Have believed that I came out from God."[1661] And how is it that we are loved of God? It says, "Because ye have loved me,"[1662] and, "He that loveth me shall be loved of my Father."[1663]

3. In order to be *loved*, *love* must be given. "Because thou desiredst me,"[1664] says His man, "my Father 'had pity on thee.'"[1665] Is this a lie? "That he might be just, and the justifier of him which believeth in Jesus,"[1666] it was the living god who ordained "his righteousness,"[1667] the righteousness of His chief apostle, "for the remission of sins."[1668]

1659 John 16:27
1660 John 16:27
1661 John 16:27
1662 John 16:27
1663 John 14:21
1664 Matthew 18:32
1665 Matthew 18:33
1666 Romans 3:26
1667 Romans 3:26
1668 Romans 3:25

4. How is the love of God pronounced? It is exposed by the gift of His Son's saying, in that from actively exercising faith on the virtue behind the illustration of him suffering the tree, his conversation's righteousness, by our faith on its intention, will be given for our inward healing.

5. A longing to silence self-righteousness and self-sufficiency to pick up His man's righteousness will secure the blessing and attention of the Father to the conversation. "Because you love my ministry's charge," says His man; that is, because you have cherished the spirit of his mind to abandon your spiritual perception for his religious character; "my Father will *love* you. You accepting my conversation will erase knowledge of all of your unhealthy inherited and cultivated tendencies, and He will see *you* as He sees *me*; 'because I live, ye shall live also.'"[1669]

6. For this cause it says, "Be ye therefore perfect, even as your Father which is in heaven is perfect."[1670] But one must ask, "How can *I* be as perfect as the Majesty of heaven?"

7. The Father Himself answers, "Perfect through my comeliness, which I had put upon thee,"[1671] and, "Perfect, as pertaining to the conscience."[1672]

8. What is this comeliness that only He gives? It says, "I clothed thee also with broidered work";[1673] "I girded thee about with fine linen";[1674] "for the fine linen is the righteousness of saints,"[1675] "and their righteousness is of me, saith the LORD."[1676]

9. The only way that "sinful" conversations may be considered "perfect" is by dawning *heaven's* conversation. Through learning of and doing the living God's commandment for mental and inward newness,

---

1669   John 14:19
1670   Matthew 5:48
1671   Ezekiel 16:14
1672   Hebrews 9:9
1673   Ezekiel 16:10
1674   Ezekiel 16:10
1675   Revelation 19:8
1676   Isaiah 54:17

one is declared to be in perfect standing with Him, even as it says, "To present you holy and unblameable and unreproveable in his sight."[1677]

10. Now, it is a depressing thought to consider the perplexity of the human heart and the natural rebellion within the mind of its *flesh*, to then think on the highness of achieving right godliness. It may be hard to know and accept that only by receiving the living God's course of learning may I then actually be accepted into His *classroom*, for to do no thing but accept, live, and learn sounds strange, but "this is the work of God, that ye believe on him whom he hath sent."[1678] This work is ordained of *heaven* that we may know His wisdom's mind to hear the counsel, "Live through him."[1679]

11. Would the living God utter some *thing* and not see to that *thing's* occurrence? Or would the living God set a precept that cannot be followed? He knows that only His act of benevolence can bestow favor to the soul, therefore "if there had been a law given which could have given life, verily righteousness should have been by the law."[1680]

12. All that was prescribed under types and figures, all that was recorded and written for instruction to follow, all of the "precepts, statutes, and laws, by the hand of Moses,"[1681] awards no good thing to them that do them, or else the living God is a liar. For it says, "Through this man"; through His chief apostle's doctrine; "is preached unto you the forgiveness of sins: and by him all that believe are justified from all things, from which ye could not be justified by the law of Moses."[1682]

13. He who actively believes on and follows after the living God's spiritual understanding is what? It says, "Are justified from all things."[1683] Why may justification fail through the religious philosophy of Moses, or through any "commandments and doctrines of men,"[1684] or through self? We read: "If I justify myself, mine own mouth shall

---

1677 Colossians 1:22
1678 John 6:29
1679 1 John 4:9
1680 Galatians 3:21
1681 Nehemiah 9:14
1682 Acts 13:38,39
1683 Acts 13:39
1684 Colossians 2:22

condemn me."[1685] Because "the law is not of faith,"[1686] and since "whatsoever is not of faith is sin,"[1687] "no man is justified by the law in the sight of God."[1688]

14. Why then should Moses' religious philosophy of *righteousness* through inventing, employing, and doing religious laws, have *justified* many who followed them? Well indeed through rites, ceremonies, traditions, and policies, freedom from *sin* existed in a figure, in that those laws "sanctifieth to the purifying of the flesh,"[1689] leaving the inward man yet without aid to overcome its error, and the error to be handled once every year by the then high priest. So we see that, in reality, there was no full work of health for the conversation participating in those ordinances, "because that the worshippers once purged should have had no more conscience for sins."[1690]

15. Works of *justification* served their purpose "until the time of reformation,"[1691] for these things once served as "our schoolmaster to bring us unto Christ";[1692] unto that knowledge in *heaven's Place*; "that we might be justified by faith."[1693] That "which stood only in meats and drinks, and divers washings, and carnal ordinances,"[1694] and with "gifts and sacrifices,"[1695] enclosed "the faith which should afterwards be revealed,"[1696] and that faith is the living God's doctrine confessing the necessary labor of His kindness to the conversation's conscience.

16. Notice how that "works" can only purify the *flesh*, yet it is the living God's will to "purge your conscience from dead works,"[1697] that is, from those same works of the *flesh*. One professing His chief messen-

---

1685   Job 9:20
1686   Galatians 3:12
1687   Romans 14:23
1688   Galatians 3:11
1689   Hebrews 9:13
1690   Hebrews 10:2
1691   Hebrews 9:10
1692   Galatians 3:24
1693   Galatians 3:24
1694   Hebrews 9:10
1695   Hebrews 9:9
1696   Galatians 3:23
1697   Hebrews 9:14

ger's spiritual understanding needs his faith's saying in order to benefit from the priestly administration of that understanding's wisdom.

17. Image begets image and the shadow begets the original. In former times, like as there were "ordinances of divine service, and a worldly sanctuary,"[1698] so too now "Christ is not entered into the holy places made with hands, which are the figures of the true; but into heaven itself, now to appear in the presence of God for us."[1699]

18. The language of the apostle reveals that the doctrine of the living God's man is "a minister of the sanctuary, and of the true tabernacle, which the Lord pitched, and not man."[1700] The only way to be received into this congregation is to have, within the mind of the *flesh* or conversation, an experience with the living God's present knowledge of creation, which is why "he hath consecrated for us"[1701] "a new and living way,"[1702] "that is to say, his flesh,"[1703] or rather, by faith in "the offering of the body of Jesus,"[1704] "he hath perfected for ever them that are sanctified."[1705]

19. From exercising faith on the living God's intention, the conversation is justified or recovered by that faith to receive His kindness. Being under the direction of this intention's wisdom, doing no *thing* for *righteousness*, justification or sanctification of the conversation's mind is given, for "whom he justified, them he also glorified"[1706] with the same righteousness as His spiritual understanding.

20. There is full hope and assurance for the conversation tired of its lame heart and paralyzed eyes. Yes the soul needs the living God's benevolence if it would have a "perfect" conversation, and because of this, he sent His chief messenger "to declare his righteousness, for the remission of sins."[1707]

1698 Hebrews 9:1
1699 Hebrews 9:24
1700 Hebrews 8:2
1701 Hebrews 10:20
1702 Hebrews 10:20
1703 Hebrews 10:20
1704 Hebrews 10:10
1705 Hebrews 10:14
1706 Romans 8:30
1707 Romans 3:25

21. No *thing* that can be done to purchase forgiveness or to forward a full spiritual experience except if that *thing* proceeds from the *heart* "through faith in his blood."[1708] If indeed we love His man, if the virtue of his offering's merits should be taken into the soul's temple and treasured, it is that the course of His education's refreshing will be given to alleviate the stain of religious error from our conversation, and as we stand before His wisdom as new creatures, it will create our conversation in His man's *image*, and "shall also quicken your mortal bodies by his Spirit."[1709]

22. The mind will regain, "through sanctification of the Spirit,"[1710] health and vigor to operate the *body* of our faith's information. With the living God's wisdom inside of this *body*, the personal religion does not retard, for His regeneration is given "to keep you from falling, and to present you faultless,"[1711] that the spirit of the mind may become that new ark holding His Ten Commandments, and that the ark of the religious character may be established upon the ordinances of spiritual justice and charity.

23. The perfect righteousness of the Father is given and is available by faith in His man's doctrine. His man saying, "Be perfect," is just as if he had said, "Take my wisdom's effect for the purging of your conversation's conscience," seeing as how one is only "perfect, as pertaining to the conscience."[1712]

24. In order for us to have that perfection pertaining to the inward *man*, it is that this wisdom must become "high priest in things pertaining to God"[1713] for us, for only then can we confess, "I delight in the law of God after the inward man."[1714] Indeed "his Spirit in the inward man"[1715] is to awaken the mind to *life* and regeneration by reformation, for "the

---

1708   Romans 3:25
1709   Romans 8:11
1710   1 Peter 1:2
1711   Jude 1:24
1712   Hebrews 9:9
1713   Hebrews 2:17
1714   Romans 7:22
1715   Ephesians 3:16

Spirit is life because of righteousness,"[1716] and this wisdom is to seal in the mind the precepts of "the word of righteousness,"[1717] certifying how it says, "All thy commandments are righteousness."[1718]

25. To be loved of the Father is to receive "the love of God, and the communion of the Holy Ghost,"[1719] for in this communion is "the grace of the Lord Jesus."[1720] The believer of His man's doctrine is justified to receive creation's power, which is grace to overcome religious error for mental and inward health. It is not just that there is forgiveness with God, but also the remedy to overcome and move on from that habit or stance depressing our heart.

26. As the believer holds dear to *heaven's* spiritual confidence, it is that they will be adopted into *heaven's* classroom and congregation to more perfectly commune with His wisdom for the health of their heart and mind. Written in the log of membership within this Church are those who subscribe and appropriate His man's saying to acknowledge that saying as their Savior and High Priest. This wisdom "is set on the right hand of the throne of the Majesty in the heavens,"[1721] shedding light on the fact that its believer is joined to His Father just as much as His man's conversation is joined to them.

27. If this is not so, then His man lies when saying, "My Father and your Father; and to my God, and your God."[1722] All things concerning the Father, due to a subscription to His religious character, belong to the personal religion. So as "God anointed Jesus of Nazareth with the Holy Ghost,"[1723] His man says to every conversation trusting his saying, "Ye shall receive power, after that the Holy Ghost is come upon you."[1724] In "being by the right hand of God exalted, and having received of

1716 Romans 8:10
1717 Hebrews 5:13
1718 Psalms 119:172
1719 2 Corinthians 13:14
1720 2 Corinthians 13:14
1721 Hebrews 8:1
1722 John 20:17
1723 Acts 10:38
1724 Acts 1:8

the Father the promise of the Holy Ghost, he hath shed forth this"[1725] blessing that we may be "sanctified by the Holy Ghost,"[1726] that is, "by the power of the Spirit of God."[1727]

28. The believer is "conformed to the image of His Son"[1728] "through sanctification of the Spirit and belief of the truth."[1729] In reality, the one professing the living God's spiritual understanding is "sanctified by God the Father."[1730] Without His righteousness, or without His kind effect over the inward person, as given by faith "through the redemption that is in Christ,"[1731] there will be no reception of "the promise of the Spirit through faith."[1732] The reformer needs to know, and to believe on the fact concerning spiritual recovery, if they would excel in fellowship with the living God's Wisdom or Spirit, for the word of truth is "that we might be justified by faith,"[1733] and by no *thing* else.

29. "The promise by faith of Jesus Christ might be given to them that believe"[1734] to "receive abundance of grace and of the gift of righteousness,"[1735] for without applying the gift or offering of righteousness, the *flesh* will offer for *righteousness*. It is that after the heart has set itself to occupy faith's ground, that being holders of creation by faith in the confidence of His man suffering the tree, the living God's Spirit or Wisdom will be given to work into the soul temple what that done by hand and *flesh* can never do. The power of this commandment is that of its fullness bestowed for mental and spiritual recovery, which fullness contains the material of grace to erase the knowledge of "sin" from the conscience.

1725 Acts 2:33
1726 Romans 15:16
1727 Romans 15:19
1728 Romans 8:29
1729 2 Thessalonians 2:13
1730 Jude 1:1
1731 Romans 3:25
1732 Galatians 3:14
1733 Galatians 3:24
1734 Galatians 3:22
1735 Romans 5:17

30. This is the love of God contained in the "mystery of his will, according to his good pleasure which he hath purposed in himself."[1736] As "the Spirit of truth, which proceedeth from the Father"[1737] is *life* because of its kind pleasure, it is that in His wisdom is "the grace of life"[1738] that we may acknowledge what is "good" of God. His man suffered in sinful *flesh* and died the *death* of the cross, and then after that, before his *name's* resurrection, tasted the pain of utter separation from *heaven*, so that the conversation of the willing could find harmony with His Father's ten precepts from learning of and proving the precepts of his doctrine.

31. This doctrine's witness testifies, "He whom God hath sent speaketh the words of God,"[1739] and of old Moses said of the event at Si'nai, "I stood between the LORD and you at that time, to shew you the word of the LORD."[1740] Whose counsel did that Prophet preach but the living God's, for His saying is "according to his good pleasure which he hath purposed in himself."[1741] Therefore now it is not Moses, but it is "Jesus the mediator of the new covenant"[1742] who will build up conversations "that come unto God by him,"[1743] that is, by the faith and confidence hidden within *his* words.

32. Who is the believer gathered to? It says, "That come unto God by him,"[1744] for he indeed suffered "that he might bright us to God."[1745] Now, to whom was the ordained priesthood of the Levites consecrated? It says, "The Levites are mine."[1746] He said, "I have taken your brethren the Levites from among the children of Israel: to you they are

---

1736　Ephesians 1:9
1737　John 15:26
1738　1 Peter 3:7
1739　John 3:34
1740　Deuteronomy 5:5
1741　Ephesians 1:9
1742　Hebrews 12:24
1743　Hebrews 7:25
1744　Hebrews 7:25
1745　1 Peter 3:18
1746　Numbers 3:12

given as a gift for the LORD, to do the service of the tabernacle of the congregation."[1747]

33. Why was this priesthood given Israel? It was known that "perfection were by the Levit'ical priesthood,"[1748] for by them, those things relating to *God* were to be carried out to serve as instruments educating on the Ten Commandments, of which every ordinance, statue, and judgment returned. The tradition of old served its purpose by "having a shadow of good things to come,"[1749] but now His man's wisdom is "come an high priest of good things to come."[1750] Just as that of old was, in relation to the violation of the precepts of *God*, a vehicle educating on the nature of "sin," so now the true Priesthood in *heaven* serves to bring His true congregation to the same respect not by works and religious laws of the *flesh*, as of old, but by active and experimental faith on His spiritual understanding.

34. It should be noticed how it also says that the Levites were given to make atonement before *God*,[1751] and no other tribe of people. This is why the Bible tells us that it is through His *man* that "we have now received the atonement,"[1752] that is, "we were reconciled to God by the death of his Son"[1753] "that we might live through him."[1754] His man's doctrine reveals the fact of devotional reconciliation, yet the believer does not hear this and quit, believing that their *salvation* is indeed personally accomplished, for they must hear, and will hear upon their honest reception of creation's wisdom, "Leaving the principles of the doctrine of Christ, let us go on unto perfection."[1755]

35. After the word of soul ransom is believed on, know that "ye were sealed with that holy Spirit of promise"[1756] to pick up the demeanor, "I

1747 Numbers 18:6
1748 Hebrews 7:11
1749 Hebrews 10:1
1750 Hebrews 9:11
1751 Numbers 8:19
1752 Romans 5:11
1753 Romans 5:10
1754 1 John 4:9
1755 Hebrews 6:1
1756 Ephesians 1:13

have suffered loss of all things"[1757] "that I may know him, and the power of his resurrection."[1758] The believer is thus born "by the word of God, which liveth and abideth for ever,"[1759] that they may know why it says, "He that doeth the will of God abideth for ever."[1760]

36. By the consolation offered through His man's wisdom, the reformer has boldness to approach the living God when admitting their religion to a living faith in His science of personal and devotional recovery. Nothing has changed, except that the former shadow has now met the figure from which it is drawn. As there were ordinances and precepts to bring the doer a higher knowledge of gratitude for the living God's religious character, so now, by His man's doctrine, the believer will come into personal contact with the living God's religious character to have His wisdom's laws engraved within their conscience.

37. That tradition old was an established waymark that led to the Ten Commandments. His chief man's faith is yet established to do the same thing by "a better and an enduring substance"[1761] poured forth from *heaven's* mind through "a more excellent ministry";[1762] this new covenant wisdom "is the mediator of a better covenant, which was established upon better promises."[1763]

38. "Verily the first covenant had also ordinances of divine service, and a worldly sanctuary,"[1764] yet by the death of His man, "he taketh away the first, that he may establish the second."[1765] Through the new covenant is "given unto us exceeding great and precious promises,"[1766] and by appropriating these promises through exercising faith on them, we may serve salvation's science in the spirit of our mind, as opposed to

---

1757　Philippians 3:8
1758　Philippians 3:10
1759　1 Peter 1:23
1760　1 John 2:17
1761　Hebrews 10:34
1762　Hebrews 8:6
1763　Hebrews 8:6
1764　Hebrews 9:1
1765　Hebrews 10:9
1766　2 Peter 1:4

works perceived to be a means for proof of loyalty, piety, beauty, and devotion.[1767]

39. The apostle John saw the Christian church turning to "the works of their hands"[1768] for *justification*, and because he knew that only One was foreshadowed to be that Minister and Son of *man*, he told them, "We have an advocate with the Father."[1769] They were again counseled by the apostles at that church at Jerusalem, "What further need was there that another priest should rise after the order of Melchis'edec, and not be called after the order of Aaron?"[1770]

40. There is only *One* ordained to continue Aaron's order, "and no man taketh this honour unto himself, but he that is called of God, as was Aaron."[1771] There is only One "after the similitude of Melchis'edec,"[1772] for "Christ glorified not himself to be made an high priest; but he that said unto him, Thou art my Son, to day have I begotten thee."[1773]

41. John saw that the church lusted after a place and a position not given to it, for in her was brewing the making of that disappointment "who opposeth and exalteth himself above all that is called God, or that is worshipped; so that he sitteth in the temple of God, shewing himself that he is God."[1774] Without the living God's doctrine, the early church existed in a very strange spirit. A new doctrine was forming in the church with creeds of faith that would teach *salvation* only through her, and with regard to the Bishops, that their word was *divine*. Because he discerned the making of a most dreadful beast, the apostle counseled, "He who loveth God love his brother also,"[1775] for the love of God was seen in that He sacrificed His benevolence for every mind,

1767 Romans 1:9; Romans 7:22
1768 Revelation 9:20
1769 1 John 2:1
1770 Hebrews 7:11
1771 Hebrews 5:4
1772 Hebrews 7:15
1773 Hebrews 5:5
1774 2 Thessalonians 2:4
1775 1 John 4:21

and John knew a love of God moved the heart to know, "We ought also to lay down our lives for the brethren."[1776]

42. The work of God for *man* did not end at the cross, but after that reconciliation is accepted and the individual moves forward in it, then the work of righteousness begins with *He* who "ever liveth to make intercession for them."[1777] By His saying of creation, we may have access to all of the riches of spiritual wisdom and knowledge concerning *heaven's* will. From simple and diligent faith on the living God's sacrifice, His wisdom will impute its virtue onto the conversation that it may be given into the hands of its course of learning for a mental resurrection, restoring to the conversation the living God's religious character.

43. What will set the sincere apart from the liar will be that their existence is not consumed in fulfilling the Ten Commandments; the spirit of man has no power to justly fulfill them. Their energies will not be spent on doing this or that handwritten *thing* for *justification*, which error is proof that they are without the teaching and sealing Spirit of the living God. Scripture says that the conversation must be "conformed to the image of his Son,"[1778] and if we would reflect that image, it is well to know that His "Christ hath redeemed us from the curse of the law."[1779] This is why His man says, "By this shall all men know that ye are my disciples, if ye have love one to another."[1780]

44. True godly benevolence is a revelation that both the commandments of God and the faith of His chief minister are in harmony within the experience. Such communion with one another can only be had if the spirit of self-righteousness is quenched. As the early church held dear to its political ambitions to support its spurious religious theory, they forsook the counsel, "Let us consider one another to provoke unto love and to good works."[1781]

45. As did the church, so too the heart may organize itself to be an impregnable empire if the virtue of His man's commandment isn't

---

1776   1 John 3:16
1777   Hebrews 7:25
1778   Romans 8:29
1779   Galatians 3:13
1780   John 13:35
1781   Hebrews 10:24

applied to. Because that doctrine expressing the living God's name was put aside for that *wisdom* emphasizing self-justification, the church did contrary to the *heaven's* will and left off unity and faithful compassion.

46. To the *professed* church of the apostles, *righteousness* came from laws of *circumcision* backed by *authority*. As time passed from the apostle John, this church would serve as the conscience of its members, for by joining to the State of Rome, she became a crowd of strangers. To say that piety was expressed from handwritten religious laws backed by the State was to call the living God a liar, and because the church existed in a spirit removing the mind from justification by faith, there was a plague among her elders and church members that confused even them that kept the old pagan Roman religion.

47. Yet remember Aaron, how that during a gross plague he "stood between the dead and the living; and the plague was stayed."[1782] The congregation of the house of *Aaron* in *heaven* is without plague, for "in the way of righteousness is life; and in the pathway thereof is no death."[1783]

1782 Numbers 16:48
1783 Proverbs 12:28

27

The Hope Of Glory

1. "Ye know that ye were not redeemed with corruptible things, as silver and gold, from your vain conversation received by tradition from your fathers; but with the precious blood of Christ, as of a lamb without blemish and without spot: who verily was foreordained before the foundation of the world, but was manifest in these last times for you, who by him do believe in God, that raised him up from the dead, and gave him glory; that your faith and hope might be in God."[1784]

2. Faith and hope are one, for without hope there is no place to bestow faith, and there can be faith in no *thing* if there is not something to bestow hope on. Faith is forwarded by a living hope, and it is because of that hope written on the heart that faith preserves the spiritual philosophy, leaving the experience in the hands of God's wisdom for purification. So then it is true that "we are saved by hope,"[1785] for it says, "Thy faith hath saved thee,"[1786] and as faith works through hope and hope stimulates faith, the mind will obey that hope in the living

---

1784   1 Peter 1:18-21
1785   Romans 8:24
1786   Luke 18:42

God's doctrine to encourage "sanctification of the Spirit,"[1787] for it says, "Have purified your souls in obeying the truth through the Spirit."[1788]

3. "According to his abundant mercy,"[1789] our Father "hath begotten us again unto a lively hope";[1790] "of his own will begat he us with the word of truth";[1791] for the faith of the believer rests in the hope that "according to his mercy he saved us, by the washing of regeneration, and renewing of the Holy Ghost."[1792] It is the hope of the faith of creation that the believer is to become familiar with, for it is by that doctrine exposed in the life, death, and resurrection of his *man* that we "by him do believe in God, that raised him up from the dead, and gave him glory."[1793]

4. What is the hope of that faith but the fact of the living God's will and wisdom, "the engrafted word, which is able to save your souls."[1794] What is it able to be saved? It says, "Your souls,"[1795] and this counsel cannot promise any other *thing* because it was confirmed of old, "He shall redeem their soul from deceit and violence."[1796] "According to the truth of the gospel,"[1797] "we might be justified by the faith of Christ"[1798] that our hope may be in what raised His *man* from the *dead*, that like as he was raised and given a continuing *strength*, so too it should be done for our conversation's conscience in similar fashion.

5. Who then raised him from the dead? Indeed it was the Father, but in truth it was "the Spirit of him that raised up Jesus from the dead."[1799] As this minister was raised from the *dead* and given a new *name* and *office*, so too it is ordained that "he that raised up Christ from

---

1787   1 Peter 1:2
1788   1 Peter 1:22
1789   1 Peter 1:3
1790   1 Peter 1:3
1791   James 1:18
1792   Titus 3:5
1793   1 Peter 1:21
1794   James 1:21
1795   James 1:21
1796   Psalms 72:14
1797   Galatians 2:14
1798   Galatians 2:16
1799   Romans 8:11

the dead shall also quicken your mortal bodies by his Spirit,"[1800] to the end "we shall be also in the likeness of his resurrection."[1801]

6. There is therefore a personal work after the heart and mind have believed on the living God's doctrine, and after the believer has been pronounced just by faith to receive the promise of that doctrine's kindness. This is why the apostle wrote, "Truly our fellowship is with the Father, and with his Son."[1802]

7. Fellowship with the Father is "fellowship of the Spirit"[1803] "and the communion of the Holy Ghost";[1804] the victory found in His words is only gained "if we believe on him that raised up Jesus our Lord from the dead."[1805] One can profess "Christ" all day and remain unchanged in their natural character. One can hear and believe the stories and doctrines sold to them on "Christ," yet it is the living God's Wisdom that breathes life into the personal religion to expose the mind to its character. Without faith in the power of His spiritual understanding, the religion will remain vain and immature, for it is that every believer should be "sanctified by the Holy Ghost,"[1806] that is, "sanctified by God the Father."[1807]

8. How is the Spirit given? It says, "We might receive the promise of the Spirit through faith."[1808] All *things* for the health of the soul are now through an experimental faith on the Bible's words for spiritual discernment.

9. The faith and hope of the believer rests on the fact that the same treatment given to His chief minister will be given to them of the Father, for as every conversation is naturally a breathing corpse, "through the redemption that is in Christ,"[1809] "God, who is rich in

---

1800 Romans 8:11
1801 Romans 6:5
1802 1 John 1:3
1803 Philippians 2:1
1804 2 Corinthians 13:14
1805 Romans 4:24
1806 Romans 15:16
1807 Jude 1:1
1808 Galatians 3:14
1809 Romans 3:24

mercy, for his great love wherewith he loved us, even when we were dead in sins, hath quickened us together with Christ"[1810] "that the body of sin might be destroyed, that henceforth we should not serve sin."[1811] Our Father would have the conversation touched by the illustration of His man suffering the tree regenerated by His wisdom that it should not serve its formerly injurious religious character, and to allow continual health to flow from *Him*, it is that the penitent should receive a covering for shame, "even the righteousness of God which is by faith of Jesus Christ."[1812]

10. "Like as Christ was raised up from the dead by the glory of the Father,"[1813] so the conversation is to be transformed "by the power of the Spirit of God,"[1814] for it says of His man, "Being put to death in the flesh, but quickened by the Spirit."[1815] This is why the reformer is told that they are "kept by the power of God through faith unto salvation."[1816] But how, for "salvation," are they kept? We ought to know that it is "the grace of God that bringeth salvation."[1817]

11. Through faith, the believer is to be kept by the power of grace. His wisdom administers righteousness' health or balm; grace; that we may "have grace, whereby we may serve God acceptably with reverence and godly fear."[1818] The faith of the believer is thus sustained and refreshed by this *power*, which power is ordained to keep them in a good and faithful spirit to remove them from troubling themselves and others, which is why it says, "By grace are ye saved through faith; and that not of yourselves: it is the gift of God."[1819]

12. As hope and faith procure recovery of soul and spirit, the reality is that from faith in the hope of being created into the likeness

---

1810 Ephesians 2:4,5
1811 Romans 6:6
1812 Romans 3:22
1813 Romans 6:4
1814 Romans 15:19
1815 1 Peter 3:18
1816 1 Peter 1:5
1817 Titus 2:11
1818 Hebrews 12:28
1819 Ephesians 2:8

of the living God's religious character, the *substance* of that character's mind will be given to replace old and damaging habits and inclinations to cultivate new and better habits for the members of the *body*. From simply actively believing on creation's present hope, grace will be given to restore the personal religious philosophy, providing us "his righteousness for the remission of sins."[1820]

13. This is why it is important to know that only those who exist in salvation's science by faith will be known of *heaven* to benefit from its current mediation. It is then not said in vain, "Whatsoever is not of faith is sin,"[1821] because "without faith it is impossible to please him."[1822] "Through the righteousness of faith,"[1823] "he that cometh to God must believe that he is."[1824]

14. By faith in creation's doctrine, that counsel will remove "us from the power of darkness"[1825] "into the kingdom of his dear Son."[1826] Scripture says that His *man* "was received up into heaven, and sat on the right hand of God,"[1827] therefore if the same wisdom that raised *him* up brought *him* before the Father to dress *him* with newness of *name* and position, should the believer refuse to consider that his or her "conversation is in heaven"?[1828]

15. His wisdom gathers every believer into creation's new covenant realm, therefore it must be known, "We have such an high priest, who is set on the right hand of the throne of the Majesty in the heavens."[1829]

16. His spiritual understanding is the only "minister of the sanctuary, and of the true tabernacle, which the Lord pitched, and not man,"[1830] and from out of this *Place* flows the precious promises of creation's science for spiritual sustenance, as it says, "Blessed be the

---

1820   Romans 3:25
1821   Romans 14:23
1822   Hebrews 11:6
1823   Romans 4:13
1824   Hebrews 11:6
1825   Colossians 1:13
1826   Colossians 1:13
1827   Mark 16:19
1828   Philippians 3:20
1829   Hebrews 8:1
1830   Hebrews 8:2

God and Father of our Lord Jesus Christ, who hath blessed us with all spiritual blessings in heavenly places in Christ."[1831] Every mental or physical sacrifice for "sin" is dethroned by faith's science, for from faith, the only righteousness that may cover "sin" is given, to the end that the living God's ordinances would be properly maintained through faith in His will and wisdom.

17. This is the instruction of faith demanding that all attention be given to hope on creation's law, and that all hope be upheld through the living God's power to purify the mind. Therefore "be not moved away from the hope of the gospel,"[1832] counsels the apostle, because he knew that "if ye continue in the faith grounded and settled,"[1833] the result would be that every believing conversation should "speak the mystery of Christ."[1834]

18. Our hope and faith in God is made plain by His man's commandment, that as he was raised by the Spirit to have "obtained a more excellent name,"[1835] so "the name of our Lord Jesus Christ may be glorified in you"[1836] to fulfill the promise, "I will write upon him the name of my God, and the name of the city of my God, which is new Jerusalem, which cometh down out of heaven from my God: and I will write upon him my new name."[1837]

19. What is His man's former *name*? It says, "That prophet that should come into the world,"[1838] because He said, "I will raise them up a Prophet from among their brethren."[1839] What then is His doctrine's new *name*? It is written, "Thou art a priest for ever after the order of Melchis'edec."[1840]

1831 Ephesians 1:3
1832 Colossians 1:23
1833 Colossians 1:23
1834 Colossians 4:3
1835 Hebrews 1:4
1836 2 Thessalonians 1:12
1837 Revelation 3:12
1838 John 6:14
1839 Deuteronomy 18:18
1840 Hebrews 5:6

20. This is that spiritual understanding who is gone "into heaven itself, now to appear in the presence of God for us,"[1841] and "to lay hold upon the hope set before us."[1842] Again, what hope? It says, "To be conformed to the image of his Son."[1843]

21. That hope of possessing His religious character's thoughts and feelings is met only by faith in the law of the illustration of His *man's* offering. By *heaven's* will, every conversation willing to hear the saying of that doctrine should joy in both the wisdom and the power of that doctrine to recover their heart from *death* and their mind from spiritual error. Truly there is thanksgiving to the living God for His good will and purpose towards us, for through His chief man is given an understanding on what the expected standard of excellence is, and there is proof that like as the Father did not leave *him* in the *grave*, so too now may every believer confess, "God will redeem my soul from the power of the grave."[1844]

22. "He that is called of God, as was Aaron";[1845] "Jesus, made an high priest for ever after the order of Melchis'edec";[1846] "made, not after the law of a carnal commandment, but after the power of an endless life";[1847] "is passed into the heavens"[1848] to bring "many sons unto glory."[1849]

1841   Hebrews 9:24
1842   Hebrews 6:18
1843   Romans 8:29
1844   Psalms 49:15
1845   Hebrews 5:4
1846   Hebrews 6:20
1847   Hebrews 7:16
1848   Hebrews 4:14
1849   Hebrews 2:10

28

Abram

1. It is true that "we say that faith was reckoned to Abraham for righteousness,"[1850] but the man was not always known as Abraham, for he was once called, Abram. Who was Abram? We know that the name of Abraham is the character of Abraham, and that the character of Abraham was one that existed "through the righteousness of faith,"[1851] but what was the "name" of Abram?

2. Abraham's heart was steadfast unwavering in faith on the living God's voice, for it says, "He believed in the LORD; and he counted it to him for righteousness,"[1852] but what was the heart or foundation of "Abram's" doctrine? Clearly the man exhibited righteousness by faith throughout his entire life, yet the Bible speaks of two specific characters with two very different doctrines.

3. "Now the LORD had said unto Abram, Get thee out of thy country";[1853] what did Abram do? It says, "Abram departed, as the LORD had spoken unto him."[1854]

1850 Romans 4:9
1851 Romans 4:13
1852 Genesis 15:6
1853 Genesis 12:1
1854 Genesis 12:4

4. This man was chosen because he was the only one of his generation that held faith in the living God's voice and doctrine above every *thing*. Herein is why the Bible says of him, "Abraham obeyed my voice, and kept my charge, my commandments, my statutes, and my laws."[1855] The living God therefore knew that He had made no wrong promise in *Abraham*, saying, "I will bless them that bless thee, and curse him that curseth thee."[1856]

5. This was that man who, although born in an idolatrous house to an idolatrous *father*, kept that faith given to him by Shem untainted. This same Abraham "was called the Friend of God"[1857] because "he staggered not at the promise of God through unbelief; but was strong in faith."[1858] And yet we find the character of Abram not fully sold on living by faith. Although "being fully persuaded that, what he," the living God, "had promised, he was able also to perform,"[1859] he counsels his wife, for example, upon entering into Egypt, "Say, I pray thee, thou art my sister."[1860]

6. Can his error be discerned? The living God had told him, "I will bless them that bless thee, and curse him that curseth thee,"[1861] yet Abram did not fully respect that promise. He said to his wife, "Say, I pray thee, thou art my sister,"[1862] and why did he say so? He continues, "That it may be well with me for thy sake; and my soul shall live because of thee."[1863]

7. Was it not the living God that had promised to bless and to curse? Wherein is Abram right to say, "I justify myself"?[1864] Although Abraham did exist by that righteousness which is of faith, the old *man* "Abram" yet knew his religion "by works of righteousness."[1865]

1855 Genesis 26:5
1856 Genesis 12:3
1857 James 2:23
1858 Romans 4:20
1859 Romans 4:21
1860 Genesis 12:13
1861 Genesis 12:3
1862 Genesis 12:13
1863 Genesis 12:13
1864 Job 9:20
1865 Titus 3:5

8. Instead of allowing his God's wisdom to work "according to his good pleasure which he hath purposed in himself,"[1866] Abram would secure his own blessing through his wife, and would even place the health of his soul in her hands. Although he attributed deliverance to his wife, in truth, Abram worked a plot for his own gain, and should this plot have granted him an escape from the supposed threat that he imagined, then his deliverance would have truly been held in his heart as from his own hand and mind, yet he must learn, "I cannot go beyond the commandment of the LORD, to do either good or bad of mine own mind."[1867]

9. A plague arose in Pharaoh's *house* because of his lie. "Pharaoh called Abram, and said, What is this that thou hast done unto me? why didst thou not tell me that she was thy wife?"[1868]

10. There is no response from Abram that Moses writes for our observation. Shame may have been the garment that Abram wore at this time, for he knew within himself that he had brought harm to the *name* of the living God by failing to experiment with faith.

11. It was the living God that caused certain events to push Abram's journey into Egypt. His wisdom knew that the Egyptians would hear Him through His minister, for from Pharaoh's response to Sa'rai, we see that the Egyptians were not quite that vile and pagan nation that should, in the future, utter, "Who is the LORD, that I should obey his voice"?[1869]

12. The living God had a message for the Egyptians, but that message was tarnished when one who claimed to serve His wisdom consciously violated His commandment to secure his own welfare. If indeed Abram honored the voice of God then he reverenced the three most blatant doctrines ordained by that voice at creation: the seventh day's Sabbath, marriage, and an experimental faith for creation. With Abram content to violate the sacredness of marriage, he could not speak on the joy, foundation, and seal of the true faith, or on the

---

1866   Ephesians 1:9
1867   Numbers 24:13
1868   Genesis 12:18
1869   Exodus 5:12

Sabbath, therefore procuring a reason to the mind of the Egyptians to cast out the full authority of the Creator, which knowledge the Egyptians needed to know.

13. Abram said not one word when convicted of his error. He would again fulfill the same scene in the future against another king, saying of his wife, "She is my sister."[1870] "I thought, Surely the fear of God is not in this place; and they will slay me for my wife's sake,"[1871] he then later confessed.

14. Again, the living God knew these people as He knew the Egyptians. This king later said to the Him in prayer, "In the integrity of my heart and innocency of my hands have I done this."[1872] "Said he not unto me, She is my sister?"[1873] To which prayer the living God responded by saying, "I know."[1874]

15. Should Abraham have remained faithful in both instances, the living God's *fear* would have strengthened in these two *nations*. He came to this king in a dream, even as He came to another in a future generation, showing that He had His eye on him, and that He cared for him to know, "The God of heaven hath given thee a kingdom, power, and strength, and glory,"[1875] to the end that king would confess, "The King of heaven,"[1876] "he is the living God, and stedfast for ever, and his kingdom that which shall not be destroyed."[1877]

16. Thus, He counsels, "I will even betroth thee unto me in faithfulness,"[1878] for there is no other way to enter into covenant relationship with Him than by faith. "Whatsoever is not of faith is sin,"[1879] for any law that the heart would obey from man, or set within itself for stillness, is of no value, for it says, "The law is not of faith."[1880]

1870 Genesis 20:2
1871 Genesis 20:11
1872 Genesis 20:5
1873 Genesis 20:5
1874 Genesis 20:6
1875 Daniel 2:37
1876 Daniel 4:37
1877 Daniel 6:26
1878 Hosea 2:20
1879 Romans 14:23
1880 Galatians 3:12

17. Because of Abram's actions, "Pharaoh commanded his men concerning him: and they sent him away, and his wife, and all that he had,"[1881] and this lesson is for us.

18. A professed experience in the living God's science without cultivating faith on it warrants the rebuke, "Depart from me, all ye workers of iniquity."[1882] As Abraham was without dispute when he was banished, without learning how to personally exercise faith on the living God's words, we will fulfill the saying, "He was speechless."[1883]

19. Why was this one individual speechless? It was said to them, "How camest thou in hither not having a wedding garment?"[1884] This person did not have on that special attire for acceptance into the family banquet, even that "garment of praise for the spirit"[1885] that fulfills the saying, "Perfect through my comeliness, which I had put upon thee, saith the Lord GOD."[1886] This is why He counseled Abram, "I am thy shield, and thy exceeding great reward,"[1887] and, "Walk before me, and be thou perfect."[1888]

20. When He said, "I will bless them that bless thee, and curse him that curseth thee,"[1889] He did not only speak literally, but "the scripture, foreseeing that God would justify the heathen through faith, preached before the gospel unto Abraham, saying, In thee shall all nations be blessed."[1890]

21. To "bless" is to kneel down before, to praise, or to salute. Should the one saluting Abraham; that is, should the conversation reverence "the faith of Abraham";[1891] then that conversation will be blessed of his God. To bless Abraham would be to uphold the spirit and law of Abraham's spiritual understanding, which law is "after the law

1881 Genesis 12:20
1882 Luke 13:27
1883 Matthew 22:12
1884 Matthew 22:12
1885 Isaiah 61:3
1886 Ezekiel 16:14
1887 Genesis 15:1
1888 Genesis 17:1
1889 Genesis 12:3
1890 Galatians 3:8
1891 Romans 4:16

of righteousness,"[1892] "even the righteousness which is of faith,"[1893] "the law of faith."[1894]

22. So then it is true, "They which be of faith are blessed with faithful Abraham,"[1895] leaving it "that no man is justified by the law in the sight of God."[1896] It is for this reason that Abraham is to be looked at not simply as a man, but also as a symbolic doctrine through whom is preached the reality of the living God's present commandment, and that reality being, "We might be justified by faith."[1897] The living God loved Abraham so much because of his active faith, for when the *earth* was trembling; as it says, "In his days was the earth divided";[1898] there stood one who "staggered not at the promise of God through unbelief; but was strong in faith, giving glory to God."[1899]

23. Abraham is a fundamental lesson for the conversation believing on the health promised by the living God. Although there may be a strong belief in His words, there will always exist, within our person, a mind to justify self before *Him*. But there is only one thing every believer should be able to confess, and that is, "Say in a word."[1900] Why? Because that word is "the commandment of the everlasting God,"[1901] and this means exactly what He has said: "My words shall not pass away,"[1902] bearing witness to how it says, "The word of our God shall stand for ever."[1903]

24. God gave His word to Abram and Abram forgot it, and the result was a plague against another person, harm against the living God's name, and inward shame and reproach against his own heart and

---

1892 Romans 9:31
1893 Romans 9:30
1894 Romans 3:27
1895 Galatians 3:9
1896 Galatians 3:11
1897 Galatians 3:24
1898 Genesis 10:25
1899 Romans 4:20
1900 Luke 7:7
1901 Romans 16:26
1902 Luke 21:33
1903 Isaiah 40:8

mind. Spiritual "desires of the flesh and of the mind"[1904] will lead "into captivity to the law of sin,"[1905] and this is our faith's naturally inherited "spirit of error."[1906]

25. But the living God has not left us without hope. "O the depth of the riches both of the wisdom and knowledge of God!"[1907] There is a purpose for faith in the living God's doctrine, and it is "that we might receive the promise of the Spirit through faith,"[1908] which Spirit is to educate the mind on how to care for the soul and *body*, engraving, within the mind, "the light of the knowledge of the glory of God in the face of Jesus Christ,"[1909] that it may be sincerely confessed, "I delight in the law of God after the inward man."[1910]

1904   Ephesians 2:13
1905   Romans 7:23
1906   1 John 4:6
1907   Romans 11:33
1908   Galatians 3:14
1909   2 Corinthians 4:6
1910   Romans 7:22

29

Faith

1. What then is "faith"? If "faith is the substance of things hoped for, the evidence of things not seen,"[1911] then what type of "substance" is "faith," or what kind of "substance" is in "faith"?

2. From the way in which Paul uses the term "substance," it is evident that faith is the reward for exercising a confidence in what is not yet seen. Paul's use of the term substance is therefore best articulated through how it says, "Thy substance and thy treasures will I give to the spoil without price, and that for all thy sins, even in all thy borders,"[1912] and, "The earth opened her mouth, and swallowed them up, and their households, and their tents, and all the substance that was in their possession,"[1913] and, "For ye had compassion of me in my bonds, and took joyfully the spoiling of your goods, knowing in yourselves that ye have in heaven a better and an enduring substance."[1914]

3. The "substance" associated with "faith" is a treasure, wealth, or "good." "Faith" is the product of exercising assurance when not

---

1911 Hebrews 11:1
1912 Jeremiah 15:13
1913 Deuteronomy 11:6
1914 Hebrews 10:34

yet given assurance, or confidence when not yet having any *thing* to be confident on, or certainty when not yet able to take full certainty. "Faith" is the by-product or merchandise of exercising hope when having no clear sign of that hope's reality, making "faith" a very important and special gift to receive.

4. When therefore exercising faith, we are exercising the confidence we possess, which if faithful to, we evince the gesture or manifestation of "faith." The question, then, is not about what "faith" is, but about what is needed in order to evince the gesture or manifestation of faith. Faith is simply the end or the result of an exercised hope. Faith is the product displayed when wavering in nothing. "Faith" must accordingly have a beginning, and a more important concern than the result of evincing the manifestation of our confidence is the source or means whereby that manifestation is empowered or inspired.

5. "Faith" is the treasure or possession of what is hoped for. When hoping for what is not yet seen, because we have no sure evidence of what is hoped for, we demonstrate faith. The act of exercising poise when life has not revealed a good enough reason to exercise poise is the definition of "faith," because when acting out poise when having no good reason to do so, we demonstrate a treasure that we are in possession of, and that treasure is "faith." How one then comes to even care to demonstrate that treasure is the science of faith's origin, opening up the mind to discern faith's value.

6. If we do not possess the ability or willingness to exercise morale when receiving no clear evidence to exercise morale, we fail to demonstrate the treasure or wealth of the ability to do so. "Faith" is the treasure or wealth of confidence, and if failing to trust on a hope that is not yet a reality, we fail to give proof of hope's balm, substance, or economy. It is then very clear to understand if we do or do not put hope in some *thing* or some one, because if we can exercise assurance when without having assurance, then our confidence on what we hope for will be revealed, but if not demonstrating assurance on what we believe to receive, then we will demonstrate an internal conflict, even like as it

says, "He that wavereth is like a wave of the sea driven with the wind and tossed."[1915]

7. Faithlessness flails the mind to and fro. Faithlessness disturbs equilibrium, which is why it says, "The wicked are like the troubled sea, when it cannot rest."[1916]

8. The "wicked" do not know peace because their inward person is not properly trusting on or exercising faith on the hope that they have. To waver in faith is to question and doubt the origin of belief, making it very important to understand the inspiration or motivation to first care for demonstrating hope's substance. Herein is the reason why it is well to know how it says, "We are saved by hope."[1917]

9. Hope "saves." What does it mean to be "saved"? We find our answer from how it says, "Through knowledge shall the just be delivered,"[1918] and, "Who will have all men to be saved, and to come unto the knowledge of the truth."[1919]

10. One is "saved," or "delivered," according to the Bible, only through knowledge. If hope "saves," and if "faith" is hope's substance, then the definitive beginning of "faith" is knowledge.

11. Knowledge is what empower or inspires "faith." Without knowledge, there can be no hope to "save," "rescue," or "deliver" the assurance from doubt. Where there is no knowledge, the heart fails and the mind has no direction of what to put hope in, making it well to know that faith's demonstration occurs only through a willing exercise of knowledge, and a willing desire to retain knowledge for exercising.

12. "Faith" is therefore not ignorant or unintelligent. "Faith" is absolutely very intelligent, because we may not have full confidence on some *thing*, but we may have knowledge of that *thing's* character, and of an experience with it. The knowledge we possess makes hope's exercise easy, which is why, if we would have faith in any *thing*, we do well to learn why it says, "I know him, and keep his saying,"[1920] and, "I

1915   James 1:6
1916   Isaiah 57:20
1917   Romans 8:24
1918   Proverbs 11:9
1919   1 Timothy 2:4
1920   John 8:55

applied mine heart to know, and to search, and to seek out wisdom, and the reason of things."[1921]

13. The "wicked" are then categorized as "wicked" because they will not apply self for knowledge to evince hope's substance. Failure to apply self for taking personal knowledge of what one is confident in will result in a troubled mind, because if possessing no knowledge of what we are confident in, then why are we confident in it?

14. Knowledge alleviates perception, which is why knowledge "saves" or "delivers." It is the mental and inward deliverance of knowledge that fortifies confidence, therefore if we should think to exercise faith on some *thing*, we should know that after a desire to put confidence on some *thing* is born, the next thing to do is to add knowledge to what we would exercise faith on. And even the apostle states this fact, saying, "Add to your faith virtue; and to virtue knowledge."[1922]

15. Our faith is a spiritual *body* that, in order to be beneficial to us, needs nourishment. "Virtue" is personal goodness or beneficence, and when adding "virtue" to "faith," we are adding what is "good" to our confidence. The greatest "good" is found in edification, which, when experienced, leads to the obtaining of knowledge to live by. "Virtue" is then beautified by knowledge, even like as it says, "The excellency of knowledge is, that wisdom giveth life to them that have it."[1923]

16. If hope "saves," and if that "saving" is through knowledge, then the *life* that is given by the wisdom retained through knowledge is newness of thought and feeling on what we are confident in. This newness of thought and feeling is what empowers and inspires the act to exercise assurance when no proof of being assured is given. The by-product of such an act is "faith," which substance is only experimented with as the person takes knowledge of what to first act on.

1921 Ecclesiastes 7:25
1922 2 Peter 1:5
1923 Ecclesiastes 7:12

30

Faith's Prerequisite

1. "Faith" is the result of a confidence successfully hoped on. If faith is then the by-product of hope, it is very possible to have a hope that does not move faith to appear. The sign of a hope perfectly believed on is "faith," and if "faith" is but a witness to a hope that is believed on, it is possible to have a hope not satisfying faith's revelation, which thought opens us up to concern our self with faith's actual prerequisite.

2. "Faith" is a state of mind demonstrated when one's hope is not questioned but examined. We can observe this fact from how it says, "By faith he sojourned in the land of promise, as in a strange country, dwelling in tabernacles with Isaac and Jacob, the heirs with him of the same promise: for he looked for a city which hath foundations, whose builder and maker is God. Through faith also Sara herself received strength to conceive seed, and was delivered of a child when she was past age, because she judged him faithful who had promised."[1924]

3. These verses reveal faith's foundation to be an experimental investigation of what is hoped for. Abraham's religious character, for its faithfulness to the living God's words, was promised a land for its offspring. Abraham, after hearing the promise, didn't sit still, but took

---

1924 Hebrews 11:9-11

courage to travel all throughout the promised area to learn about the actual fulfillment of the vision he not only received, but also examined. Abraham, by continually and actively checking for the promise, demonstrates hope's substance, revealing the confidence he had in the promise made for his religious character, even if the vision wasn't yet apparent.

4. Sara also demonstrates hope's substance by raising an inquiry against the promise she received. The act of her not only judging the promise, but also the mind behind the promise, added strength to the hope that she possessed. Seeing as how "wisdom strengtheneth,"[1925] her investigation gave her enough wisdom take confidence on the promise of her conception, even if she believed the possibility of that promise's fulfillment to be unlikely.

5. These examples show that if faith should ever be demonstrated, and if the person should possess hope's wealth or bounty, active examination for knowledge of what is hoped for should commence. Abraham and Sara would not have had faith to exercise if they didn't first actively judge the character of the hope that they had, and the character of the mind promising that hope to them. By judging the faithfulness of their hope and the mind magnifying their hope, they both retained enough wisdom to let their understanding see or perceive what they naturally could not.

6. Herein "faith," because of its reliance upon obtained knowledge, is understood to be a trait transcending the natural character or state of mind. Faith doesn't move unintelligently, but operates through the knowledge retained by investigation. In order to have faith, it is then necessary to put self, in the hope of better understanding what is hoped on, in uncomfortable circumstances.

7. Because the goal is the hope that is desired, in order to have enough energy for reaching that hope, understanding is the fuel encouraging activity to perform what is desired. Both Abraham and Sara, by placing self, due to their belief on what was hoped for, in very uncomfortable circumstances, received knowledge of their belief's certainty.

1925 Ecclesiastes 7:19

This knowledge became the means whereby they never grew tired of continually hoping for what they knew to be true, even if reality did not then provide evidence of what they knew to be true.

8. Knowledge of what is desired allows the hand of our confidence to paint the picture of our belief on hope's canvas. This canvas is naturally empty and blank, but knowledge adds a colorful and precise image to it, giving us, although not yet physically apparent, a clear vision of what to exercise faith on. There is then no such exercising of faith without knowledge of what to exercise faith on; that knowledge informs our thoughts and feelings of the vision we need to pay close attention to. To therefore simply say, "Have faith," is but empty or useless if not also advising, "Acquaint now thyself with him, and be at peace: thereby good shall come unto thee. Receive, I pray thee, the law from his mouth, and lay up his words in thine heart."[1926]

9. Peace and stillness of mind occurs as the conversation's mind takes knowledge of the living God's words. It is our responsibility to exercise faith on those words, but there can be no exercising of faith on those words if we are not at peace with them. Both Abraham and Sara found peace with the words of their promise by examining them, and through their examination, became mindful to exercise faith on the mind behind the promise they hoped on. This mindfulness to engage with what is not yet apparent is the "good" that the book of Job states will come when taking knowledge of what is hoped on, which "good" is but the substance of what is hoped on.

10. Faith is the "good" of knowledge, or is but the "virtue" of wisdom. Without taking knowledge of what we hope on or believe in, we cannot receive a vision of it to exercise faith on. Taking knowledge of what is hoped on is a labor verifying both our desire and belief, allowing us to know the certainty of our hope. The experience of verifying our hope is the fuel satisfying the output of energy for what is hoped on, making the exercising of faith, seeing as how it is supported by proven and increasing knowledge, no task at all.

1926 Job 22:21,22

11. This is how Abraham and Sara could demonstrate hope's substance. Because they took the time to take knowledge of the hope that they had, they grew rich in their understanding, possessing a storehouse of confidence to keep their hope alive. Their record teaches us that faith is but a bank of knowledge holding proven information on what is hoped for. The greater our bank account is, or the more knowledge we have on what is hoped for, and on the mind or *person* behind that hope, the greater our joy and confidence to exercise faith on what is hoped for, even if we do not yet have what is promised.

12. So then we must raise the question: "Is the reception of the promise more important than the hope of that promise's reception, or is faith on that promise's reception more important than the actual reception of it?"

13. It is always pleasing and satisfying to receiving what is hoped for and desired. There is nothing wrong with a promise being fulfilled, but the fulfillment of a promise means the end of hope, which means the end of faith, which means the end of knowledge. It would then be better to exercise faith on a major hope than on a promise that is easily met, because the exercising of faith, adding knowledge to the person, also purifies the personal and devotional character, allowing that character to become the best version of its self.

14. This is why it is well to know the Bible's spiritual understanding, and also the promise that it promises to its doer, even as like it says, "That we might receive the promise of the Spirit through faith."[1927] There is a very real promise within the Bible's present doctrine, even the promise "that ye might be filled with the knowledge of his will in all wisdom and spiritual understanding."[1928] Why is such a promise made? It is made so that this wisdom of His will may "purge your conscience from dead works to serve the living God."[1929]

15. The living God promises our conversation's conscience mental and spiritual health, growth, and development. This promise is only received when exercising faith on His spiritual understanding,

---

1927 Galatians 3:14
1928 Colossians 1:9
1929 Hebrews 9:14

meaning that if our conversation's mind should receive this promise, it first needs to be filled with "the spirit of wisdom and revelation in the knowledge of him."[1930] When therefore talking about faith, we are but talking about the labor of taking knowledge for an understanding to live by. Hope's substance can only be released as knowledge fuels a consistent belief on what is hoped for.

16. So then what is a more important exercise: faith or knowledge? No matter what we do, in every *thing*, and in all *things*, we exercise faith for knowledge and knowledge to stimulate faith. Abraham and Sara exercised confidence in what was promised because through their taking knowledge of what they perceived, they were also exercising faith on what they examined. By taking knowledge on what they had hoped for, they exercised faith on their hope for knowledge to live by, so it doesn't quite matter how it is viewed, because both faith and knowledge depend on one another to exist.

17. Faith may be the substance of hope, but hope is the substance of knowledge, and without knowledge's substance, there can be no faith in what is hoped for. We cannot therefore begin any *thing* in life at faith, but at hope, because our hope forces us to take knowledge of what we would exercise faith on, so that we may exercise that knowledge for obtaining hope's substance.

18. So then I have faith because I first have knowledge. "Faith" is but the conclusion of hope, but hope is the result of knowledge, making it possible for faith to exist.

19. Without knowledge, the heart is not soft enough for exercising faith. Faith rejuvenates the heart, but the heart fails if it is without wisdom and knowledge, even like as it says, "My people are destroyed for lack of knowledge,"[1931] and, "Fools die for want of wisdom."[1932]

20. If, then, we should have faith, we first need to have knowledge. Knowledge makes our confidence bold enough to hope on what isn't yet apparent. If possessing personal knowledge of what we hope for, we actually have the assurance we need to exercise faith, but if without

1930 Ephesians 1:17
1931 Hosea 4:6
1932 Proverbs 10:21

assurance, or if without understanding what to hope for, how can we think to ever begin exercising faith? Faith's exercise therefore doesn't begin with faith, but with knowledge, and with an experience in the vision we hope to achieve.

31

Faith's Work

1. If, then, the conversation is "justified by faith,"[1933] but it says, "By his knowledge shall my righteous servant justify many,"[1934] it is then a fact that before faith can justify, knowledge must first prepare the way for the justification that is to be received by faith. Our faith is to justify, cleanse, or better our conversation's conscience, but if there is no knowledge of what to have faith on, must we then think that we have faith in what we have faith in, and that we have a justifying faith in what we have faith in?

2. Our faith can only justify because of the knowledge first justifying. Knowledge justifies because understanding reveals fact from fiction. Having the revelation of truth and error, or of what to put confidence on and what not to put confidence on, we may exercise faith on the data accumulated through experimentation. This data, when lawfully and consistently exercised, is the means whereby our thoughts and feelings are bettered, allowing us, because of the knowledge we have, to put faith in what we first took knowledge of.

1933   Romans 5:1
1934   Isaiah 53:11

3. Our personal and devotional inward person is justified, cleansed, or alleviated through faith, but only through a faith that is knowledgeable. Justification occurs by faith because justification first occurs by knowledge, meaning that the first act of faith isn't actually belief, but is rather examination. Such a proposition sends the mind to think on how it says, "And the scripture was fulfilled which saith, Abraham believed God, and it was imputed unto him for righteousness: and he was called the Friend of God. Ye see then how that by works a man is justified, and not by faith only."[1935]

4. What are the works that justified Abraham? The Bible is making a very clear distinction between "belief" and "faith." Paul would tell us "that faith was reckoned to Abraham for righteousness,"[1936] and that "they which be of faith are blessed with faithful Abraham,"[1937] but James is telling us that Abraham was not only justified by "faith," but also by the "work" of "belief." What then is belief's labor?

5. The "work" of "belief," if all Abraham did was believe on the promise he was told, is the labor of taking knowledge. Because Abraham believed on the promise he was told, "by faith Abraham, when he was tried, offered up Isaac."[1938] Why did he do this? He did this to prove the Mind uttering that promise, and to take knowledge of the certainty of his confidence in that Mind and promise.

6. Abraham was told, "My covenant will I establish with Isaac."[1939] What then did Abraham do? Did he simply trust this saying? Did he sit back and lethargically wait for this saying to be fulfilled? How should Abraham know to put faith in the confidence this saying gave him? The only way to know the certainty of this saying would be to prove its value, or to take knowledge of the *character* within it. Abraham therefore, believing on the words of the promise, thought it well to sacrifice his *son*, because if the covenant should continue through Isaac, then surely he will not be allowed to kill the covenant's *child*.

1935   James 2:23,24
1936   Romans 4:9
1937   Galatians 3:9
1938   Hebrews 11:17
1939   Genesis 17:21

7. Abraham's faith on the living God's promise was exposed by the "work" of offering his *son* as a sacrifice. By consenting to sacrifice Isaac, Abraham was taking knowledge of the living God's character, and also of the validity of whatsoever passes out of *His mouth*. This act of proving his belief made Abraham favored of the living God because Abraham put his belief through the ringer, pressing his own heart for knowledge to exercise faith on.

8. This level of faith so caught the living God's *eye* that He moved on Abraham's conscience, saying, "Lay not thine hand upon the lad, neither do thou any thing unto him: for now I know that thou fearest God, seeing thou hast not withheld thy son, thine only son from me."[1940] Herein we learn that although we fail to please *heaven's* promise without faith, if ever failing to take knowledge of that promise for understanding the character within it, we fail to actually please the conditions for developing and displaying faith.

9. The "work" of faith is knowledge. Abraham didn't just put faith on a promise. Abraham, by proving the Mind uttering that promise, and by growing familiar with the spirit of that Mind and promise, educated his belief, allowing that belief to graduate into faith. So it is not faith alone that alleviates the inward person, but knowledge, when it is sincerely and honestly sought after and applied to, prepares the inward person for the alleviation their confidence should attract.

10. The entire point of faith is to attract what we believe or have confidence on. It is impossible to receive what we have confidence on if we do not apply self to take knowledge of what we believe is worth exercising faith on. The lesson we learn through Abraham is that we attract our belief when taking knowledge of our hope, seeing as how Abraham was "fully persuaded that, what he had promised, he was able also to perform. And therefore it was imputed to him for righteousness."[1941]

11. Again, how was Abraham persuaded that what the living God had promised was able to actually happen? The answer is that he always took knowledge on what was promised. Abraham's confidence came from him challenging the promises that were told to him. This man,

---

1940   Genesis 22:12
1941   Romans 4:21,22

by learning of and proving the value of those promises, had evidence of the Mind promising them. This evidence is what he used as fuel to receive what was promised, making the saying true, "Seest thou how faith wrought with his works, and by works was faith made perfect?"[1942]

12. There is only one acceptable "work" for faith, and that is the labor of knowledge. Abraham took knowledge of what was promised, and by taking knowledge had proof of belief, which proof he used to strengthen his confidence. Abraham's faith did justify, alleviate, or advance his thoughts and feelings, but his faith perfected the data or evidence he obtained through knowledge, which knowledge perfected the faith he had in what was promised.

13. There is no separating faith from knowledge, or knowledge from faith. The science of faith is taught through Abraham to reveal the importance of taking knowledge on the living God's promise. This is why it says, "Now it was not written for his sake alone, that it was imputed to him; but for us also, to whom it shall be imputed, if we believe on him that raised up Jesus our Lord from the dead."[1943]

14. The living God has, "having abolished in his flesh the enmity, even the law of commandments contained in ordinances,"[1944] given us a promise. This promise states: "A new heart also will I give you, and a new spirit will I put within you: and I will take away the stony heart out of your flesh, and I will give you an heart of flesh."[1945]

15. "As Christ was raised up from the dead by the glory of the Father, even so we also should walk in newness of life,"[1946] meaning that there is a level of newness of thought and feeling our conversation is to presently know and resurrect into. If the promise is a new heart and spirit or mind, then the goal of the promise is a resurrection from an old or former heart and spirit or mind.

16. The Bible's spiritual understanding teaches the promise of a personal and devotional service according to the living God's religious

---

1942 James 2:22
1943 Romans 4:23,24
1944 Ephesians 2:15
1945 Ezekiel 36:26
1946 Romans 6:4

character, and to receive the promise by faith, the inward person must first take knowledge of the character within that promise. We can only receive this promise by faith, therefore the example of Abraham is ever relevant, seeing as how this man learned of and received the promise not "through the law, but through the righteousness of faith."[1947]

17. We today live in the age of Abraham's religious character. Herein is the reason why the living God had to annihilate the philosophy of *righteousness* and *favor* by the religious law, "nailing it to his cross."[1948] Why figuratively nail this religious philosophy to the cross? It says, "And he fastened it with nails, that it should not be moved."[1949]

18. The illustration of the man's *body* of knowledge separating from the cross is so important because it reveals the separation of the living God's religious character from a false religious philosophy. To observe that *body* not only separated from the cross, but also brought into the living God's direct presence within the heavenly Sanctuary, is to observe a religious conversation saying, "And be found in him, not having mine own righteousness, which is of the law, but that which is through the faith of Christ."[1950] Today, it is our responsibility to exercise faith on the living God's promise, but we cannot begin to do so without taking knowledge of that promise's character.

19. Abraham's example is for our present learning. The living God has given every age some *thing* to exercise faith on, and the promise of today is a new and healthy personal and devotional heart and mind by exercising faith on that promise's instruction. Abraham teaches us that we cannot exercise faith without applying to faith's higher employment. Until we learn of and prove the living God's promise, taking knowledge of its force, we will never have confidence to believe that He is able to perform what He promises. Knowledge is therefore the substance of hope, allowing hope to release the substance of faith, which faith we can never possess if not willing to first take knowledge of what is promised.

1947   Romans 4:13
1948   Colossians 2:14
1949   Isaiah 41:7
1950   Philippians 3:9